RCA and the VideoDisc:
the business of research

STUDIES IN ECONOMIC HISTORY AND POLICY
THE UNITED STATES IN THE TWENTIETH CENTURY

Edited by
Louis Galambos and Robert Gallman

Other books in the series:
Peter D. McClelland and Alan L. Magdovitz: *Crisis in the making: the political economy of New York State since 1945*
Hugh Rockoff: *Drastic measures: a history of wage and price controls in the United States*
William N. Parker: *Europe, America, and the wider world: essays on the economic history of Western capitalism*
Richard H. K. Vietor: *Energy policy in America since 1945: a study of business–government relations*
Christopher L. Tomlins: *The state and the unions: labor relations, law, and the organized labor movement in America, 1880–1960*
Leonard S. Reich: *The making of American industrial research: science and business at GE and Bell, 1876–1926*

RCA and the VideoDisc: the business of research

MARGARET B. W. GRAHAM

The right of the
University of Cambridge
to print and sell
all manner of books
was granted by
Henry VIII in 1534.
The University has printed
and published continuously
since 1584.

CAMBRIDGE UNIVERSITY PRESS

Cambridge

London   New York   New Rochelle

Melbourne   Sydney

Published by the Press Syndicate of the University of Cambridge
The Pitt Building, Trumpington Street, Cambridge CB2 1RP
32 East 57th Street, New York, NY 10022, USA
10 Stamford Road, Oakleigh, Melbourne 3166, Australia

First published 1986

Printed in the United States of America

Library of Congress Cataloging-in-Publication Data
Graham, Margaret.
RCA and the VideoDisc:
The business of research.
(Studies in economic history and policy)
Bibliography: p.
1. Video disc players – Design and construction.
2. RCA Laboratories.   3. Radio Corporation of America.
I. Title.   II. Series.
TK6685.G73 1986   338.7'621388332'0973   86-2241

British Library Cataloguing in Publication Data
Graham, Margaret

RCA and the VideoDisc: The business of research (Studies in economic
history and policy: the United States in the twentieth century)

1. Video discs   2. Optical storage devices

I. Title   II. Series
004.5'6   TK7895.V

ISBN 0 521 32282 0

All photographs and charts are reproduced by permission of RCA.

Contents

v

TO FLOYD, HARRY, EVERETT, DICK, AND LOU –
A PRIDE OF MENTORS

Editors' preface

American business has been on an economic and political roller coaster in the years since World War II. Although business emerged from the war triumphant and profitable, the adjustment to a peacetime economy was conflict-ridden and painful for many American corporations. But then, in the 1950s and 1960s, the nation's businesses were so successful at home and abroad that they prompted discussion of the American Century, a century in which this country's efficient giant enterprises would dominate the world economy. Other nations would, it seemed, be forced to master American business techniques and organizational modes if they were to remain competitive. By the late sixties some doubts about this prophecy were beginning to emerge. In the seventies intense international competition, inflation, the energy crisis, and labor problems crushed the dreams of dominance and left Americans uncertain about the future of their business system.

It is in this setting that Margaret Graham places her penetrating analysis of *RCA and the VideoDisc: The Business of Research*. One of the key elements in American business success has been the mastery of modern science-based technology. One of the salient aspects of the business system's recent time of troubles has been competition from foreign firms that have frequently bested U.S. corporations in technological innovation. Graham's book helps the reader understand this transition and the complex problems of managing research and development in a corporate setting.

RCA, as Graham shows, was for many decades a remarkably successful, high-tech business. Under the leadership of David Sarnoff, the relationship between the research and development organizations and the rest of the corporation was managed with great skill. When, for a variety of reasons that Graham describes, that managerial task was no longer performed successfully, the firm experienced serious problems in translating sophisticated technological concepts into profitable products. The VideoDisc experience was symptomatic of those problems, and the author uses that episode in the corporation's history to provide us with the best analysis we have read of the contemporary "business of research." We are delighted to add this innovative volume to the series *Studies in Economic History and Policy: The United States in the Twentieth Century.*

Louis Galambos
Professor of History
The Johns Hopkins University

Robert Gallman
Kenan Professor of
Economics and History
University of North
Carolina

Preface and acknowledgments

The project out of which this book grew began in 1976 at the Harvard Graduate School of Business Administration. It was an exercise in a type of applied history that was rare then, but has since become far more common. Professor Richard Rosenbloom, the David Sarnoff Professor and then Director of Research at the Harvard Business School, took advantage of a rare opportunity to investigate a major consumer electronics project still under development at RCA. VideoDisc was then wrongly believed to be at the point of final transfer from RCA's corporate research laboratory in Princeton to two RCA consumer divisions, Consumer Electronics and Records, in Indianapolis. In the belief that there would be value in studying a science-based innovation for which the outcomes were still uncertain, Rosenbloom arranged to document the experience at the time. That way, the learning could not later be distorted by participants' natural tendencies to revise their memories to explain the ultimate success or failure of the project.

When I joined the project with newly completed degrees in history and business, our objective was simply to get as accurate an idea as possible of the various nontechnical considerations that helped to shape VideoDisc technology. Our original intention was to produce a teaching case or two, perhaps an article.

It took much negotiation and persuasion to convince all interested parties at RCA that our research intentions were honorable. Corporate executives are naturally fearful of allowing academic researchers to observe their work in "real time." On the other hand, scholars must always be wary of an organization's tendency to want to control or influence their interpretation of the facts. Both sides are anxious that the facts themselves not be misrepresented, but what "the facts" are is open to debate. For the VideoDisc project a format was devised that, although complicated and time consuming, satisfied both parties. On the basis of open and candid access to all present and former participants and company documents that could be located, I prepared a factual narrative of the VideoDisc project from its inception through 1975. The company had the right to review and correct the narrative itself, and all parties quoted therein were given the chance to correct, and comment on, what was said. The corrected factual narrative, entitled "RCA's VideoDisc: Technical Development and Business Development," is located in the archives of Harvard's Baker Library. It serves as the major source document for Chapters 4 through 8 of this book, as well as for interpretive material that others will publish.

From 1976 to 1978, I consulted every available document collection concerning videoplayer research at RCA that I could find, both at the company and in private hands, from laboratory logs and departmental file collections to personal files and even some extensive unpublished memoirs. I also interviewed more than forty people who either worked for RCA or had worked for the company in the past, all of whom had played a role in some phase of the VideoDisc or related videoplayer projects. A list of those interviewed appears in the Appendix. Some were researchers, development engineers, planning staff, project administrators, senior executives, and industry observers or even RCA's competitors. They were located at corporate headquarters (30 Rockefeller Center, New York), at the David Sarnoff Research Center in Princeton, New Jersey, at any of several RCA divisions and offices from Los Angeles, California, to Burlington, Massachusetts, and at other companies. All these people gave generously of their time to speak with me, and many went far beyond to furnish more documents, to write letters, and later to comment on drafts of the narrative.

It soon became clear that the questions under study required more than a case or an article to treat them properly. Cases focus on one or two key decisions, and articles are limited to a few themes, but VideoDisc could not be treated as just a sequence of individual decisions or isolated episodes. It took form out of the fabric of RCA corporate life. From a simple account of the VideoDisc project, my work expanded to a monograph covering the entire innovation as an outgrowth of earlier innovations, and treating the RCA company context as a critical determinant of the technology.

The scope of the project expanded several times as I encountered different groups of participants. When interviewing at the RCA Laboratories, for instance, I discovered that several researchers from two predecessor projects, Holotape and Phototape, were still at work on ideas derived from their videoplayer work, now directed at different product objectives. Some remained convinced that their alternative technical approaches would have been preferable to the one that had been selected for development, and these rejected alternatives became part of the story.

I redefined the project again at the consumer divisions, for these organizations had only recently lost out in their effort to induce RCA to adopt a proprietary magnetic tape videoplayer as RCA's main videoplayer project. It was obvious that the consumer divisions had a different philosophy concerning technically based product innovation from that of the Laboratories, one that stressed incremental technical developments carried out by advanced development groups. Many of the engineers who had been involved with Selectavision Magtape, as RCA's magnetic videotape recorder project was called, had been reassigned to work on the VideoDisc, only recently introduced out of the research center at Princeton. The decision had been imposed on them by corporate headquarters, and they had yet to be converted to the new cause. Here again, it was apparent that losing projects had affected the course of the VideoDisc innovation in countless ways and could not be dismissed, although history written after the project had concluded might well have ignored them as dead ends.

Outside competition had also played an important role in influencing both the direction of research and the course of business planning for the VideoDisc project. Key project turning points could be classified according to the foremost competitors that influenced RCA managers at the time they occurred: CBS, Teldec, Philips-MCA, Sony, JVC, and Matsushita, to name only the most important, had all made their mark on RCA's videoplayer projects, most of them long before their own products had even entered the marketplace. When the scope of the project threatened to include the whole international electronics industry, Richard Rosenbloom and I divided the project. He took the emerging videoplayer industry as the focus of his work, while I concentrated on the videoplayer innovation at RCA alone.

A new set of questions arose when I began to write the narrative. When I asked why RCA had pursued VideoDisc, the stock answer was always that the consumer electronics industry needed an act to follow television. But why RCA? And why a videoplayer rather than some other product? Why not another acquisition to accompany the string of acquisitions RCA was making during the later 1960s? When I pushed for more illuminating explanations, my informants would launch into stories about RCA of the previous era. Even executives who had been at RCA only for a few years explained current events in terms of past history. They told of mistakes that had been made with previous products, of the way things were managed at RCA under David Sarnoff, of successes that showed RCA's former greatness. But while company history obviously contained explanatory power, the links with the past were not obvious. I learned that David Sarnoff, RCA's leader for more than four decades, had done his best to control, and in some instances even to create, the history that had been written about him and about the company. History had mattered so much to him that he had devoted a substantial part of his later career to building the image of himself that he wanted preserved at his own memorial library at the RCA Laboratories. It was in pursuit of more objective historical explanations, therefore, that I assembled, from public sources, internal documents, and interviews with RCA veterans, the history of RCA and its research traditions that form Chapters 2 and 3 of this book. For the first time, I learned why the Laboratories that I knew as a low-key, friendly place filled with RCA loyalists had sometimes been mistrusted and resented by people in other parts of the corporation, why David Sarnoff's style of managing innovation was mentioned whenever people discussed the management of contemporary projects, and why the television experience of the 1950s still seemed so often to be used as a yardstick when evaluating current new products.

As Chapters 9 and 10 of the book indicate, the VideoDisc project took far longer than anyone had expected to reach the marketplace. Although I updated the research to 1977, I was not able to do the extensive interviewing and document research for the final phases of the project that I had done for earlier phases. The account of the ultimate launching of the project and of what happened when VideoDisc reached the market is therefore based largely on key interviews and on published sources. Again, the facts have been checked for accuracy with the same executives who reviewed the principal narrative. For this piece as for all earlier sections of the book, the interpretation, right or wrong, is wholly my own.

Any book project that takes nearly ten years to complete is likely to have involved many people, if only to encourage and strengthen the author in what sometimes seems an interminable process. For this book I am indebted to the Research Division of the Harvard Graduate School of Business Administration for providing the money and release time to support an expensive kind of work and to a large group of people who helped in so many ways that a chapter could be devoted to their efforts. I owe special thanks first to Richard Rosenbloom, who suggested that I write the book to begin with, and who acted as sponsor, hardworking critic, and friend throughout the entire process. As the list of interviews indicates, numerous people connected with RCA gave me their cooperation, but I am especially grateful to William Hittinger, William Webster, Richard Sonnenfeldt, Kenneth Bilby, and Phyllis Smith for many hours of reading, discussion, and comment. From their personal commitment to accuracy and fairness and their strong support of the integrity of my project I learned more about the meaning of academic freedom than I ever learned in the academy. From my colleagues at the Winthrop Group, George Smith, David Allen, and Davis Dyer, I received encouragement, many useful suggestions, and a deepened understanding of what it is to do applied history. Thanks are due also to academic colleagues at the Harvard Business School and at the Boston University School of Management, and to fellow members of the Society of the History of Technology, many of whom provided encouragement, read sections of the manuscript, and discussed lines of argument in seminar sessions. Chief among these were William Abernathy, Hugh Aitken, David Allison, Alfred Chandler, Kim Clark, Raymond Corey, Karen Freeze, Mel Horwitch, Jeffrey Miller, Robert Stobaugh, Richard Tedlow, and Abraham Zaleznik. I had the help of skilled and patient editors at several phases of the book's preparation – Max Hall, Kathleen Spivack, Judith Gurney, Frank Smith, and especially Louis Galambos. Finally, I had the encouragement and help of Father Thomas Shaw and other members of the Society of St. John the Evangelist, who gave me the use of their hermitage to write in, and of Susan McWade-Patten, who at several stages did much of the preparation of the manuscript. Without these, and many other friends, who here go unnamed, but whose contribution is no less appreciated, this book would not have come to pass.

Introduction

This is the story of RCA's VideoDisc, a systems innovation by a company, once an industrial pioneer, that was trying to innovate again after a generation of inactivity.

VideoDisc was in two senses a "systems innovation": its technology was founded on several interdependent science-based products and processes, and the coordinated efforts of several different RCA product divisions were required to bring it to market. Like other innovations that originated as science-based systems – the telephone, radio, television, and more recently, videotex – once the elements were in place, parts of it could be sold as individual products, but no piece of it could exist alone in the marketplace.

An innovation is considered to be science based when either the components that it comprises, or the configuration of the innovation itself, require scientific research to bring them into being. Such innovations are generally dependent on some form of industrial research organization either to generate the missing knowledge or to apply already existing knowledge to the problem raised by the innovative system concept. Many argue, for this reason, that science-based systems innovations can best be carried out in a large corporate setting. Few small companies have the resources, the varied production capabilities, or the necessary technical support required for this type of project. Nor can small companies, however innovative, develop and manufacture the specialized components and materials, or assemble the complicated business relationships, to market technology-based systems. Joint ventures, which sometimes attempt to mount systems innovations by combining the complementary skills and resources of several companies, are

1

notoriously cumbersome and difficult to coordinate and are rarely flexible enough to bring uncertain projects to completion.

Innovation in large companies

Most of what is known about innovation as a managerial activity accurately reflects the experiences of small companies but is wholly unrepresentative of the experience of most large companies. This is unfortunate, for by far the lion's share of the spending for research and development (R&D) and much innovative activity in the United States is performed in large corporations. How does the process of innovation differ in large companies, and what does it take to manage that process effectively?

The standard notion of the innovation process is that it matches a technical capability to a market need. In a small company, where most successful innovations take place, the match between a technical capability and a market need is undertaken and pushed to completion by an individual entrepreneur. A small company rarely has more than a few novel technical capabilities; it is therefore the role of the small-company entrepreneur to identify and define a market need that his or her enterprise can meet with the technical capabilities at its disposal.

The differences between the small-company version of innovation and what passes under that name in large companies are more than simply matters of scale; they are qualitative in nature. In a large company, particularly a diversified one, many considerations intrude upon the simple act of matching technical capability to a market. The large technology-based and diversified company has manifold technical capabilities, often represented by specialist engineering and research organizations, and it frequently has two or three different technical approaches for any given problem. One reason that large companies have in-house research organizations is to acquire or create technical capabilities not already available within the corporation; often rival parts of the company's technical community are behind different technical approaches. Under such circumstances, the choice of technical approach to a given innovation often relies more on the internal needs and preferences of various parts of the corporation than on a sense of a need in the marketplace. Jobs, retention of key skills, use of readily available equipment, shared characteristics with other projects, and fulfillment of individual organizational goals all are legitimate internal needs that can influence the choices made about a technology as much as, or more than, information about the market.

In any case, if a proposed innovation is really new, little information about the market can be trusted. Often other factors, such as the behavior of key competitors, or the predictions of the press, provide the only information available. It may be distorted, but it is in some sense real. The more diversified a company becomes, the more competitors there are to influence behavior and to filter or distort market information, and the more interested the press is in reporting, and possibly influencing, the innovation process.

Documented examples of the development of science-based systems innovations are rare. Large-scale innovations of any kind, from first inventive idea to full-scale commercialization, are such major undertakings that only a few are carried to completion in any industry. Moreover, because systems innovations generally involve the efforts of several organizational entities within a company and frequently take place over a prolonged period of time, even people who have managed pieces of such projects for years often are surprised to learn what has gone on at other periods or in other parts of the company.

Examples of innovations that have not succeeded are even rarer than those of successful ones, though the former category is many times larger than the latter. Companies, like individuals, are often unwilling to allow themselves, or anyone else, to learn from their experiences. Yet such is the perversity of existence that plans gone awry can teach us more about the way things work, and the way they ought to work, than plans fulfilled without a hitch. We are indebted, therefore, to RCA for allowing this inside look at one large and very complex

3

systems innovation that lasted nearly twenty years, involved the efforts of thousands of people, required the investment of hundreds of millions of dollars – and ultimately failed.

The research organization

An industrial research organization can be found at the source of many science-based innovations, but relatively little is known about this peculiar corporate institution. Research has been an in-house activity in a few leading American companies since before the turn of the century, and most large companies have had some form of research laboratory since World War II. Yet research remains an enigma in most management circles. R&D is a broader term, encompassing the activities of several forms of technical organization: research laboratory, advanced engineering group, product engineering, process engineering. It is partly because most major science-based innovations in industry involve so many different institutions, even within the same organization, that the process of innovation, from first inventive idea to full-scale commercialization, can take as long as it does, often more than a decade. The popular impression that an invention, once made, should be available for use within a few months' time, reflects public lack of awareness of the operating aspects of R&D. In fact, the act of invention, whether research based or spun off from some other activity, only begins a lengthy and complicated process of embodiment, design, and refinement collectively termed "development." Even in technology-based companies, non-technical employees or employees who work outside the R&D organizations can be unaware of the many ways that research feeds into and draws upon other more visible productive activities. For this reason we are concerned here with the role of the research organization. How has it evolved inside the corporation? And how has it contributed to the process of innovation?

In RCA it was David Sarnoff, the head of the company from 1930 to 1967, who created the corporate research center in a sense as his surrogate, to stand up for the long-term interests of the corporation and to generate major new business opportunities based on technology. It was to carry out this mission that managers of RCA Laboratories became the wholly committed sponsors of the consumer videoplayer product during the 1960s, and during the 1970s chose to back one technical approach to that product, the capacitance videodisc system.

To manage a corporate R&D division is to encounter daily some of the central tensions of industrial life. Inside his or her own organization the director of an industrial research laboratory must manage research, an act of human creativity and perseverance, but the director must also make objective judgments about technologies, their quality and their utility. At the same time the director must manage the relationships between the research organization and all the different operating entities it serves. This is a delicate balancing act, for there is a natural and unavoidable tension between the immediate demands of current operations, often responsive to short-term profit needs, and the no less important but wholly different requirements for long-term research.

The case of VideoDisc illustrates well the contradictions between managing research and managing intercorporate relationships. The successive heads of RCA research for years had to orchestrate a competition between several videoplayer technologies inside the Laboratories, unsure which one would, or should, win out. At the same time, they had to promote the idea of a videoplayer system to top corporate management and to try to build support in the product divisions for whatever technologies the Laboratories ultimately selected for transfer. The latter task was made all the more difficult because several product divisions preferred videoplayer systems of their own devising, despite the fact that, from the corporate point of view, the Laboratories had primary responsibility for corporate technical decisions.

Why take a risk?

A project involving large-scale innovation would be too wrenching and too dangerous for any responsible corporate management to undertake if new products were not central to the process of industrial renewal. How and when to renew its products and its organization is a major strategic choice that each company must make. Should it take the initiative, and be a pioneer, or should it wait until most uncertainty is gone and adopt a less risky me-too strategy? In some U.S. industries with a strong technology base, the role of pioneer has belonged historically to one company, one with strong in-house technical capabilities and structured to lead.

A rapidly changing scene has been an abiding feature of life in the consumer electronics industry since the early days of radio. New products based on new technologies diffused rapidly throughout the economy, saturating the market within a few years. Each new decade seemed to bring with it the need for a new generation of products with the potential for renewing and sustaining a multitiered industry. Each major product transition brought with it the need for industrial transformation; that is, the whole complex of related industries that had been created to produce, operate, and maintain radio, and then television, had to transform itself with new facilities, new operating technologies, new components, new products, and new types of software to stay in the market.

For decades, it was RCA that took the lead whenever an industrial transformation was required. It is in light of this pioneering legacy that RCA's experience with VideoDisc is especially interesting. For while VideoDisc was under development in the RCA Laboratories, RCA's corporate management was reconsidering and debating the company's role in future industrial transformations. The ambivalence within the organization led RCA to pursue the paths of leadership and followership at the same time. The course of the VideoDisc project reflected this internal schizophrenia.

The VideoDisc experience also demonstrates the problems of managing an important corporate resource, the central research laboratory. Paradoxically, the RCA Laboratories was both the chief agent of innovation and the major conservative force. Faced with the sole responsibility for RCA's future, but with little corporate direction and in the face of major uncertainty, the Laboratories pursued a course in VideoDisc innovation that was shaped very much by RCA's earlier experience. The constraints placed on videodisc technology reflected the Laboratories' interpretation of RCA successes and failures with other science-based systems products, such as television and magnetic videocassette recorders.

One of the most intriguing things about VideoDisc was the project's tenacity – its ability to survive several changes in top management as well as several revampings of RCA strategy. Yet each threat it survived had its effect on the project. The struggle that the VideoDisc caused to be waged inside RCA raises questions critical to the effective contribution of all research organizations. What is the proper role of the research function in the formulation and execution of corporate strategy? How can research be integrated into the mainstream of corporate life without sacrificing the long-term interests of the corporation? How can the corporate research organization be protected from the negative operating effects of shifts in corporate strategy, yet remain responsive to its changing needs?

VideoDisc was an important part of RCA life for more than fifteen years, especially in the Research Laboratories and in the divisional engineering groups. RCA has extended and applied in countless ways to many other RCA products and processes the knowledge and the know-how, technical and managerial, that came out of the project. This multiplier effect is a characteristic of R&D that is often forgotten, yet few long-term R&D projects are so specific that they do not generate learning for further applications.

It is the purpose of this book to examine aspects of the VideoDisc innovation experience from a management standpoint. The case of the VideoDisc has much to say about four major related themes: the nature of industrial research and how it differs from other forms of industrial activity; the role of the corporate laboratory as an industrial institution; the skills required to manage research and a research laboratory, particularly as it relates to other parts of the corporation; and the problem of integrating research and development into mainstream corporate activity.

1

Selectavision VideoDisc: opportunity and risk

It was a highly improbable match between promoter and product. RCA Chairman Edgar Griffiths was not by nature a keen risk-taker, and Videodisc was certainly not the product he would have chosen to make his first deliberate and large corporate wager. Yet in February 1981, Griffiths led the parade of RCA executives who appeared in front of NBC closed-circuit television cameras to announce the introduction of Selectavision VideoDisc to 14,000 RCA distributors and dealers, assembled in seventy-five cities across the United States via satellite.

The Selectavision launch was the result of more than fifteen years of painstaking effort and investment in technology and business development. RCA had embarked on its round of videoplayer development in 1965, in the midst of the "golden age of color television," partly because color TV had become a $3 billion industry and the mainstay of RCA's consumer electronics business only after a prolonged delay. From 1954 to 1960, the market had not welcomed color television, and RCA had spent most of the 1950s at a low level of profitability as a consequence. Only during the 1960s, when color TV finally caught on, did the company enjoy a period of prosperity comparable to its blue chip era of the 1920s.[1]

Naturally, after this experience, a major goal of RCA's top management in 1965 was to find a way either to sustain the prosperity of its television business through extensions to the product line or to identify a substitute product line that could be started up without putting the entire company through another intolerable period of austerity. In theory, it should be possible, for the company had superior technical resources, including 6,200 engineers and scientists. Yet the problem of

RCA's VideoDisc preview for the retailers via satellite from NBC studios.

renewing RCA's core business by selling new technology, never a simple one, had become more complex than it had been in the period when David Sarnoff was building the company. RCA's relationship with the industry and its ability to dominate the direction of development in its core technology had changed.

9

The computer failure

RCA had enjoyed a de facto monopoly in technology-related aspects of the industry up until World War II.[2] Its technical dominance was grounded in a pool of key radio-related patents that allowed it to influence the rate and direction of development of first radio, and then electronics, technology. In addition, RCA's integrated organizational structure, which gave it a presence in all aspects of consumer entertainment businesses, from hardware manufacture for consumer and professional broadcast markets to radio and television broadcasting, made it possible for the company to bring about systems innovation in entertainment technologies.

In the aftermath of the war, RCA experienced the losses of both its patent monopoly and its unique status as an entertainment systems company. In the battles over color television, RCA for the first time faced domestic competitors who rivaled its technical supremacy as well as its systems structure. Other areas of electronics technology had also attracted competitors. New entrants came from among the leading airframe companies, which had benefited, just as RCA had, from government support for R&D during the war. They were cutting deeply into the military electronics market and beginning to go after commercial markets as well.

RCA was successful in defending its position of leadership only in the entertainment market. After abortive attempts on the part of CBS and others to build a fully integrated, technology-based capability, RCA was still the only U.S. consumer electronics company able to pursue a pioneering strategy in a systems business during the 1960s, by combining R&D, manufacturing, marketing, and entertainment software. Other companies with equivalent integrated structures and leading-edge research could only be found in Europe and Japan. These included N.V. Philips, headquartered in the Netherlands with manufacturing divisions spread over Europe, Thorn based in England, Thompson Brandt based in France, and Telefunken and Siemens in West Germany. Several major Japanese firms, such as Matsushita and Toshiba, were in the process of attaining a large, integrated structure,

10

but the possibility that they might become more than swift imitators and eager purchasers of technology from Europe and the United States was only dimly perceived at that time.

In 1965, RCA was a company with $2.5 billion in sales, and it was still headed by David Sarnoff, its leader for nearly forty years. It was riding the crest of the boom in two of the three sectors in which electronics technology had made its initial impact – consumer entertainment and defense – but it was having trouble with the third, computers for the commercial sector. A portion of its sales, and an even larger share of its profits, were related to color television in some form (NBC, Professional Broadcast Equipment, Home Instruments, RCA Service, Electronic Components). It also had important businesses making defense-related products such as missile systems, space and communications satellites, and computers. Roughly 30 percent of its revenues derived from the government contracts. Indeed, it was with its government businesses that RCA had established a reputation for leading-edge computer technology.

RCA had had difficulty adjusting to the new, postwar competitive environment, particularly in trying to start non-government businesses. Color television failed to pay off on schedule on what was a $132 million investment, and the company was late in entering the electronic data processing business. In time, the computer business seemed to be on track and, in 1965, computer orders were doubling. RCA was projecting computers to be a major profit generator by 1970, although capital requirements for this product line were exceptionally high because of the leasing approach adopted by IBM. Moreover, although RCA's leading-edge technology in computers and computer communications gave it an advantage, it could never seem to gain ground against a deeply entrenched IBM. Its efforts to make a frontal assault on the computer marketplace under the leadership of John Burns, a computer industry expert appointed president of RCA in 1957, did not pay off. His tenure ended in 1960 before his four-year contract ran out.

It fell to Robert Sarnoff, former president of NBC and his father's handpicked successor, to improve the RCA position in computers and to make good use of the profits finally generated by color television. He spent his first four or five years reformulating strategy and thoroughly revamping the company's management style and public image. Robert Sarnoff departed from previous company practice by expanding overseas and by diversifying into businesses peripherally related to electronics and, in some cases, wholly unrelated. In anticipation of competing in the newly integrated and standardized European Common Market, RCA under Robert Sarnoff set up manufacturing joint ventures in England, France, and Italy and hired a former ITT executive to head its international division. Meanwhile, its acquisitions were widespread. From early forays into publishing and graphics, where the relationship to its existing businesses was straightforward, the company made extreme departures, until RCA subsidiaries were making carpets (Coronet) and frozen foods (Banquet), as well as renting automobiles (Hertz).

Robert Sarnoff also spent millions modernizing RCA's image, changing the RCA logo from the old Radio Corporation of America lightning flash to a symbol that was supposed to suggest the integrated worldwide system that RCA would become. Portrayed in starkly modern graphics, RCA's new image was that of a unified, rationalized, sophisticated communications and service systems company. Gone were such familiar symbols as the dog "Nipper."

There were also profound alterations in the company's style of management. A new, sizable corporate staff was responsible for making the key decisions about long-term planning and resource allocation, and most of its senior members came from other companies, such as Ford and IBM, known for their "professional" approaches to management. The expertise these outsiders brought with them tended to be in the areas of finance, marketing, and strategic planning. RCA operating divisions were given targets for growth, market share, and profitability, and resources were allocated in terms of a top–down overall company perspective after extensive market research and portfolio analysis.

The new structures and systems were hardly in place when a severe economic downturn in 1970 hit the entire electronics industry and seriously affected RCA sales and earnings. Bad times focused reaction inside and outside the company against the changes in strategy and management style. At a special stockholders meeting in February 1971, called to approve an increase in authorized stock, one elderly woman seemed to express the feelings of many towards RCA's "conglomeration" strategy. Addressing Robert Sarnoff, she said, "We have already gone from soup to nuts. Tell me, mister, where is it going to end? You are going to build an empire and look what happened to all the empires."[3]

The worst effects of the recession in the early 1970s were sustained by RCA's computer business. It was hemorrhaging money after being reorganized at the beginning of 1971 and refocused into a new aggressive mode in a more narrowly defined segment of the market. In the fall of 1971, having only recently invested in new production facilities for peripheral equipment, having just completed a $16 million computer business headquarters in Massachusetts, having just hired a new group of employees away from Honeywell, and having made solemn promises to customers about its intention to stay in the business, RCA abruptly pulled out of computers, taking a write-off of $250 million.

The computer withdrawal had deep and far-reaching consequences throughout the company. More than 4,000 people lost their jobs. At the research center 40 percent of the staff had been involved in computer support efforts, and these had to be either transferred to operating divisions, laid off, or reassigned to other research work. Overseas licensees of RCA computer technology, Siemens and ICL, were left without the crucial technical support that they needed. In the rigorous cost cutting and consolidation that followed withdrawal, businesses related to information technologies were also phased out, leading to an overall force reduction of 13,000. Ironically, the corporate staff that had pushed for the computer write-off received much of the blame, and it was effectively dismantled.

Although Robert Sarnoff survived the immediate aftermath of the computer business write-off, it was a black mark from which he was never able to recover. In 1975, he ran afoul of the RCA Board and was succeeded by Anthony Conrad, then

13

president, and a veteran of RCA from the service side of the business. Conrad's term of office lasted less than a year, for the embarrassing and potentially compromising discovery was made that he had failed to file personal tax returns for several years. His successor in October 1976, was Edgar H. Griffiths, another RCA insider who determined to put RCA back on a stable financial footing.

Nevertheless, there were benefits from the computer pull-out. The removal of a serious financial drain freed up top management's attention for other things and also created renewed interest in new consumer products. The research center management was able to devote a significant portion of its effort to consumer electronics support and to videoplayers. Among other things, it was able to turn its attention to long overdue improvements in color television – solid-state products and the processes to support them. The Videodisc project likewise benefited from the materials research expertise that was freed up.

Focus on the VideoDisc

After the computer failure, the company looked to video-players in general as the product with which RCA might recoup its technological image. Between 1971 and 1979, several different videoplayer technologies were publicly proclaimed as RCA's next consumer entertainment product. The Video-Disc project as such went through ups and downs inside the company.

RCA's Selectavision VideoDisc system was one of several disc systems to surface during the 1970s. It was part of a broader category then loosely defined as prerecorded video players. As a technical genre, the various videoplayer systems shared key system elements, a loose product concept, and performance requirements that had to be met.

At the simplest level, the videoplayer system began as the video analog of an audio system, several forms of which, magnetic tape or record, were available during the early 1950s. The videoplayer provided a means of storing, retrieving, and playing back visual and audio images through a television set. It was a more challenging achievement than audio because the amount of information involved was 200 times as great as that stored on a long-playing (LP) record.

The elements involved in any videoplayer included a high-density storage medium capable of accommodating the vast amount of information required in a manageable space, a mastering process capable of storing the information as a signal or an image on the medium, and an electronic retrieval device capable of detecting and playing the information back with high resolution comparable to other available visual-image technologies such as television and film.

Each element of the system could be approached in several possible ways. Media alternatives included film, magnetic or nonmagnetic tape, and hard vinyl discs, either grooved or ungrooved, of various sizes, coated or uncoated. Information could be stored in several different formats, but the main options were photographic images, optical images, or signals. The storage had to involve a mastering method, since the purpose was to replicate prerecorded programs many times over.[4] This could be electromechanical, as in traditional audio recordings, photographic, electron beam, or optical, using a laser beam. The pickup device could be a magnetic head, an electromechanical needle in a groove, an electronic capacitance sensor, a piezo electric needle (pressure pickup), or a laser optical device.

Although these elements were not completely interchangeable, there were enough combinations and permutations to afford a wealth of options to research and advanced development groups trying to produce the most effective form of a videoplayer system. For each group, product effectiveness was defined slightly differently, as it considered product performance and cost, coupled with the need to capitalize on the capabilities and proprietary technologies of its own institution.

RCA worked on several versions of videoplayers in its RCA Laboratories in Princeton and in its Consumer Electronics Division in Indianapolis. At one point in the early 1970s it had announced that it would introduce a Selectavision family of videoplayers to suit all needs and pocketbooks. But in the end

RCA VideoDisc System

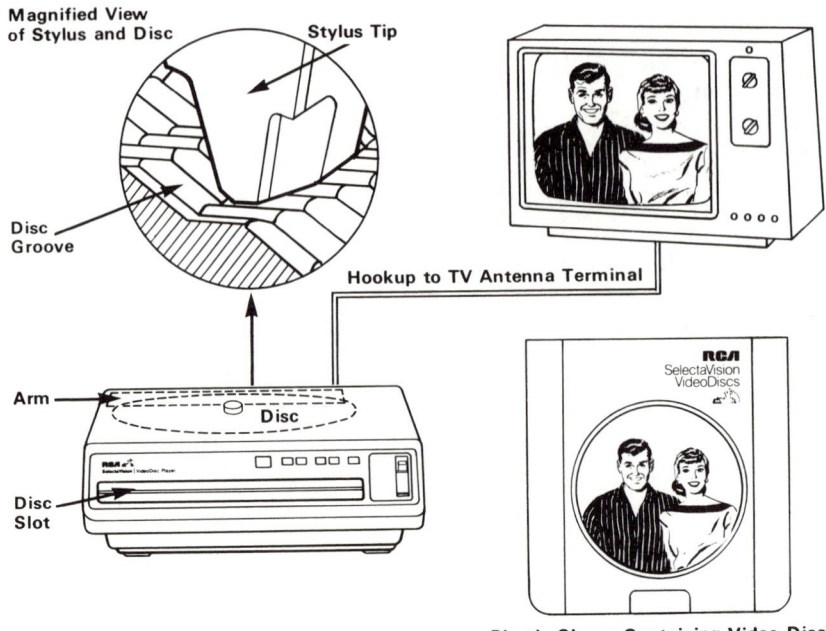

RCA VideoDisc system and how it works.

the only videoplayer technology that RCA actually brought to market that was a product of its own technical effort was the Selectavision VideoDisc, a twenty-pound, fully enclosed player capable of spinning a twelve-inch vinyl disc at 450 revolutions per minute (rpm), thirteen times as fast as the regular LP record. The player extracted the disc from a plastic cassette, or "caddy," inserted in a slot in its front, and employed an electrode on the end of a stylus to sense the variations in capacitance (defined as the relationship between charge and voltage of two adjacent electrical conductors) on a grooved spinning disc. It also employed advanced solid-state circuitry to decode the signal picked up from the disc and to display it on a television monitor. The picture it displayed was of superior resolution to any picture received over the airwaves at that time and considerably better than most pictures received via cable. It was also superior to pictures played back from magnetic tape.

Each element of the system embodied research and engineering performed at several different levels of the company's R&D organization. Some pieces required new technology, based on advanced scientific methods rarely before employed in consumer products. Others involved state-of-the-art technology pushed to its furthest limits. In general, after the initial development of the concept and the prototype, the RCA Laboratories took responsibility for further development of materials and systems, while advanced engineering groups in the product divisions worked out the necessary circuitry and handled product design, mastering, and manufacturing. Both the final product and the processes that were put together to manufacture it were compromises among many technical options backed by different parts of the RCA organization in support of complex technical and commercial agendas.

Considerably more sophisticated than any previous RCA consumer hardware, the player was nevertheless the most straightforward element of the videodisc system. Important research successes were involved in the linear tracking arm assembly that housed the cartridge and stylus and moved them across the disc, in the complicated sensors used to keep the stylus on track, and in the tiny diamond stylus that transported an even smaller electrode that sensed changes in distance between the peaks and undulations of the grooves and sent them to the player. Research was also involved in the very stable high-speed turntable, the microprocessor control, and the decoding circuitry that broke down and reprocessed the signals containing audio and video information, synchronizing instructions and other data. The design of the player and "caddy" posed challenges for consumer product safety, such as preventing flying or cutting discs, and disc protection (avoiding damage from dust, humidity, wear, and user negligence). The most demanding challenge of all for R&D was to come up with a product so easy to manufacture at volume that RCA could make money at a selling price of $500.

The disc presented other problems. The information density required to play two hours of programming on a twelve-inch disc was considerably greater than the density achieved at the time in computer discs used for information storage. The capacitance approach required that the disc be conductive and the information storage needs meant finely spaced grooves that were exacting to make and very difficult to keep free of impediment. The mass-production volume and quality requirements meant that millions of discs would be produced each year; the need for conformance to strict standards would require a production process then common in the semiconductor industry, but still not used in the record business, where the discs would be made. For a company that had done relatively little with advanced automation in its consumer product business until recently, videodisc production represented a quantum jump in process innovation and process control.

Early performance goals for the disc compared to the final Selectavision version that went to market show a great difference. The first requirements were for a disc to play twenty minutes per side of black and white pictures at a signal-to-noise ratio (measuring picture quality) of thirty-six decibels (db). Early prototypes were discs with three microscopically thin coatings – of metal, a nonconductive plastic material, and oil – applied in a vacuum chamber. In the end, the Selectavision disc was made of conductive vinyl, a patented composition of plastic and carbon with a single layer of thinly deposited lubricant. It had a playtime of two hours and a signal-to-noise ratio of forty-six db. Its production process was computer controlled to meet purity requirements for the material that were higher than many of those in the pharmaceuticals industry.

The "mastering" process used to enable the replication of discs was a highly advanced version of the electromechanical cutting method used to make audio disc masters. To achieve real-time mastering (i.e., storing the program material on the master at the same rate of speed that it would play back) it employed a new, microscopically small diamond cutting tool and cutting speeds twelve times as great as conventional mastering. The master started as a copper-coated fourteen-inch aluminum disc spinning at 225 rpm on a special recording turntable mounted on air cushions. The disc when cut was electroplated, coated with nickel, and used to make nickel molds, which were in turn used to make stampers. While these were essentially incremental innovations, achieved mostly by extending existing audio recording technology, RCA also developed high-resolution mastering methods using lasers and electron beams that involved new technology.

Selectavision's chief technical challenge was the system problem that it posed. Even at the earliest prototype stage it was impossible to work on each part of the system in isolation, for all elements were interdependent. Though individual pieces of a working laboratory model might be considered "off-the-shelf" items (i.e., not requiring further fundamental research), the uncertainties associated with the functioning of the components when they were combined in a system gave the project as a whole an element of extraordinary technological reach. RCA researchers were familiar with this problem from television days, but this did not make it easier when individual elements of the development program were scattered geographically and organizationally throughout RCA's far-flung R&D community.

Selectavision debut

The February 1981 VideoDisc showing for distributors was exotic, a show mounted by a company in the entertainment business that mingled images of the past and the future in a dazzling display of light, sound, and color. The glittering advertising theme, "Bring the Magic Home," was represented by Radio City Rockettes and NBC "Today" stars. Selectavision VideoDisc, it was promised, would bestow on the American consumer magical powers – the ability to have pictures in the home, selected no longer at the will of an aloof television executive in New York, but by each individual member of RCA's long-standing target market, the mass-entertainment audience.

Hand in hand with the emphasis on a magical future were visual images and spoken reminders of an almost-forgotten

19

RCA past. In countless ways RCA's leadership seemed to be using the occasion to reassert the company's historical claim to the industrial entrepreneurship and technological supremacy it had all but abandoned during the 1970s. Posters of "Nipper" hearing "His Master's Voice" in the gramophone were seen for the first time in more than a decade. The new product bore many of the hallmarks of a traditional RCA systems innovation. It was priced low enough to appeal to a mass market. Its videodisc player, Model SFT 100, could be attached to a television set by cable, and its two-hour capacitance electronic discs (CED) were encased in hard plastic caddies, sleeves that served as colorful record jackets and protected fragile disc surfaces from direct consumer contact. The player was priced at $499, and discs were set at $14.98 to $24.98 retail. At first the hardware and software would be sold by the same RCA dealer network that sold televisions. Discs would contain such mass-entertainment fare as feature movies, past television hits, sports, music, and self-instruction programming.[5]

According to Roy Pollack, RCA executive vice-president in charge of all electronics businesses, Selectavision's outstanding features were its simplicity, reliability, ease of use, and low-cost appeal to a mass market. The product might have some advanced features such as pause, fast search, and stereo in the future, but these were not aspects of the product that RCA wished to promote. Fundamentally, Selectavision was aimed at RCA's favorite customer, the average television viewer who did not want to be bothered or confused by fancy features that might not work but who wished to sit in front of the television set and be entertained. It was the fulfillment of a promise RCA made long ago to its public. In a sense it was the product that David Sarnoff, RCA's legendary leader, had imagined would free television viewers from commercial broadcasting, the part of the entertainment electronics industry he himself had helped to create but had long despised.[6]

In the beginning, said Herbert Schlosser, executive vice-president of VideoDisc programming and former president of NBC, Selectavision software would be heavily oriented toward movies, but later, programming would be created especially for the system. An initial catalog of 100 titles would be augmented

20

quarterly, he promised, with additions of twenty-five titles each time. In a significant departure from previous practice, RCA had ensured softward availability by inviting the participation of other familiar American entertainment companies in the production and sale of videodiscs. Included among these was RCA's oldest rival, CBS.

That Selectavision was a major technical achievement was something RCA wanted to promote, for the company's lack of visible innovations in its core business had been noted on Wall Street and elsewhere. A product involving the storage and retrieval of billions of elements of information on a single disc was a triumph of research ingenuity worthy of earlier RCA radio and television research successes. Moreover, RCA had overcome significant hurdles in product design and manufacturing process to make the player reliable and easy to use and to make the discs error free. In less than two years RCA had created a manufacturing organization of unprecedented sophistication for one of its consumer products. Clean-room facilities and advanced materials control, combined in an automated plant, provided the capability of producing and automatically testing 4,000 discs per day.

RCA Chairman Edgar Griffiths did not play down the magnitude of the risk RCA was taking with VideoDisc. Indeed he underscored the commitment RCA would make to the new product. He assured RCA dealers, and by extension the home entertainment electronics industry at large, that RCA's investment was not just a short-term commitment to a product, but a commitment to a new business. RCA would remain in this business, he asserted with a degree of emphasis that went beyond his prepared text, not just for this generation, but for the next and the next. Coming from a man who had previously earned a reputation as RCA's first bottom-line-oriented leader, the remarks had an incongruous ring. In fact the whole episode seemed strangely risk seeking for a company that had spent its last decade trying to live down the computer business write-off. Yet the stress on the size of the commitment RCA was making to the product, like the points about the sophistication of the Selectavision manufacturing process and the integrated systems strategy, were all intended to remind the market of competitive advantages RCA's strategists believed it to have over other versions of the videodisc concept that had already been, or were soon to be, introduced to the U.S. market by foreign competitors.

The competition

The "magic in question," as one press observer called Selectavision at the launch, was the first videodisc player to use the capacitance approach to information storage and retrieval, but it was not the first videodisc player on the market. In fact, videoplayers in general (videodisc and videocassette) had ushered in a new competitive era for RCA, especially in the business of research. For the first time, the company was competing for its pioneering status in an industry that was international.[7]

During the 1960s and 1970s, RCA and its competitors developed as many as ten different videoplayer systems for consumer use, each involving a different technical approach. By the time RCA introduced Selectavision, two major categories of consumer videoplayer system had emerged to dominate the rest. They were magnetic tape players in two distinct formats, VHS and Beta, and two disc formats, optical and capacitance, with a third, VHD, in the wings. Several technical approaches had already failed in the marketplace during the mid-1970s. Most were earlier versions of magnetic videocassette systems, like the Avco Cartrivision system, but other approaches were also tried. CBS had introduced a photographic image system called the Electronic Videorecorder (EVR) and Teldec, a joint venture between Telefunken and Decca Records, had introduced a disc system in Germany. In most cases the reasons for failure had been complex, seldom strictly technical. Often it had been the problem of coordinating multiple enterprises, for most of the systems had involved joint arrangements between different companies, each supplying one or more elements of the technology. Occasionally failures yielded important new information about the market. Teldec, for instance, found that the industry in general had underestimated the amount of programming likely to be demanded per player sold.

Of the magnetic tape players, or videocassette recorders (VCRs), Sony's Betamax, a consumer version of its earlier successful institutional Umatic was the first product to have the look of staying power. By 1981, it had been on the market selling at respectable volumes, for a luxury electronic product, for more than five years. There was also Matsushita's VHS format VCR, sold, in fact, in the United States by RCA's Consumer Electronics Division. Both VCRs were high-priced products compared with Selectavision, selling for around $900 retail in 1980. Blank videotapes could be purchased for as little as $20, but prerecorded tapes were much more expensive. A great attraction of VCRs was undoubtedly their recording ability that allowed consumers not only to select their own prerecorded programming, but to take any programming they liked that was available over the airwaves. The opportunity to see favorite sports events that would otherwise have been missed, or to watch "Wall Street Week" at midnight, might not be a mass-market desire, but it certainly appealed to wealthy consumers. The beauty of this feature for manufacturers was that it took the pressure off the need to guess the type of programming consumers would be willing to buy a machine to see. They were buying the ability to record an already familiar type of entertainment fare and there would be few surprises. Other disc players were also on the market in 1981 and appeared to have some chance of success, although again for a well-to-do consumer. North American Philips, using technology derived from its Dutch parent, had teamed up with MCA and Magnavox to make and market an optical video-disc product, Discovision. Several Japanese firms had also announced their intention to produce and sell their own versions of the Philips system (generically known as Laservision), and Pioneer's LaserDisc had appeared in time for the 1980 Christmas buying season. All the optical products were available in very limited quantities selling for more than $750, and their discs were priced at $39 and up. Another videodisc format was under development in Japan, the VHD format disc, product of the combined efforts of Matsushita and its subsidiary, Japan Victor. It was a CED system incompatible with RCA's that used an ungrooved disc. Although it had yet to reach the open market, it was advertised as having the versatility of the optical systems at a price closer to that of the RCA system.

The consumer electronics trade had been hearing for some time that the optical disc technology was technically superior to RCA's. Optical systems were designed to have interactive capabilities and were supposedly indestructible. Priced at levels roughly comparable to magnetic tape recorders, they provided superior access over VCRs to prerecorded programming, for any individual frame on a disc holding an hour of programming could be retrieved through an indexing feature.[8] Because the optical disc system used a laser pickup device coupled with a disc containing optically encoded information embedded beneath a transparent layer of hard plastic, optical discs were supposed to be impervious to normal wear and tear. Consumers had found the reality disappointing, however, for owing to early production problems, the quality of the optical discs on the market had been marred by a tendency of the laminated discs to buckle. Moreover, the two-hour versions of the discs were, for technical reasons, not indexable in the same way as the original hour-long versions.

The RCA sales pitch

RCA VideoDisc presentations in February and March 1981 were calculated to convince the trade of specific advantages the CED technology could offer the consumer. As the only video-player offered under what was believed to be a psychological cutoff of $500, it was the first mass-market product. Competitors predicted falling prices in time, but how low or when was anybody's guess. Selectavision players would be available immediately through thousands of RCA dealers across the country, while several of the competitive systems were only offered in certain cities. The RCA emphasis on simplicity and reliability was meant to point out weaknesses in competing models, while advertising their technological sophistication.

24

Anything involving exotic laser technologies, complicated ser-vomechanisms, and multiple features, it was suggested, was bound to be unreliable. Finally, and perhaps most important of all, RCA stressed the size of its disc selection catalog and the availability of discs through the same vendors who sold the players. Owners of other disc systems were reported to be having trouble getting programs, and prerecorded material for magnetic tape machines was very expensive, around $100 for a full-length movie. RCA's offering of 100 items immediately with the promise of twenty-five additions to the catalog at frequent intervals was expected to be a significant attraction.

Jack Sauter, RCA group vice-president, said at the presenta-tions that market research had indicated that at a price under $500, three million, or 7 percent of all households, would be interested in Selectavision VideoDisc in the first three years. This was a market worthy of the fabled television market, which at the time was selling roughly 15 million units per year. The point was to turn the three million interested households into solid buyers of hardware, and thereby consumers of discs, as soon as possible. Sauter predicted sales of 200,000 players in 1981, rising to 2 million for the entire industry by 1983. Unlike its competitors, RCA would not test the market first or "roll out" gradually. Instead, it would employ its full marketing might to create the Selectavision business. To achieve instant recognition and to stimulate primary demand, the company was launching a major advertising and consumer education campaign, estimated to cost $20 million in the first year. Expensive television commercials had been lined up on all three networks to appear on a "saturation schedule." In the early summer there would be "happenings" at dealerships. Print media ads would appear to provide more detailed in-formation about such questions as "What is it?" "What does it cost?" "How does it work?" and "What can I see?"

At the same time RCA would provide its dealers with the necessary support in training and product supply to ensure that when consumers were ready to buy, dealers had product available and would be prepared to support it. To execute this ambitious plan within a few months would be a monumental task, for a minimum of 5,000 dealers would be needed to create the nationwide network RCA envisioned. Sauter assured his audience, not a few of whom were veterans of past wars in which campaigns had not always gone smoothly, that RCA had carefuly considered all the ramifications of its plan and was prepared to execute it.

What was at stake

RCA in 1981 was still a large, although scarcely still a leading-edge, American electronics company, with a strong presence in its traditional businesses and rather more diversified in service businesses than the average electronics company. Despite the trauma of the 1970s recessions, its sales had grown from less than $3.5 billion in 1970 to $8 billion in 1980. Electronics – consumer, commercial, and government – comprised 40 percent of its sales, broadcasting nearly 20 percent, transportation services – primarily Hertz Corporation – 15 percent, and communications less than 4 percent. Financial services – CIT Financial Corporation – and assorted other businesses, including RCA Records and Coronet Carpets, accounted for the remaining 21 percent. In 1981 RCA ranked 35 on the *"Fortune 500"* list of largest American companies. Its manufacturing plants were scattered from one end of the country·to the other, although it had shed its overseas plants during the 1970s. It had a corporate research center, located in Princeton, New Jersey, satellite research laboratories at several operating sites, and advanced engineering development groups in its various divisions. Its total R&D budget in 1980 was $430.6 million, of which more than half was provided by government and private customers. Corporate research consumed more than a quarter of RCA's total R&D spending.

At the time of its launching, VideoDisc represented more than $200 million of investment for RCA and untold human effort. During the course of its development, it had involved several RCA businesses directly or indirectly. As the expected generator of $7.5 billion in annual retail sales by 1990, it was the legitimate hope for the future of all RCA. The chief institutional protagonists in the program were the Consumer Electronics

26

Division in Indianapolis, which manufactured the players; the Records Division, which produced the videodiscs; and the David Sarnoff Research Center, which not only provided ongoing technical support for the program but was also committed to providing successive generations of upgraded VideoDisc systems.

The Consumer Electronics Division had a long history of innovation in television and had recently recaptured the position of number one domestic supplier in the television industry, having overtaken Zenith for the first time since the mid-1970s. The Division had not welcomed the VideoDisc player wholeheartedly, however; rather, it had fought unsuccessfully to continue development of its own magnetic-tape version of a videoplayer system, and when that fight was lost in 1975 it had looked for outside players to sell. In 1977 it introduced the VHS videocassette system produced by Japan's Matsushita. The Records Division, on the other hand, which had originally taken a lead position in planning for a disc system, had fallen on hard times, with sales having slumped drastically and unexpectedly in 1979. But it was the RCA Laboratories and the related licensing operation, that were the two organizations that had the most to gain from VideoDisc. The Laboratories had acted as institutional champion and entrepreneur throughout the program. When the computer pullout freed up a large chunk of RCA's technical staff, it was the Videodisc project that soaked up and put to good use the talents of the former computer researchers. It was the existence of such a visible new business opportunity that gave public force to the claims that the RCA Laboratories was essential to RCA's long-term future.

In attempting to start a new consumer entertainment business, RCA was taking on what was recognized to be a significant commitment, perhaps even a "bet the company" proposition. Some consequences of failure, like the loss of perhaps 1,000 jobs, could be easily quantified. Less easy to measure would be the possible marring of managerial records, the possible damage to the company's reputation with its dealers. Most important for the long term would be the probable undermining of RCA's technical position and reputa-

27

tion and the effect of this on licensing possibilities for the future.

It might be hard to predict precise financial repercussions, but their magnitude could also be anticipated. The company stood to lose outright hundreds of millions of dollars in investment not recouped and in licensing revenues forgone. Perhaps just as important, other opportunities for growth in other businesses could be starved of capital where they needed it, just as the computer business had been starved in the critical early growth period of the 1950s. Poor financial performance would not only affect such measures of corporate well-being as stock price and bonus, it could even threaten the company's existence by subjecting it to the risk of a takeover. A low stock price could attract the attention of companies that might recognize an opportunity to purchase RCA and break it up for the value of undervalued assets.

But why take such risks, and why do it in such a way that the risks were magnified? At the time, the answer to such questions would probably have hinged on two points: the opportunity was unparalleled, and management believed it was doing well something that it knew how to do. Predictions of a $7 billion business by 1990 implied that as much as 30 to 50 percent of RCA's entire sales revenue could come from the VideoDisc business within a decade. There was a chance to turn back the clock and take back from the Japanese worldwide leadership in consumer electronics. The company had gone much further than most of its competitors to cover all its bases. Market research was encouraging, its product had been tested exhaustively, and its distribution channels for new products had only recently performed splendidly when marketing the VHS videorecorder. To the highly successful people who had been given the responsibility to carry out the program, it seemed only a matter of careful execution of a well-planned campaign. Yet in hindsight another factor was probably decisive, and it requires a longer explanation: the risk of backing out was highest of all.

Taken at face value, the brief description we have given of RCA as a company during the period when VideoDisc was under development may seem to justify the decision to complete the innovation and take it to market. But second thoughts make us probe further. How could a continuing image as an innovative company, and a tarnished image at that, be so important to RCA that it was willing to risk another computer debacle? To understand the matter in those terms we need to go deeper into the company's experience, to examine the place of innovation in the company's history, and to understand the roles that different organizations in RCA's corporate hierarchy played in the innovation process. Historically, one person and one organization had the most to do with RCA's focus on innovation and with the organizational structure that perpetuated that focus. They bore the same name. The man was David Sarnoff, RCA's senior executive from 1930 through 1969, and the organization was the David Sarnoff Research Center.

2

David Sarnoff:
industrial entrepreneur

It was David Sarnoff who had made RCA into an effective context for innovative activity. It is impossible to understand how RCA attempted the task of innovation at any stage of its history without first coming to grips with Sarnoff's pivotal role in the company. Sarnoff's career with RCA and its predecessor company, American Marconi, extended over a period of sixty years, by any standard an extraordinary tenure for someone at the head of a major American corporation.

Sarnoff's style of leadership was not only engraved in the minds of those who worked for him, it was embedded in the structures of the organization. His ambition extended far beyond the confines of his own company, embracing the entire electronics industry, and for many years his drive and acumen matched his ambition.

In a speech entitled "Message to Broadcasters" delivered in Atlantic City in 1947, Sarnoff expressed his vision of what it took to lead in a technology-based industry that was perpetually in a state of renewal:

Let me assure you, my friends, after more than forty years of experience in this field of communications and entertainment, I have never seen any protection in merely standing still. There is no protection except through progress. Nor have I seen these new scientific developments affect older businesses, except favorably, where those who were progressive gave careful thought and study to the possibilities of new inventions and developments for use in their own business.[1]

During his career, Sarnoff had witnessed or played an active part in three industrial transformations. He had seen the early days of wireless transform international communications, he had assisted entertainment radio to emerge from the wireless communications industry, and he was in the process of forcing the birth of commercial television. He had also taken control of RCA and turned it from the subsidiary of the giant corporations, General Electric, Westinghouse, AT&T, and United Fruit, to a pioneering firm with a stake firmly planted in the future.

Sarnoff's early career can be divided in two parts. He spent the first thirteen years from 1907 to 1919 in the infant wireless industry working mainly for American Marconi, a subsidiary of the original British Marconi. During the second part from 1919 to 1931 he rose swiftly through the ranks to the top of the company that succeeded American Marconi, the Radio Corporation of America. The first phase gave him familiarity with the rudiments of radio technology and several years of direct contact with the marketplace; the second gave him a chance to apply what he had learned in a larger industrial arena.

American Marconi

David Sarnoff had found a job in the newly formed wireless industry only seven years after arriving in the United States from Russia in 1900, aged nine, with his family. He was hired as an office boy by the Marconi Wireless Company of America. The Italian-born inventor Guglielmo Marconi had given his first public demonstration of long-distance wireless only a decade earlier, in 1896. Since that time, the enterprise he had founded had become multinational, with transmission stations and small operating subsidiaries in several parts of the world. Yet however farflung its operations, the company was still struggling financially, for when Sarnoff joined it there had never been a profit.

During his time with Marconi, Sarnoff became a skilled telegrapher and an able, though self-taught, engineer. By all accounts, he spent much of his time on the New York and New Jersey waterfronts comparing information about wireless techniques and equipment with other wireless operators. A succession of assignments, both at sea and on shore, broadened him socially and professionally. He soon became active in the

31

fledgling Institute of Radio Engineers where, according to a biographer, a membership of young men much like himself eventually chose him as its president.[2] His IRE membership gave him a strong sense of professional identity and a lifelong ability to communicate with technical experts who were pushing forward the fields of radio and electronics. It also gave him a valuable network of contacts throughout the wireless, then radio industry.

Sarnoff advanced quickly inside the Marconi operation through the ranks of radio inspector, chief radio inspector, and assistant chief engineer, achieving promotion to contract manager in 1914. In the years before World War I, he was known among his superiors for his frequent memoranda suggesting improvements to Marconi operations or equipment. He leveled criticisms at Marconi apparatus compared with competitive offerings, criticisms that were well founded, since Marconi was pursuing the risky course of concentrating on growth and neglecting technology.[3]

As he achieved higher rank, Sarnoff became interested in finding new applications for wireless technology. A memorandum he sent to the Marconi Company's chief engineer, for example, looked at the way wireless might supplant telegraph as the main means of railroad communication. It contained a detailed proposal for equipping freight trains with wireless sets in order to make radio contact between cars.[4]

Another Sarnoff memo from the same period identified what was to turn out to be a far more significant commercial opportunity in applied radio science. Sarnoff called it the "Radio Music Box," a term he may have picked up from his friend A.N. Goldsmith:

I have in mind a plan of development which would make radio "a household utility" in the same sense as the piano or phonograph. The idea is to bring music into the house by wireless. . . . The "Radio Music Box" can be supplied with amplifying tubes and a loudspeaking telephone, all of which can be neatly mounted in one box. The box can be placed on a table in the parlor or living room, the switch set accordingly, and then transmitted music received.[5]

Sarnoff was to develop the idea over the next few years. He suggested that the Marconi Company could derive benefits from such a project in two ways, by manufacturing and selling the "music boxes," and by using the transmission as a form of advertising. The sets would sell at the moderate price of $75, complete with antenna, which, Sarnoff conjectured, if manufactured in quantities of a hundred thousand or so would yield a "handsome profit." He did not conceive of advertising as support for the costs of programming, nor was the "music box" to promote other companies' products. Marconi would provide the programming as a public service, gaining for itself "national and universal attention."

No such new business was destined to see the light of day in the Marconi operation. To people whose careers had been devoted to operating a long-distance maritime communications service, the home radio idea sounded like little more than a gimmick. Besides, American Marconi's vice-president, Edmund Nally, was having a hard enough time reconciling the demands of his British parent company with the needs of his American market without paying attention to wildly speculative propositions. But to Sarnoff, who was in close touch with radio buffs, the idea of entertainment radio was the next logical step. Radio amateurs were already devising forms of experimental equipment, and talk of various ways of broadcasting entertainment for public consumption was a favorite topic of conversation in amateur circles.

Perhaps the most important benefit of Sarnoff's early career with Marconi was exposure to Guglielmo Marconi himself, a model creative systems entrepreneur. As an office boy, Sarnoff had observed Marconi's urbane figure from time to time at first hand; later the two men would become close confederates. Marconi had started his international enterprise by persuading the British Royal Navy in 1899 of the feasibility of long-distance wireless telegraphy for maritime communications.[6] He had parlayed the business he developed, with the Royal Navy as his first customer, into a virtual monopoly in the areas he served by controlling all elements of the wireless system. The Marconi enterprise was a systems business.[7] The Marconi organization formed operating subsidiaries everywhere that wireless communications appeared to have potential for profitable operation. Not only did it manufacture wireless apparatus

33

David Sarnoff and Guglielmo Marconi at RCA's Rocky Point transmitting station in 1933.

and rent packages of equipment and operators to its users but, to secure its leadership, it followed a policy of nonintercommunication with other radio systems. It attempted to control wireless technology by constructing an ironclad patent position to cover all parts of the wireless system that Marconi had not himself invented.

34

Directed research was also part of the plan, for in Britain, Marconi employed a group of researchers whose work was dedicated to continual improvement of the existing wireless system. The flaw in the scheme, and the one that ultimately led to its undoing, was the failure to maintain real technical leadership by keeping ahead of competing developments in wireless research. Marconi paid so much attention to geographical expansion and incremental improvements of his existing technology that he failed to take seriously enough the host of other radio inventors whose efforts were stimulated and focused by his success. Men like Lee deForest and Ernst Alexanderson were not simply improving the existing wireless system, they were inventing around it. The young David Sarnoff had encountered evidence of this problem on the waterfront when, for instance, his wireless cronies told him that the German company Telefunken was supplying the U.S. Navy with wireless apparatus superior to the equipment Marconi had to offer.[8]

The Marconi company awoke to the precariousness of its technical position only shortly before the start of World War I. Not only were the original Marconi patents on the verge of expiration, but a new transmission technology threatened the guts of Marconi's system. In 1916, Marconi opened negotiations with General Electric for exclusive rights to its powerful Alexanderson Alternator, but U.S. entry into the conflict overtook the company. By the time hostilities had ended, circumstances had altered to such an extent that Marconi had irrevocably lost its lead.

Sarnoff's years with American Marconi gave him firsthand experience of the potency of changing technology. Later he was to interpret the lessons of the experience as a cautionary tale. A company had to be willing to risk early obsolescence of its own products, however costly, if it intended to reap the benefits of technological leadership. Many times in his later career Sarnoff expressed this philosophy, as in a speech in 1928 at the Harvard Business School in the headiest days of commercial radio. "No industrial organization devoted to radio could hope to survive," he said then, unless it "travelled with the art." The way to ensure business success in a technology-based business was not only to control all parts of the system, but to keep pushing the state of the technology so that future developments could be channeled in directions beneficial to the leading enterprise.[9]

When the United States entered the war, Sarnoff worked for the navy, as American Marconi, along with all other privately owned long-distance wireless facilities in the country, was taken over intact. Naval control had a positive impact on the American wireless industry, for it cut through the tangle of patents that had restricted technological development and rapid commercialization of wireless before the war. It also brought into the industry the large electrical manufacturers whose mass production facilities were the only available means for satisfying the large military demand for wireless equipment.

Nevertheless, when Secretary of the Navy Josephus Daniels proposed legislation after the war to consolidate all wireless communications under government control, David Sarnoff was the member of the American Marconi operating staff who testified most forcefully against the proposal at the hearings.[10] He was convinced that bureaucratic control of any kind had an inhibiting effect on technological innovation. Speaking before the House Marine and Fisheries Committee, he warned that under naval department control, experts in radio science would not have access to equipment used in the field, and that this would have the effect of slowing down development in the radio art. The importance of early and extensive exposure of researchers to actual operation of equipment in the field was to remain a critical concern of Sarnoff's throughout his career. In the end, powerful antigovernment and antimonopoly sentiment in and outside of Congress killed the proposal to nationalize American long-distance wireless.

Formation of RCA

American Marconi escaped naval control, but it did not escape other control. In 1919, with the active encouragement of key naval officers and the compliance of other parts of the government, General Electric arranged to purchase American Marconi and transform it into a completely American wireless telegraphy company, the Radio Corporation of America – RCA.[11] It was to be jointly owned by General Electric, some American holders of Marconi stock, and by 1921, Westinghouse, AT&T and United Fruit, all companies that held radio-related patents that were important to the international operation and defense of a complete wireless telegraphy system.[12]

The Radio Company, as it was known for many years, had a threefold mission: to wrest control of wireless communications from Britain; to hold, administer, and also expand the radio-related patent pool on behalf of its corporate stockholders; and to act as merchandising agent for whatever radio equipment the parent companies wanted to sell on the open market. GE's Owen D. Young, a financially oriented lawyer and a negotiator experienced in the complexities of electrical systems and public utilities, arranged a unique cross-licensing setup for RCA with its corporate owners. The company would have no manufacturing capability and its independent research and development would be confined largely to test facilities in support of its sales effort. Its key advantage would be that no other company would be able to sell radio tubes or some other kinds of wireless equipment without violating one of RCA's patents, assuming that its patents were upheld in court. Its patent pool contained more than 2,000 patents along with mutual rights for RCA parent companies to future developments in radio. The RCA board consisted of Young as chairman, two officers of the Marconi company representing the original domestic owners, and one officer representing the U.S. Navy. During the decade from 1919 to 1930, when RCA was thus controlled by outside corporate owners, Sarnoff rose from the position of commercial manager to general manager. His superiors, president Edmund Nally and chairman Owen Young, were largely preoccupied with external affairs and were frequently absent overseas. Sarnoff had nearly complete operating control of the company.

In later years, Sarnoff was to foster the notion that he had personally been responsible for creating commercial radio in each of its several aspects, just as Marconi had created commercial wireless. He buttressed this claim by citing his several

"Music Box" memos to superiors at American Marconi and later at GE. But although Sarnoff promoted his idea with unrelenting enthusiasm, he actually found no one who would go along with his scheme at the time. His own authority was severely limited when it came to investing in any form of activity outside the scope of long-distance communications. It was only in late 1920, after two stations had been licensed for regular broadcasting, that Sarnoff was finally able to convince the RCA board to allow him to allocate $2,000 for development and sale of an improved radio receiver equipped with numerous accessories. About the same time he also convinced his superiors to allow him to begin broadcasting on an experimental basis. RCA duly set up WJZ, a broadcasting station jointly owned by RCA and Westinghouse.

The radio manufacturing industry

RCA was ill-prepared to cope with the huge instant demand that the start of scheduled broadcasting stimulated.[13] Young had structured the new company to operate a wireless communications service as a privately owned utility in a field in which there was no domestic competition. Now Sarnoff wanted to use this inappropriately structured organization as a vehicle with which to dominate the entertainment radio business. Moreover, while in theory RCA's commanding patent position in radio entitled it to property rights in all radio equipment sold, both tubes and receiver assemblies, actual market domination proved to be anything but automatic. For several years after RCA's formation, its patent position was under challenge in the courts, and patent violators were immune from prosecution during that period. If RCA intended to dominate the market, it simply had to meet the demand for radios.

The demand turned out to be far larger than anyone had anticipated. Sarnoff had predicted in his early "Music Box" memos that total demand might be one million units selling at $75 each. In actuality, radio sales were $60 million in 1922 alone, $130 million in 1923, and $358 million in 1924. Sarnoff met the demand with the only tools at his disposal. He increased the size of RCA's sales organization from fourteen people in 1921 to a nationwide network of 200 offices in 1922. As a result RCA's sales grew to $11 million in 1922, $22.5 million in 1923, and $50 million in 1924.

Entertainment radio became RCA's largest business by 1922, much larger than the maritime communications business. Sarnoff was rewarded with promotion to the position of vice-president and general manager. His immediate superior, Nally, faced with the sudden transformation of the operation he had headed for years, and still unable to live down his previous association with the British in a now fiercely nationalist company, resigned in 1923 and was succeeded by General James G. Harbord.

Hundreds of firms entered the radio manufacturing business during the first five years. Scores of amateur radio buffs had taken the opportunity to convert their hobbies into businesses. Most made short-term profits with their first generation of receivers and then collapsed at the first sign of a plateau in sales. Of more than 900 companies, nearly 600 shut down before 1927.[14] Changing technology was the most common reason for company failures, for companies often found themselves with stocks of obsolete radio receivers when receiver and tube designs changed.

Even though RCA had a more stable financial base than the rest, RCA's operating arrangements made it quite vulnerable to the problem of technological obsolescence. Because of the fixed merchandising arrangements with GE and Westinghouse, it was unable to control either the costs of its merchandise, the amount or quality of its supply, or the nature of the designs it wanted to sell. Moreover, it had to pay its owner-suppliers a generous 20 percent margin, making it difficult to compete with small garage assemblers. Worst of all was the problem of trying to coordinate with GE and Westinghouse, which were both geared for mass production of relatively mature products. They produced receivers and tubes the way they produced their other products. At Westinghouse, for example, one model of a receiver might be produced in several different plants to several different specifications.

39

As radio technology began to stabilize, design and standardization committees were formed with representatives from both GE and Westinghouse. The first of these, the Tube Committee, was formed in 1924. Writing in the late 1930s, John Warner, head of RCA's Radiotron Division, described the cumbersome arrangement that existed when RCA had to rely on facilities owned by its parent companies:

The Radiotron Standardization Committee was made up of representatives from East Pittsburgh, Cleveland, Schenectady, Bloomfield, and Harrison – two, sometimes three, from each. It met once a month round the circle and attempted to arrive at agreements on tube designs, ratings, characteristics, and even some production problems. It had no direct representation from the receiver divisions so the coordination with them was supposedly handled by the East Pittsburgh and Schenectady tube representatives, and the ideas and needs of the receiver engineers carried to the tube meetings. The main committee carried with it a train of subcommittees and coordination groups intended to handle specific technical items. . . . The loss of time inherent in the inter-company committee method of coordination was a major handicap to progress in engineering, manufacturing, and sale. . . .[15]

Package licensing

With his aspirations for RCA to dominate the industry, Sarnoff was discovering that radio technology, especially in the case of receivers, was too permissive to maintain leadership through mere patent domination. Until the courts declared RCA's patents valid, a process that took several years, it was not even possible to prosecute illegitimate competitors. And when it was possible, the cost of prosecuting so many people was prohibitive.

For a time RCA tried to enforce its patent position where it had the most technical leverage, through its vacuum tube technology, as vacuum tubes involved the sophisticated technology from a production standpoint, and there were fewer competitors. RCA adopted a policy of allocating tubes only to distributors that agreed to handle its entire product line, and a clause was inserted in contracts forbidding distributors to supply unauthorized assemblers. This policy infuriated the independent radio assemblers who complained to Congress of the activities of what was becoming known as the Radio Trust: RCA and its electric company owners. In 1924 the Federal Trade Commission (FTC) launched a four-year investigation into charges that RCA was restraining trade. RCA's standard distributors contract was eventually held to violate the Clayton Anti-Trust Act and RCA's share of the vacuum tube business subsequently fell to less than half of total industry sales.

Once the validity of its patents was established in court, RCA adopted a restrictive form of licensing called "package licensing" as a way of imposing order on the industry. This was to be a major source of revenue to the company until 1958, when package licensing was found to be in violation of antitrust laws. In the beginning, RCA issued licenses to twenty-five large competitors, giving them nonexclusive rights to produce and sell completed tuned radiofrequency receivers. In return for RCA's legal recognition, each licensee not only paid past damages of $1.3 million, but agreed to pay substantial royalties on all future radio sales. At first this amounted to 7.5 percent of the sales value, with a required minimum of $100,000 per year. From $136,000 in 1926, RCA's royalty income jumped to over $3 million in 1927. In 1929 and 1930 RCA's licensing returns hit a ten-year peak of more than $7 million.[16]

The package-licensing policy won no friends for RCA in the industry. Package licenses were eventually extended to smaller enterprises, and fees were reduced; nevertheless, a number of companies were forced out of business during the late 1920s. Perhaps the most important enduring consequence of the policy was that it made it uneconomic for most other companies to do radio-related research, because they could not recoup their investment. This left control of the rate and direction of technological change in the radio industry largely in the hands of RCA. For RCA, the effect was to make licensing fees the major payoff of its research activity. RCA was effectively in the business of selling research.

Sarnoff defended RCA's control of radio technology as its birthright, justified because of its importance to the nation's defense. But he also claimed, and passionately believed, that RCA's control of technology benefited both the radio industry and society at large. RCA's large size and its access to several major research laboratories, in addition to its in-house capability, gave it unparalleled qualifications to coordinate research into all aspects of radio science. RCA was, Sarnoff maintained, collecting license fees and plowing them back into a focused research program that helped the entire industry.

The licensing policy was Sarnoff's first step in constructing a continuing corporate commitment to technology, which was henceforth to characterize RCA's relationship to the rest of the industry. The idea was consistent with favorable public attitudes toward technology in general in the 1920s, but it was also Sarnoff's very personal commitment, and it would endure even when public attitudes towards technology became much more negative during the 1930s.[17]

To Sarnoff, the business executive who promoted the advancement of technology was a breed apart from the ordinary manager whose bureaucratic tendencies and risk-averse behavior he came to abominate. "Other motives than mere economic gain are beginning to influence industrial leadership," he told his audience at the Harvard Business School in 1928:

Men are contending not so much for a share of the public dollar as in the endeavor to develop and perfect those unlimited possibilities of achievement which science is breeding in the laboratory and executive genius exploiting in the promotion offices of modern industrial organizations.... The needs of time will bring forth, perhaps, a new type of executive, trained in a manner not always associated with the requirements of business management.[18]

Diversification in entertainment

Meantime radio sales, which had continued to grow through the 1920s, hurtled upward in the boom years of 1928 and 1929, when sales of radio receivers were 75,000 per week. RCA accounted for $282 million in sales and $31 million in profits out of total industry sales for the two years of $7\frac{1}{2}$ million radios and $1.5 billion in sets and components. The dark side of this spectacular performance, as Sarnoff was all too well aware, was that the demand was soon going to be satiated. With the number of radios in American households approaching 14 million by 1930, radio had achieved mass-market penetration that neither household electricity nor telephone had achieved.

Sarnoff's solution to this threat to RCA was to try to diversify into businesses with better future growth potential, like broadcasting. For a time his tentative moves in this direction were blocked by AT&T, which had joined the group of companies that controlled RCA in order to protect its own wired network from potential threats by wireless.[19] As the developing potential in broadcasting became evident, AT&T insisted on prerogatives that gave it control of transmission technology. Sarnoff could experiment with broadcasting if he chose, but AT&T would not allow RCA to use telephone lines to link its stations, and RCA's broadcasting had to be done as a public service. Meanwhile, AT&T, which had inaugurated toll broadcasting in 1922, expanded its network of stations rapidly. In March 1925, it broadcast President Coolidge's inauguration ceremony over 22 stations coast to coast, reaching an estimated 18 million listeners. On the same occasion, RCA could link up only four stations reaching 5 million listeners; it had to use inferior Western Union telegraph lines and could sell no advertising.

AT&T agreed in 1926 to resolve the serious conflicts it was having with members of the Radio Trust over the broadcasting issue. In May 1926, RCA purchased AT&T's entire broadcast network for $1 million. The Telephone Company thus withdrew from the radio industry altogether, divesting its RCA stock holdings at the same time. The following September, RCA formed the National Broadcasting Company held jointly with GE and Westinghouse. Under the NBC umbrella, RCA consolidated its own chain of stations with those it had acquired from AT&T to form two networks, the red and the blue. NBC would have a monopoly of network broadcasting until a year later when CBS formed its rival network.

This was the beginning of unquestioned RCA domination in its related industries. A few years later Sarnoff took advantage of the glamour status of RCA's stock to acquire a number of companies in the entertainment business. In 1929 he purchased Victor Talking Machine together with its enduring trademark, the dog "Nipper" listening to "His Master's Voice." Victor had suffered severe inroads on its business from radio, and it had been unsuccessful in its own attempt to enter radio manufacturing. At the same time RCA entered the talking picture business by commercializing the Photophone system of sound recording that had been developed at GE Laboratories. This in turn led to the formation of Radio Keith Orpheum, of which RCA owned a minor share.

Sarnoff was assembling for RCA the integrated business systems structure that would characterize the company for many decades. He stressed the complementary nature of the entertainment businesses he had acquired, adding that diversification was intended to provide RCA with security in a saturated market, and the various pieces of the business would be operated in a complementary fashion. The strategy differentiated RCA from its leading competitors in radio manufacturing, which would ride out the Depression by emphasizing a particular specialty in radio production, design, or features. RCA's approach to diversification was not just a defensive posture. It gave RCA such breadth of operation that almost no radio-related opportunity its own research staff or that of one of its parent companies could produce would in theory fail to find a home in one of RCA's operations.

The acquisition of Victor Talking Machine did more for RCA than to add to its line of entertainment products. It formed the cornerstone of Sarnoff's plan to gain independence for RCA from its electric company owners.[20] Victor owned extensive manufacturing facilities in Camden, New Jersey, complete with R&D facilities where it had made both phonographs and radios. Victor also brought with it important assets for the entertainment side of the business, for it had a stable of recording stars that RCA inherited.

In 1930 the Justice Department filed suit (*United States* vs. *Radio Corporation of America et al.*) against all parties in the so-called Radio Trust, charging "unlawful combination and conspiracy in restraint of trade in both domestic and foreign commerce."[21] The defendants were said to be able to "dictate by agreement among themselves the terms upon which any competitor or potential competitor" could use any of the 4,000 patents RCA had by then amassed. When the action was still in the wind, David Sarnoff convinced RCA's corporate owners to allow him to turn RCA into a fully integrated and self-contained operation, manufacturing its own tubes and receivers, and controlling its own research. Under the new arrangement, Sarnoff became RCA's executive vice-president. He then spent several years consolidating and rationalizing operations into a holding company structure. RCA absorbed manufacturing plants formerly owned by GE and Westinghouse. GE's Harrison, New Jersey, plant became RCA Radiotron; Westinghouse's lamp plant gave RCA mid-western manufacturing capacity in Indianapolis; and Victor became the RCA Victor Company, which produced and marketed home and industrial equipment. Since Sarnoff's ultimate ambition was to free RCA from anything that interfered with its core entertainment radio business, he even tried to sell the communications business to ITT, but the federal government blocked the move on antitrust grounds.

The suit might have ended in RCA's disbanding, but instead a consent decree in 1931 provided that GE and Westinghouse divest their RCA stock and agree not to compete in the radio business until RCA could be independently established. The settlement left the crucial cross-licensing agreement intact, and with it RCA's right to continue to share in further radio-related developments in technology that might be produced by any of the great electric companies' laboratories. By the mid-1930s, RCA was structured as a holding company, with operations including two broadcasting networks, an international communications service, manufacturing of components and final assemblies, and a unified R&D organization embracing several major locations. The company grossed over $100 million in 1936 with profits after tax of more than $6 million on a fixed asset base of $38 million.

Sarnoff, as RCA president, publicly lamented the hardships RCA faced at being cast adrift from its owners at a very bad time for the economy, but privately he was elated at the outcome. In later years he was to portray RCA's separation from its owners as an emancipation. Independent operations for RCA meant personal independence for Sarnoff himself and freedom from all the trappings of large company operation that had so limited RCA's flexibility. For the rest of his lengthy career David Sarnoff was to express an abiding distaste for bureaucracy in all its forms – committees, corporate staffs, formalized planning procedures, and organization charts were all objects of scorn at one time or another. Even after RCA had grown much larger, Sarnoff would continue to proclaim that RCA was "a company of men, not of charts."

In the space of one decade Sarnoff had assumed control of a company created for the purpose of operating an international wireless telegraphy system and had transformed it into the self-appointed leader of the new entertainment radio industry. During the 1930s, he put such overwhelming emphasis on technological leadership that *Fortune* magazine referred to his "missionary approach to the science of electronics."[22] Writing in the RCA Annual Reports, Sarnoff claimed technological leadership of the entire developing field of electronics as the founder's responsibility. RCA would maintain its broad coverage of all phases of radio while extending its activities to "other allied electronic arts."

To transform a large, well-endowed, but cumbersome, organization into a creative climate for technology-based innovation was a task that required leadership. Sarnoff led by publicizing his disregard for formal routines and barriers, and by keeping the RCA organization off balance, personal, and fluid, often to the discomfort of the new generation of managers. His contempt for much that was formally managerial kept RCA from developing the kinds of systems that were needed for a larger company to become a highly profitable enterprise, and his behavior, which grew increasingly autocratic as time went on, discouraged the development of strong managerial personalities under him. In a sense, the only replacement for his own entrepreneurial role that he was ever to regard with enthusiasm was his beloved RCA Laboratories.

The critical thing about Sarnoff's particular vision was his ability to relate to technology as an industrial force, and to technologists as creative people, without being himself a technocrat. From his early days as a wireless operator, he had learned to regard technology as the chief dynamic element in industrial life. He understood fully the risks that it posed – the swift eclipse, sometimes the destruction of businesses, and the possible dislocation of whole industries. But he also believed that technology could be a controllable asset. Given an organization with the right set of talents and properties – scientifically trained researchers, inventive engineers, adequate financing, and market power – he believed that technological change could be induced, channeled, and contained.

3

Research as prime mover

David Sarnoff marked the occasion of his forty-fifth anniversary in radio in September 1951, with a ceremony at the RCA Laboratories in Princeton, New Jersey. Less than a decade after the research center's founding, Sarnoff renamed it the David Sarnoff Research Center. The gesture was significant in two senses: it indicated Sarnoff's extraordinary degree of personal identification and involvement with RCA's research community and its activities, as well as the beginning of a change in his role in RCA that would gradually work itself out during the next decade.

"The General," as he was universally known after World War II,[1] never gave up his role as RCA's innovative leader, but he institutionalized part of it by creating a corporate research organization to which he gradually turned over many responsibilities associated with his leadership. As a consequence, the RCA research community underwent profound changes in its relationship with the rest of the company and with the industry it had been established to serve.

By the early 1950s, the RCA research center was one of the largest and most respected corporate research organizations in the United States. Sarnoff boasted that it was the "largest radio electronics laboratory in the world." Electronics, a term that had barely been used before World War II, had replaced "radio art" as the basis for the industry, and the scope of the research that pertained to the field had expanded considerably. To maintain mastery of every facet of electronics research was an ambitious task, but it was indeed an "all-electronics research focus" that Sarnoff asked of his corporate research center.

Sarnoff was a familiar figure at the Laboratories during its first decade. He made weekly visits during the height of the color television activity during the late 1940s and early 1950s. It was his practice on those occasions to dine with the leading scientists, drawing out of them in animated informal conversations an assessment of their progress, and assuring them of his confidence. Seldom had a group of researchers employed in a large corporate research center had such close contact with a chief executive.

The speech Sarnoff delivered at his anniversary celebration in 1951 has been best remembered for his flamboyant request for three anniversary presents to be developed by the Laboratories in time for his fiftieth anniversary, five years later. Less often quoted is the passage in his speech in which he gave researchers his personal view of their mission and of the role that scientific research had come to play at RCA since its integration into the life of the company twenty years earlier.

In RCA we do not fear or resist change. The ghost of obsolescence that some folks see stalking around the corner of their industry does not frighten us. To those who believe, as we do, in research, invention and pioneering, obsolescence often means progress rather than decay. Instead of a wicked ghost that threatens extinction, we see a beneficent wraith, whose proddings stimulate opportunity, advance prosperity and raise the standards of living. Let the Chairman and the President and the Commercial Vice Presidents worry about obsolescence. You keep on researching and inventing.[2]

Evolution of the research community

When RCA was founded, the only activity that could have been termed research consisted of two people housed in a tent at a spot near Riverhead, Long Island, conducting experiments in radio transmission and reception. For several years after radio became a business for RCA, the company purchased much of its supporting R&D from outside sources. It contracted with A.N. Goldsmith, a professor at the City College of New York and a close personal friend of David Sarnoff's, to do sales-support testing in his electrical engineering laboratory.

In 1924, RCA hired Goldsmith and his staff on a more formal basis to set up the RCA Technical and Test Department at Van Cortlandt Park, New York. For a company that had nominal access to several of the most impressive industrial laboratories worldwide during the 1920s, such an arrangement might have seemed an act of absurd redundancy. But RCA needed a facility of its own to provide ready and convenient access to work done on its behalf. R&D in support of radio was then a very low priority to GE and Westinghouse, which had other bigger fish to fry. In addition to its original main responsibilities for testing and modifying equipment supplied by GE and Westinghouse, the Van Cortlandt Park facility soon added side investigations into acoustical studies, circuitry problems, sound motion picture equipment, and later television.

As surveyed by the National Research Council (NRC) in 1927, RCA's in-house research capability then consisted of Alfred N. Goldsmith, three physicists, five engineers, six assistants and mechanics, and other supporting staff, for a total of seventy full-time employees. The group devoted half its time to researching radio receiving apparatus and half to testing equipment. Small though it was, Van Cortlandt Park served as a breeding ground for RCA executives and became the backbone of the strong technical community that was to dominate RCA for at least thirty years.

Technical assistance for licensing

Licensing support, the first major RCA research-related activity, was influential in defining the later character of the RCA research organization. Licensing became a long-standing priority of RCA's research program and a major generator of revenues. When RCA began its policy of technology-sharing through licensing in 1927, Van Cortlandt Park undertook to provide the technical assistance that RCA's licensees required to support the technology they had purchased. In 1930, when corporate RCA integrated other operating functions, it reorganized the research facilities, and licensee assistance went to a separate RCA License Laboratory in New York City. The License Laboratory served as a counseling service, a testing facility, an advanced development organization and an engineering facility. Its most important role was to disseminate

RCA's advances in the radio art to its licensees and to serve as a collection point where field information could be gathered in aid of further development. It held clinics, issued bulletins and pamphlets, systematized measurement procedures, and developed many new testing devices. It also allowed licensees to share information with each other and provided expert trouble-shooting for the industry. Had things developed differently, with manufacturing receiving R&D support first, RCA's entire research community would almost certainly have been different in character.

Effect of consolidation

The manufacturing facilities that RCA took over from GE and Westinghouse in 1930 came equipped with their own research operations. RCA consolidated its communications researchers with the newly acquired R&D forces in two separate locations. One was the former GE Electric Tube Plant in Harrison, New Jersey, and the other, the former Victor Talking Machine Company facility in Camden, New Jersey. Both organizations were placed under a new research director, Elmer Engstrom.

It was difficult enough for RCA to consolidate and rationalize new manufacturing facilities, but merging research groups whose work involved a high degree of personal interaction and cooperation in a relatively informal environment, was an even more sensitive matter. Each group brought its own technical preferences, its own particular style of research management. In theory, the multiplicity of technical approaches was a great asset for RCA, especially in view of the new product work it was taking over from GE and Westinghouse. It did make possible the systems approach to research that eventually characterized RCA's particular strength in electronics. But focusing and coordinating the work took time and tact.

By the end of the 1930s, research at Harrison's RCA Radiotron employed 210 people working on the fundamentals of vacuum tubes, with the objective of developing high-performance tubes, as well as on basic materials research. Some thirty-four scientists and eighty-four engineers were

51

members of the scientific research staff, while the rest were technicians. For the prewar era, it was a high proportion of scientists. At RCA Victor, there were only twenty scientists with 319 engineers in a total complement of 604 people housed in three different buildings. Common early experiences in Harrison and Camden formed strong bonds that developed into networks throughout the corporation after World War II. These networks served as channels of communication and often led to enduring political alliances that were sometimes reflected in technical choices.

The challenge of television

Television was the first project to take full advantage of RCA's consolidated research capability. The two forms of television that RCA pioneered, black and white, and later, color, were not only innovations for which RCA is best known, but also served as yardsticks within the organization by which all later innovations were measured.[3]

Sarnoff singled out television in 1923, as the ideal new technology-based business for RCA to pursue. Writing in the 1923 RCA Annual Report, he predicted that television would be the next major development of the radio art after point-to-mass (then the term for broadcast) entertainment radio. Sarnoff was an early promoter of video communication and perhaps the first nontechnologist to back an all-electronic approach.

Three different strands of television research were proceeding independently during the 1920s at Van Cortlandt Park, GE, and Westinghouse. Van Cortlandt Park set up an experimental television station with FCC approval, while GE's Ernst Alexanderson was doing experimental broadcasting for "moving pictures by radio." Both projects were pursuing mechancial approaches, using a rotating disc to break down the image into a high-speed scanning sequence. However, Vladimir Zworykin at Westinghouse was trying an electronic approach with a device called the iconoscope. In 1928, hearing of Zworykin's iconoscope, Sarnoff agreed to fund this research using RCA money even though the project still formally belonged to Westinghouse.

In 1930 all three projects came together in Camden, with instructions to cooperate toward the common goal of a practical television system. The first phase of the newly consolidated research program was an attempt to merge the best elements of each approach. It produced a hybrid system using a mechanical scanning and transmitting system with an electronic receiver. When Zworykin demonstrated his iconoscope in 1933, it moved all-electronic television into the realm of commercial possibility. By scanning a picture electronically, the iconoscope made it possible to do away with the previous hybrid aspects of the system.

When Sarnoff had asked Zworykin in 1928 how much it would take to produce a commercial television system, his answer was four men and $100,000. Of course this was a vast underestimate. RCA was to invest some $9 to $10 million before television reached acceptable entertainment quality, and another $4 million before the company actually began to realize profits. Several other companies were also to invest millions in television, though individually smaller sums than RCA.

The difference between predicted and actual cost had much to do with Sarnoff's different idea of commercialization. Zworykin assumed a free-market approach in which early introduction of individual components would induce the remaining pieces to fall into place. Philo Farnsworth, for example, was known to be working on a key element of electronic television, a form of cathode ray camera called the image dissector. But Sarnoff rejected the free-market approach to television systems innovation in favor of the approach that Marconi had used to commercialize wireless communication. Rather than market television sets as high-priced curiosities, giving every television inventor a piece of the business, he chose to wait until RCA could install a complete television system. While development and field testing were going on, effort could also be directed at improving the production process and paving the way for industrywide acceptance, albeit perhaps reluctant, of television.

Sarnoff's substantial investment in television was particularly striking because it occurred in the Depression era when sales were down. Beginning in 1935, RCA mounted an

53

extensive program of system field testing in New York City. Among other things, this involved building a television transmitting station atop the Empire State Building. The New York field test employed a large group of technical experts and many extra operating people. RCA plant and equipment were allocated to manufacture receiving and transmitting apparatus and special programs were prepared for transmission. At the same time, other substantial expenditures were involved, including an increase in RCA's patent department activity in order to obtain strong patent protection for television and to conduct patent interference proceedings.

Sarnoff took a personal interest in the progress of television development during the field test period. Charles Jolliffe, who joined RCA as chief engineer of the RCA Manufacturing Company, recalled that his relationship with Sarnoff was unique. "We didn't work with Sarnoff in the normal Boss–Employee relationship; it was as if he became one of the group in those early stages...." Even men who were junior on the project felt Sarnoff's personal interest and were intensely affected by it. One young television engineer on the project recalled years later:

> The General used to come down to Camden about once every six months to see what we had done. He would stand under those terrifically hot lights in the studio, perspiration pouring from him, and say: "Boys, it's remarkable what you've accomplished in the last six months!" ... Sometimes we had and sometimes we hadn't, but you have no idea what that did for our morale.[4]

Sarnoff yielded to no one in his determination to make RCA the company that decided the shape of the evolving radio industry, and the direction radio-related technology should take. To achieve successful commercialization of television, he had to manage a regulatory environment that was not pro-RCA. FM radio was a serious problem, as much of the rest of the radio industry was pushing adoption of this much less radical change that promised to yield substantial performance improvements in entertainment radio. FM's chief promoter, Edwin Armstrong, was an old friend of Sarnoff's, but when it became clear that a commercialized FM system would occupy the same VHF area of the radio spectrum that RCA wanted to use for television transmission, Sarnoff used his considerable clout to block further FM development by persuading the FCC to reserve the VHF portion of the spectrum for television.

There was another serious regulatory obstacle as well. The lock-and-key nature of television transmission and reception required industrywide agreement on a standard if full commercialization were to take place. Whereas the FCC's role in radio was to allocate the spectrum, it had to approve more specific standards for television. Some members of the industry complained that RCA had too much influence over the standard that was proposed to the FCC by the Radio Manufacturers Association. Sarnoff tried unsuccessfully to force acceptance of the standard by commencing regularly scheduled broadcasting at the New York World's Fair in 1939 and by marketing a limited number of television receivers before FCC hearings were due to begin. When the FCC tried to block premature operation, Sarnoff took his case before a Senate investigating committee and charged that the FCC had behaved in a dictatorial and bureaucratic manner. The technical issues that divided the industry were resolved by the National Television Standards Committee (NTSC) established by the FCC under Walter Baker of General Electric. The NTSC standard was a stiffer version of the proposed Radio Manufacturers Association standard that RCA had advocated, but it was essentially RCA's approach. World War II suspended all further progress toward commercial television while radio firms turned their full attention to defense. The prewar NTSC standards continued unchanged after the war even though war-related research made considerable contributions to the state of television technology.

Support for research

During the early 1930s, while RCA's status as a company remained unclear, research at RCA was funded and controlled largely by the manufacturing divisions. Sales were down drastically from the highs of the late 1920s, reinvestment in production facilities and their consolidation was an urgent and costly priority, and RCA's operating managers were not enthusiastic about funding longer-term research.[5]

The lack of operating support for research and the uncertainty it engendered in the research community would almost certainly have killed longer-term projects like television if Sarnoff had not decided in 1934 to allocate RCA corporate funds to a unified RCA research program. A large portion of corporate R&D funds came from royalties assessed from RCA licensees, and RCA divisions paid equivalent assessments. Sarnoff chose Otto Schairer, whose strong commitment to R&D was well-known, to be in charge of coordinating R&D with the patent department. Schairer was expected to focus research away from existing business and toward leading-edge projects that could be licensed or that could provide long-term opportunities for new businesses within RCA, and these priorities amounted to the first mission that corporate research had at RCA.

RCA's first corporate research budget totaled $880,000, of which $500,000 went to Victor in Camden, $240,000 to Radiotron in Harrison, and $140,000 to RCA Communications Research in Long Island.[6] Central funding not only stabilized the research community's source of support and level of effort, but it also gave the RCA corporate office a chance to control the areas to which resources were allocated.

The new source of funding was only a beginning of the kind of corporate research program that Schairer and Engstrom, who reported to him, both favored. RCA still lacked a formal general, not product-related, research program. Facilities were still physically dispersed and researchers were still expected to perform manufacturing support functions.

The inauguration of corporate research at RCA during the Depression turned out to be especially opportune, for it came at a time when many other companies had cut back their research budgets, laid off researchers, and in some cases closed facilities altogether. Good researchers were looking for jobs. Sarnoff's support for research under the circumstances was viewed inside and outside the company as an extraordinary commitment at a time when all sections of RCA were making major sacrifices. Interviewed years later, Sarnoff remembered

David Sarnoff displays his skill with the radio telegraph key by tapping out a message from his office in the RCA Building, Radio City, New York, in October 1936.

that during the Depression "we cut costs, we cut salaries, we cut everything but research while the storm was going on."[7] His commitment earned him and his company the undying personal loyalty of many talented researchers who had seen their colleagues laid off at other companies.

As the research effort at RCA gathered momentum during the late 1930s, RCA research managers tried desperately to convince Sarnoff that the company needed a separate research facility, removed from the encroachments of the manufacturing environment and similar to the prestigious Bell Laboratories and General Electric Laboratories, which had developed most of the radio patents then controlled by RCA. The opportunity came with the 1940 Lend-Lease Act, for both RCA's research

57

and its manufacturing facilities had to be expanded quickly to accommodate the sudden surge in government defense contracting. Orders for RCA government research contracts jumped from $100,000 to $700,000 in just three months in 1940. Early the next year Sarnoff consented to the purchase of a large tract of land in Princeton, New Jersey, and the building of a modern research facility there. The plan had the twin advantages of freeing up space for manufacturing at Camden and Harrison and of improving security for classified research.

Research became a separate department called RCA Laboratories, "a service of the Radio Corporation of America," in March 1941, even before the special laboratories building was completed. The new department had responsiblity for "all research, original development and patent and licensing activities of the Corporation and its associated companies," and financial control over all of RCA's research work. It was to allocate funds to other RCA companies "only for such original development work as can be effectively conducted by them under the direction of the laboratories."[8] Corporate resources would form only part of the R&D budgets funded by the individual parts of the company, but the new arrangement allowed the RCA corporate organization to coordinate what was done where.

The Princeton location was equidistant from Camden and Harrison, and within easy reach of corporate headquarters in New York City and the setting, with its many acres of land and its rural character, was meant to simulate the atmosphere of a university campus. Close ties were established between the Laboratories and the university.

As a result of wartime expansion and the addition of numerous scientific specialists, the RCA research staff became one of the top groups in the United States working on tube design, high-frequency techniques, electron optics, acoustics and luminescent materials. Highly specialized and costly equipment purchased partially at government expense gave RCA researchers the capability to pursue any area of advanced electronics research on a self-contained basis. Urgency and secrecy were paramount conditions of the work. General Harbord, RCA's chairman, speaking to a small group of guests gathered for the Laboratories opening in 1941, announced that the facility was to be an important part of the national defense. "It is to be considered as a fort," he said.[9]

Defense work soon absorbed most of the research staff. During the war RCA became the fourth largest recipient of contracts from the Office of Scientific Research and Development.[10] RCA's pioneering work on radar and high-frequency vacuum tubes made it the obvious source for engineers and scientists to participate in top priority projects such as radar, sonar, navigation systems, and electron optics. For years at a time, RCA researchers had the heady experience of working with large project teams that combined research engineers and scientists from universities with other industrial research laboratories all over the country. Some RCA researchers field tested their devices under combat conditions, while others served as government technical consultants and observers, and as members of the planning task forces in the Office of Scientific Research and Development.

Television comes into its own

Television technology benefited from the five-year hiatus imposed by World War II. Defense-related research into television led to the replacement of the iconoscope with the much more sensitive orthicon that became the basis for postwar camera technology. Other wartime developments that benefited television included the high-power vacuum tube, other special tubes as display devices, mass production techniques for cathode ray tubes, and better network relay and microwave techniques.

The war also contributed immeasurably to production technology. Had electronic television receivers been sold in the mid-1930s, they would have contained handmade cathode ray tubes and would have been priced at between $500 and $1,000. When they appeared after the war they were mass-produced and sold at less than $500 per set, for roughly 30 percent of the cost of a set was the large, funnel-shaped picture tube. Toward the end of the war, RCA acquired a fully mechanized tube

59

manufacturing facility at Lancaster, Pennsylvania, from the government. Sarnoff bought the plant over the objections of his senior manufacturing executives, who, like many others in the radio industry, were content to produce radios. They feared that television demand would not justify the investment.

Aware of this in-company resistance, Sarnoff did not risk letting television be commercialized by the existing RCA leadership, and he also took the precaution of bypassing some of the company's most important interest groups. Insisting on immediate introduction of black and white television, Sarnoff appointed Frank Folsom, a prewar mass merchandiser from Montgomery Ward, as head of RCA Victor. With Folsom's aggressive leadership RCA introduced its mass-market version of the black and white television receiver, the 630 TS, at $375, a year after the end of World War II. Despite the objections of its dealers, RCA insisted that each receiver was sold with a service contract that provided for installation and maintenance by RCA's service company, rather than by the local dealers. To complete its integrated system approach, RCA staffed the service company with 2,200 ex-servicemen who had received electronics training.

In keeping with its practice of technology sharing, RCA involved its competitors in television manufacture and sales as quickly as possible. Soon after introduction of the 630 TS, the company held industry seminars, adding manufacturing know-how to the package of television patents it was making available. The objective was to encourage manufacturers such as Emerson and GE that had done little television research of their own, to market their own branded sets equipped with RCA picture tubes.

On the market in time to benefit from postwar consumer demand, television sales climbed even faster than radio sales had twenty years earlier. In 1947, RCA sold $40 million worth of television-related goods, more than the rest of the industry combined. In 1948, it still had one-third of the market and was turning out about 2,500 sets per week at each of its plants, in Camden and Indianapolis. When manufacturing sales began to level off during the early 1950s, RCA's NBC network, which had taken a $3 million loss in its early television operation, began to make a handsome profit of its own from television broadcasting.

The advent of color

In 1955 *Fortune* called color television a "monumental achievement embodying more research and engineering at the time of its debut than any other product offered to the public."[11] This technical triumph for the David Sarnoff Research Center was nevertheless little short of a commercial disaster for RCA until seven years after its market introduction. The successes and the problems RCA had with color television reflected the changing structure of its technical community and its relationship to the industry in the postwar period.

Research on color television began immediately after the war. Charles B. Jolliffe, RCA's head of the Research Laboratories at the time, assigned color television the highest priority because it seemed to be ideal work for the Laboratories to pursue. It was sufficiently large in scope and complexity to justify retaining the impressive collection of scientific and engineering talent that the Laboratories had assembled during the war. Also, since many of the researchers had been working on related projects under defense contracts, it seemed to be the kind of project that would make the transition to commercial end-product research relatively painless.[12]

The research took on a sense of urgency when CBS petitioned the FCC to adopt its field sequential color system, developed under the leadership of its research head, Peter Goldmark, before the war. The running battle that ensued with CBS made the color research program a different experience from that of black and white television. Unlike prewar challengers, including CBS, postwar CBS was a systems competitor. By acquiring a tube manufacturer, Hytron, and by reorganizing into a six-part divisional structure that included radio, television, records, tubes, sets, and research, CBS had achieved the capability of carrying out broad systems innovations in the style of RCA.

The CBS proposal to the FCC was a partially mechanical system that involved spinning color wheels in front of both

61

camera lens and receiver. It was not compatible with the black and white system that RCA championed, and it appealed to promoters of FM because it located color television in the UHF range of the spectrum.

RCA based its case on compatibility between its color and black and white systems, both using the NTSC standard. Sarnoff also made much of what he claimed was the inherent superiority of an all-electronic television system, on the grounds that mechanical technology had far more limited potential. RCA proposed to crowd the color signal into the same channel space in the VHF part of the spectrum that the FCC had allocated to black and white television. But the system that Sarnoff proposed to the FCC in 1947 was still very much in the concept stage. Nevertheless, the same year after a "crash" research program, RCA demonstrated to the FCC a crude, highly unstable, but all-electronic system, using three separate coordinated color tubes. Pointing to flaws in the CBS proposal, RCA convinced the FCC to deny the CBS petition.

Three years later, however, CBS sought FCC approval for a much improved version of its "field sequential system" modified to fit into the VHF range. The picture quality it demonstrated was excellent, greatly superior to that of RCA's system, still in the early stages of development.

For an entire year after the first news of an improved CBS system, the RCA television research team endured what was later described as "an exhausting ordeal during which the RCA teams were probably subjected to heavier pressure than any industrial research group had ever before known in peacetime." Much of the systems work had to be done near the FCC in Washington D.C. It was, Charles Jolliffe noted, "like doing research in a goldfish bowl."[13]

In April 1950, RCA displayed the results of its effort. It was a disaster of legendary proportions. Even Sarnoff admitted that the monkeys were green and the bananas blue. The single tricolor kinescope that RCA had used for its dot-sequential color system was not ready, and the results were predictably poor. Citing RCA for poor color fidelity, misregistration, undesirable dot structure, lack of brightness, and complexity of equipment, the FCC in 1951 ruled in favor of CBS.

At the time much of the industry saw this FCC decision as perverse. Not only was RCA's electronics system obviously improving rapidly, but by 1950 a large base of black and white sets was in place throughout the country. Because the CBS color system, unlike the RCA proposal, was incompatible with existing black and white standards, periods of color transmission on the new CBS standard would simply blank out black and white reception. Sarnoff, moreover, refused to concede defeat. RCA filed suit in November 1950 against the FCC in the federal courts, charging that the failure to consider the compatibility problem made the FCC's ruling illegal. The case eventually reached the Supreme Court which concurred with lower courts in upholding the FCC's ruling in favor of CBS.

Meanwhile Sarnoff rallied his research and engineering teams and redoubled RCA's efforts to improve the all-electronic system for color. Major improvements were made to the RCA-based system in the 1950s through work not only in the RCA technical community but also by researchers at Hazeltine.[14] Rex Isom, an engineer at RCA's Camden television plant, who later became chief engineer at Indianapolis, vividly recalled Sarnoff's actions immediately after the FCC delivered its verdict. Summoning the members of the color project to a large meeting, Sarnoff congratulated the group as a whole on the remarkable progress they had made and promised them that he had no intention of giving up the fight for the RCA standard. Forming a lengthy receiving line and calling each man by name, he presented all members of the team with envelopes containing sizable bonus checks. "It was," said one recipient later, "the largest single check I ever received from RCA."[15]

The Korean War saved CBS from almost certain embarrassment, for it had scarcely begun to manufacture experimental color receivers and to do trial programming of color before the U.S. government put a lid on the use of electronic material during the war. By 1950 there were 9 million monochrome sets in the field, and 12 million in mid-1951, so that the compatibility issue had become a critical concern.

The FCC set up a second NTSC in June 1951 along lines similar to the first prewar committee. Again it was headed by

David Sarnoff leaps for joy upon being informed on December 17, 1953, that the FCC has approved the standards for compatible color television.

GE's Walter Baker. After two years of work involving 200 engineers from ninety-one companies in the industry, the committee produced proposals for a television system that were compatible with, though not identical to, the system RCA had proposed in 1949.

FCC approval of the second standard came in December 1953. Without delay, RCA ran enormous advertisements, signed by David Sarnoff and Frank Folsom, claiming complete victory for RCA in color television, and making no mention of the contributions made by other companies. This outrageous gesture infuriated RCA's competitors, for one of the biggest obstacles to agreement had been the unwillingness of industry members to concede to RCA the same power to control color television patents as it had to control patents relating to radio and black and white television. It was widely believed that Sarnoff's insistence on speedy commercialization of color stemmed from a wish to replenish the RCA licensing base, since its large collection of original radio-purpose patents was due to expire in 1954. Another motivation was certainly the wish to begin recouping the $65 million RCA had invested in the color system.

The task of transferring receiver technology from the Laboratories into production fell to the Systems Research Laboratory under George Brown's leadership. The all-out effort was organized along lines similar to those of the wartime interdisciplinary projects. The color project was authorized to draft support from any specialist or support service it needed. The complete commitment that the project had from the top of the corporation was seen by the technical staff as the right way to implement a transfer.

Commercialized color broadcasting began in January 1954. RCA marketed its color receivers under the slogan "Big Color Is Here" at $900 to $1,000 per set. Other manufacturers' offerings ranged from $695 to $1,100. An obligatory service contract added $100 to $150. Early sales were so poor – a total of 50,000 sets for all manufacturers – that GE, CBS, and Zenith all withdrew their color models from the market.

It did not pay for RCA to alienate the rest of the industry. The buying public and the industry took seven years to decide that color was ready for them and that they were ready for it. While competitors enjoyed the proceeds from strong black and white sales, RCA bore the entire burden of keeping the color system alive. The company's integrated structure had contributed immensely to its profits from monochrome television

65

because all parts of the company benefited, but the same structure was now a liability, for all parts suffered. Unable to attract advertising support for color, NBC paid a substantial premium to broadcast color programming; the RCA manufacturing organizations carried large unabsorbed overheads for color tooling; and the drain on finances robbed other new enterprises, such as computer development, of necessary capital.

The $10 million that the RCA Laboratories alone was said to have invested in color had yielded an impressive device from a scientific point of view, but from the standpoints of production and performance it left much to be desired. The RCA shadow-mask picture tube was so difficult to manufacture that it accounted for $300 of the full cost of the receiver. It required precision assembly techniques, for instance, to line up 350,000 pinpoint holes over one million colored phosphor dots. Moreover, RCA sets were so hard to keep operating reliably in the home environment that a GE head of research once joked, "If you have a color set you've also got to have an engineer living in the house." The color set picture was not as bright as black and white and viewers had to watch it in subdued light. A significant commercial problem was that the picture tended to degrade when transmitted over long distances.

RCA was a victim of the classic "chicken and egg" problem that threatens any would-be systems innovator, and it no longer had leverage over the rest of the industry to bring it along. A few other manufacturers adopted the RCA kinescope, but major holdouts, such as GE and CBS, kept making well-publicized efforts to produce a cheaper and better alternative to the shadow mask. As long as they believed cheaper alternatives to be in the offing, consumers held off, and advertisers refused to sponsor color programming until the color set owner base was large enough to justify the extra cost. Zenith finally broke the industry boycott of color in 1961 as monochrome sales fell off. By 1962 a million color sets were in use, at an average price of $600.

For the RCA Laboratories the color television experience was both a model of what could be done with all-out commitment and a reminder of the considerable costs to a research organization of conducting such an effort. The crash program had demonstrated that, with top management backing and a clear sense of priorities, the impossible could be achieved. But RCA's research staff was changing. The postwar research staff, with its growing number of discipline-oriented specialists, was becoming geared to a different kind of research.

Sarnoff's leadership, especially his ability to judge the value of a potential innovation and to make the connections between the research community and the divisions, was becoming less effective in the 1950s. "The General's" request for three specific products as fiftieth-anniversary presents from the RCA Laboratories underscored this dilemma. The proposed presents were a light amplifier, an electronic air conditioner, and what Sarnoff called a "videograph" – a mechanism by which to record video information on magnetic tape. Although the press coverage of the request made it sound as though Sarnoff was engaged in pulling rabbits out of a hat, there were indications in the Laboratories that work on the three "gifts" might yield results in time.[16] With his penchant for the attention-getting gesture, Sarnoff used a public occasion to stimulate and channel the Research Center's efforts along lines that he believed would have value for the corporation. He perceived his role as corporate entrepreneur to be to capture the imagination of both researchers and the marketplace in such a way that the market might be prepared to accept a new product when the Laboratories had developed the technology for it.

None of the three presents became pioneering successes for RCA, however, although the work advanced the company's electronics know-how. Sarnoff had overstepped that invisible boundary between preparing to exploit a new technology that is in a state of readiness, and forcing the unforcible. He had created a glare of publicity that hampered the research community's ability to work. Moreover, two of the items, the light amplifier and the electronic air conditioner, were unrealistic products. The light amplifier, while feasible in principle, was too costly to produce, although the work led to further research on flat-screen television. The electronic air conditioning unit became a small thick-walled refrigerator that produced what was jokingly referred to at RCA Laboratories as the most expensive ice cube in the world.[17]

The videotape recorder was an entirely different matter, for it showed clearly how competitive the business of research in the postwar era had become. The Acoustical and Electromechanical Research Laboratory spent years trying to perfect videotape recorders for professional and consumer use, but were hampered by Sarnoff's insistence that the equipment accommodate both black and white and color. In the end, a small engineering group led by Charles Ginsberg, in a small California company called Ampex, commercialized a usable professional videotape recorder in 1956.[18] RCA was eventually able to come to a cross-licensing agreement with Ampex, by exchanging its color know-how for Ampex's quadruplex approach to videorecording, and the two companies effectively split the professional market, two-thirds for Ampex and one-third for RCA. But the payoff for RCA was much less than it would have been for pioneering, and the Laboratories suffered intense embarrassment over the project that was to color their later assessments of magnetic tape as a fit technology for further development. Rather than expend effort on technologies in which the scientific principles involved were believed to be understood and in which a small group of bright people could potentially have an advantage over a more cumbersome organization, they gravitated toward fields less well inhabited, where a large company with a highly specialized staff of scientists and breadth of coverage could expect to maintain proprietary advantage.

Shift to fundamental research

The fact was that electronics was a different kind of research field after World War II, one that no single company could hope to dominate and one that also needed major infusions of new knowledge. The great interdisciplinary projects and other wartime activities had nearly exhausted the store of existing knowledge. They had also taken the field out of the hands of one or two industrial enterprises and spawned a variety of new research competitors similar to Ampex. Philco, for instance, having enjoyed free wartime access to patents that it previously would have had to license, was not willing to leave research to

RCA after the war. GE and Westinghouse both became more heavily involved in electronics R&D, and several smaller organizations merged to form larger units with adequate resources to support continued activity. Public criticism focused on RCA's patent position as having inhibited radio-related research during the prewar period by depriving other members of the industry of the incentive to do research. The government responded by deliberately encouraging more competition in research.[19]

The national research climate after the war tilted firmly toward more basic science research in industry as well as in academia, and government funding for industrial research continued in peacetime through such agents as the Office of Naval Research.[20] Elmer Engstrom, RCA's director of research and engineering in 1945, readily acknowledged the necessity for more fundamental research – research, often theoretical in nature, that aimed to uncover the scientific principles in fields that were believed to have commercial applicability. He wanted to rebuild the inventory of scientific knowledge in electronics and recommended that corporate management devote a sizeable effort to this. Engstrom was convinced that all fundamental scientific progress related to electronics would ultimately yield commercial advantage for RCA, for "by doing work in this field of a quality which will command the respect of scientific investigators in universities, we will stimulate work there which will, in effect, enlarge the scope of the work done within RCA Laboratories, and thus bring about more rapid progress."[21]

The impetus toward fundamental research also came from RCA's licensing interests, for the company's position depended on its continued leadership in electronics. To remain in the forefront, RCA had to add specialists in disciplines it had not previously covered. Solid-state research, for example, required a buildup of all the disciplines related to materials, partly because appropriate materials were not commercially available and had to be synthesized in the Laboratories. Another compelling argument for shifting the Laboratories more in the direction of basic science was the dire shortage of qualified researchers created by the new research competition coupled with the wartime hiatus in university training of scientists. RCA hired Douglas Ewing, a former physics professor who had worked on the large government air navigation project in Camden during the war, to head a recruitment program from colleges and universities. The company also cooperated with Princeton and MIT to make graduate training available to current employees and new recruits. After a decade of concentrated recruiting of graduate trained scientists, the Laboratories staff comprised 270 scientists and engineers, and the composition had shifted from 30 percent theoretical scientists in 1945, to almost 50 percent in 1955, including metallurgists, chemists, physicists, and mathematicians.

For the kinds of researchers RCA hired after the war, government-funded projects often provided an attractive alternative to work funded by the company, for several reasons. Government contract research was often more exploratory, and it could lead rather rapidly to the kind of published results that built scientific careers. By contrast, research related to RCA's commercial end products, or carried out on behalf of other companies, had to be cloaked in secrecy and was seldom publishable until years later, if at all. Government research contracts administered by the research contracts department at the Laboratories accounted for a growing percentage of the entire research budget, from 20 percent before the Korean War, to 25 percent in the later 1950s. At first the RCA policy was to accept government funding only for work that the company had no internal reasons for pursuing. Toward the end of the Korean War, however, it became RCA practice to seek out military research contracts that would lead to procurement orders for RCA businesses, especially in military systems.

Gradually the changing composition of the RCA Laboratories created divisions in the staff and contradictions between different ideas of what RCA's corporate research mission ought to be. The "scientists," who were young, highly trained from a theoretical point of view, but inexperienced in business terms, cared chiefly about working on problems defined by their disciplines. Because they were in demand, they could insist on doing primarily discipline-oriented work such as they would have done in universities. They kept close contact with specialists in their fields and valued highly the rewards and recognition that came with publishing articles in leading professional journals.

RCA research center veterans, on the other hand, typically had backgrounds that bore little resemblance to those of their younger colleagues. Few held advanced degrees, but most had a good deal of practical experience. Some thought of themselves as inventors. Because most had worked in RCA research departments at a time when they were still attached to manufacturing divisions, they were familiar with manufacturing activities and concerns. For these veterans it was still problem-solving that was exciting, and company loyalty mattered more than professional loyalty. There were bound to be tensions between such different groups, just as there were in research organizations all over the country at the time.

In fact, the RCA Laboratories served three separate constituencies, each with its own orientation and its own set of demands. For the American scientific community, the Research Center was a gathering of distinguished technical staff, including many prominent contributing members of professional societies and journals, and holders of numerous patents. For RCA headquarters and the rest of the electronics industry, the center was the cornerstone of RCA's identity as the pioneering technical company in its industry and the concrete rationale for RCA's privileged licensing position. But for RCA operating divisions, the corporate research center was coming to be known as "the country club," a place where RCA resources were squandered on exotic or impractical ideas. As time went on, the younger generation of researchers moved into positions of authority and the balance tipped more in the direction of theoretical work. The Laboratories became something of a corporate counterculture, dominated by people with whom the rest of RCA had, or thought they had, very little in common.

The building block research strategy

Potential electronics applications went far beyond the bounds of RCA's existing businesses after the war. The discovery of the transistor effect with its implications for miniaturization expanded the limits of the technology to an unimaginable degree. Sarnoff's dictum, that RCA ought to follow the electronic art wherever it led, caused RCA product divisions to investigate a wide range of new markets, from industrial television to computers to semiconductors. The increasing technical diversity caused demands to be placed on the Laboratories that it simply could not meet. The task of identifying revolutionary products when new markets were multiplying was, in itself, complicated. Moreover, competition was increasing to such an extent that keeping track of potential competitors in each segment of the market was a herculean task.

The RCA Laboratories management eventually responded to the problem of increasing complexity and market diversity by adopting a "building-block" research strategy. This involved deemphasizing product development and concentrating primarily on fundamental research in electronics and related fields. Except for work on projects that were considered corporate in nature – that had generic applicability or that were long-term and would not fit any existing business – product-related R&D was shifted out of the Laboratories to advanced development departments within the divisions to which it pertained most directly. The building-block strategy became a structural reality at RCA following an overall corporate restructuring that took place in 1954. Douglas Ewing, who was named administrative head of the Laboratories, moved the research center away from its former project focus toward a modified functional organization. Individual laboratories were dedicated to disciplines such as physical and chemical research, electronics research, or acoustical and electromechanical research. The new arrangement did not eliminate project groupings altogether but provided for them to be set up on an ad hoc basis. Researchers whose work was in a particular area of product development were given the option of redirecting their work, or relocating in the divisions. Each division formed its own advanced development group, substantially enlarging the size of the RCA technical community overall. The quality of these groups varied as they were hampered by the scarcity of available scientific talent and enjoyed varying degrees of support from their local managements.

The research reorganization had two major consequences. First, the clear emergence of a hierarchy of research priorities, with the highest status accorded to fundamental research as practiced at the Laboratories, fueled intense competition inside RCA's greater technical community. Whether the research center was the first among equals, or the undeserving recipient of credit for work performed elsewhere, became a matter for dispute. In some areas of RCA, the movement of product R&D to the divisions effectively foreclosed new product development altogether for a decade.

Had the restructuring taken place in a corporation that was still fairly geographically concentrated, it might have had less drastic consequences. But from 1954 on, the corporation spread out geographically. The consumer division was located in Indianapolis, at the site of former Westinghouse facilities, while activities related to the space program moved to Massachusetts and California. The corporate research center was no longer accessible to many of the product divisions and this widened the gap that had opened with the shift to a building block strategy.

Had Sarnoff's leadership continued in the style of the television era, he might have compensated for some of the changes. But Sarnoff became an increasingly active spokesman for the Cold War and a symbolic figure in what his friend, President Eisenhower, termed the military industrial complex. He was also heavily involved in RCA's legal affairs concerning patent policy and he was struggling to keep color television alive on behalf of an industry that preferred to defer its introduction.[22] In such circumstances it was hardly surprising that he gradually lost touch with objective technical reality and relied more on the layers of managers beneath him to filter the information he received.[23]

Sarnoff never lost interest in research, however, nor did he lose faith in innovation as the main avenue to corporate prosperity. To the end of his long active career he maintained his very special relationship with the research center and its staff, which he called his "loyal corps of scientists." In one of the major laboratory expansions that occurred during the 1950s, Sarnoff ordered a suite of rooms to be built especially for him, complete with a formal dining room. He talked of retiring there, and in the 1960s, when he became concerned about his place in history, he set up his memorial library at the research center in a style reminiscent of presidential libraries. In later years, his visits became less frequent but, when he appeared, executive committee in tow, he could still be observed walking through the laboratory corridors and stopping often to examine a new piece of apparatus or to talk with a member of the technical staff.

Central role of research

R&D was central to RCA's corporate identity even when the company had only token research facilities. But Sarnoff elevated research to corporate status, made it a separate division, and eventually gave it its own institutional identity. The interaction between Sarnoff and the Laboratories that bore his name was RCA's primary long-range planning during the late 1940s and early 1950s. Sarnoff saw corporate research as the key to the steady flow of new product ideas based on technical advances in electronics that RCA needed to remain preeminent in a business based on self-obsolescence, and he knew that operations managers rarely made provisions for the long-term future of their operations.

As a separate entity, the Laboratories served several constituencies and developed its own agenda and its own interpretation of the proper role for corporate research. After World War II, this view was heavily influenced by national research priorities and by the changing requirements of the electronics field. A need for basic research to replenish the inventory of scientific knowledge ready to be applied, the increasing competition for competent research personnel in the industry, and the demands of the new-style technical people created very different conditions from those in the prewar era when RCA's technical community had been fashioned from the remnants of GE and Westinghouse.

Research as prime mover

RCA's two different experiences with television illustrate the effects that changes in RCA's research community had on the way innovation was conducted. As successor products to radio, black and white and color television became "pattern innovations" for the corporation – experiences that served as yardsticks for future attempts at innovation. They were both the kind of large-scale systems engineering projects that Sarnoff regarded as RCA's particular area of competitive advantage, requiring technical depth and diversity within a comprehensive business system. But black and white television was a product of the prewar decentralized research configuration with its close links to manufacturing, with a tremendous amount of its manufacturing development funded by the government during wartime R&D projects. By contrast, color television emerged from the unified corporate laboratory where research was beginning to dominate and would eventually be divorced from manufacturing. As a consequence, color television had the benefit of much greater scientific expertise but was plagued with design and manufacturing problems that kept the price high and the quality low for a long time. The lesson that the RCA research organization took from its color television experience showed up later in the stringent economic goals and the stress on simple design and minimal features that governed the Videodisc project from its inception.

Had corporate research funding depended on RCA divisions in the 1950s, little, if any, building block research would have been funded. But outside sources – government research support and the continuing proceeds from RCA's patent pool – gave RCA's corporate research center the latitude to pursue its own interpretation of long-term interests. Enjoying Sarnoff's still powerful patronage, but lacking the firm direction he had once provided, it was perhaps inevitable that the Laboratories chose to define the company's long-term needs in terms of its own needs and capabilities as an institution. It was out of just such an exercise that the Videodisc project emerged.

4

Laboratory as entrepreneur: videoplayer research begins

James Hillier, vice-president of RCA and head of RCA Laboratories, was the keynote speaker at the Institute of Electrical and Electronic Engineers (IEEE) Consumer Electronics Award Dinner in October 1964. It was clear from his speech that he had been giving much thought to forging a strategic role for the technical community in a large electronics company. He entreated his audience to look beyond the limited confines of the present industry, defined by a mature and familiar television technology, to the creation of other consumer electronic devices that could transcend entertainment. The building blocks were now in place, but how, he asked, would the industry reach the point of mass production of new electronic systems for the home?

> What is needed at this juncture ... is more of the daring Entrepreneurship that we saw in the founding of our industry.... Entrepreneurship in our context must occur in the companies that have the necessary technical and economic resources. In these companies engineers have a vital role to play as part of management – a role, by the way, that seems to get more lip service than real attention from management and engineering. You can perform an important function as interpreters of research results and the opportunities they create not only in home entertainment but in the whole consumer electronics products field. You can keep the systems concept of the possible explosion in consumer electronics before your management.[1]

What Hillier had in mind would be as much of a change of institutional behavior for his own RCA Laboratories as for any other. For the David Sarnoff Research Center to become RCA's corporate entrepreneur would require a radical shift away from the building-block research mission of the previous era, as well as a profound change of attitude. Hillier was discovering that to reform a research center from within was no mean feat.

76

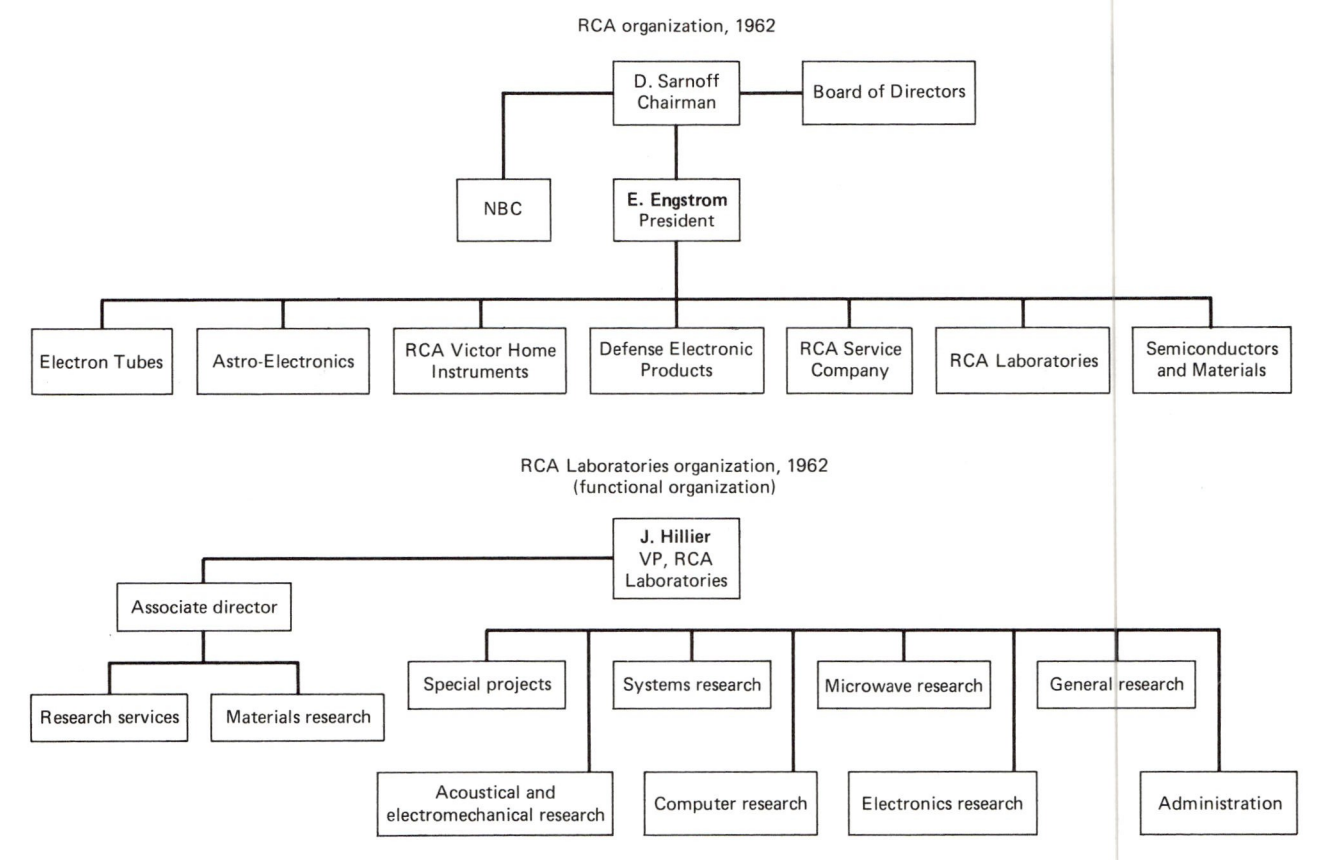

RCA organization, 1962

D. Sarnoff
Chairman

Board of Directors

NBC

E. Engstrom
President

Electron Tubes

Astro-Electronics

RCA Victor Home Instruments

Defense Electronic Products

RCA Service Company

RCA Laboratories

Semiconductors and Materials

RCA Laboratories organization, 1962
(functional organization)

J. Hillier
VP, RCA Laboratories

Associate director

Research services

Materials research

Special projects

Systems research

Microwave research

General research

Acoustical and electromechanical research

Computer research

Electronics research

Administration

RCA and RCA Laboratories organization charts, 1962.

In the end, perhaps the most significant outcome of Hillier's attempted reform movement was a by-product, the Laboratories' identification of a major new end-product project for RCA, consumer videoplayer technology.

At the time, RCA's corporate research organization was in no danger of losing its funding. The company was flush with prosperity as the belated but copious returns from earlier investments in color television rolled in. Moreover, there was no pressure for reform from top management. In David Sarnoff and Elmer Engstrom, its creators and staunch defenders, the RCA Laboratories enjoyed uncritical support. What Hillier feared was the longer-range prospect. From the point of view of the rest of the company, the Research Center was becoming dispensable.

In the 1964 volume of the internally circulated Annual Report of the David Sarnoff Research Center, Hillier noted that the costs of doing research, including salaries and the increasingly intricate and expensive capital equipment needed to support the work, were rising more sharply than the overall rate of inflation. The Research Center's portion of the corporation's overall R&D activity had shrunk from 20 percent during the postwar period to 6 percent. Yet it still consumed its former share of the corporate R&D budget, in 1964 nearly $20 million. The trend seemed likely to continue. At the same time there were distinct signs that the center would soon become much more dependent on company support rather than on outside money. The government largesse that had originated at the time of the space program in the 1950s had just about run its course. Government-funded research, like government sales, had fallen back from earlier levels of 30 percent to 25 percent of the RCA Laboratories' operating budget. Meanwhile, the cost of doing government contract research had increased, with tighter reporting requirements consuming more and more administrative overhead and management time.

Perhaps even more serious than the funding issue for Hillier was the divergence he foresaw between RCA's future needs for research and what the David Sarnoff Research Center on its present course was preparing to provide. Building-block, or fundamental, research had been appropriate during the 1950s

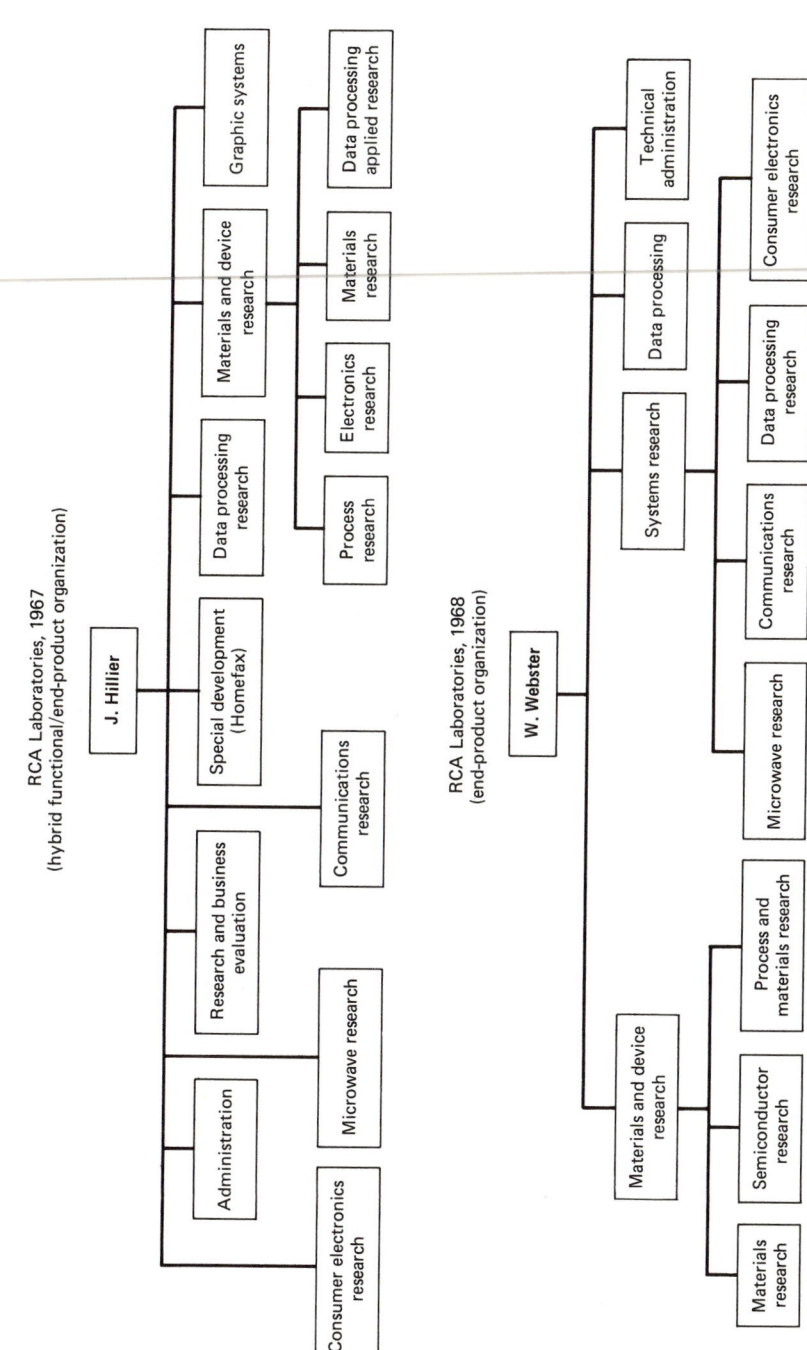

RCA Laboratories organization charts, 1967 and 1968.

as bedrock electronics technology had been changing from the vacuum tube to the semiconductor, and major systems work had been necessary to develop new transistor-based circuitry. But the advent of integrated circuit technology in the early 1960s was shifting the focus of effort back again from fundamentals to applications. Hillier faced the dilemma of all research managers in such a time of transition, how to redirect the work of a research center without changing its staff and seriously disrupting the critically important stability of its organization. Hillier had already lived through one episode of attempted reform at the Laboratories during the late 1950s, and he knew what a difficult experience it could be.

Watershed for RCA research

During the building-block research era, the research center had concentrated on linkages with those RCA product divisions that had development interests consistent with its own research directions – mainly Government Systems and Electronic Components. Government Systems, in particular, competed on the basis of new technology, receiving funding and often follow-on business for introducing new products and systems, RCA consumer divisions were struggling under the burden of color television from the mid-1950s on, and they wanted no part of further scientific discoveries.[2]

RCA's loss of "package" licensing revenues in the mid-1950s had, for a time, threatened both the Laboratories' external funding base and its semiautonomous mode of operations. While licensing revenues did not come directly to the RCA Laboratories, they were clearly identifiable returns to research. Elmer Engstrom, head of the RCA Laboratories, knew very well that loss of this large external source of funding would result in demands from RCA's divisions for the research center to justify its existence in ways that were more closely allied to immediate divisional interests. RCA's profits had then fallen to such a low point that resources allocated to research must inevitably be viewed as depriving the divisions of investment for other, more visible, purposes. To prepare for a possible loss of funds, Engstrom instituted a budgetary process in the Laboratories that considered only revenues assessed from the RCA divisions as a reliable planning base. The budget's introduction was a memorable event in the life of the research center, for it was the first time since the founding of the Laboratories that limits on the resources devoted to research were visible to the research staff.

When the antitrust litigation in 1958 resulted in an unfavorable judgment against RCA, the RCA Laboratories encountered the very pressures Engstrom had anticipated. In principle RCA now had to pay with its own money for research it had previously viewed as being supported by the entire radio and electronics industry. By law any patents that could be regarded as pertaining to "radio-purpose" electronics would now cease to be sources of domestic licensing revenue for RCA, but newer application areas of electronics, such as business computers and medical electronics, were not covered under the term "radio purpose." If RCA was no longer entitled to claim licensing revenues for maintaining the whole state of radio-related research, the obvious question for the company was, what kind of research should it continue to support, and at what level?

Attempts by RCA management to resolve that question during the next several years plunged the Laboratories into a sudden and disorienting reform movement imposed from above. When, surprisingly, John Burns and not the anticipated candidate Elmer Engstrom, succeeded Frank Folsom as RCA president in 1957, the Laboratories saw a powerful ally moved aside. The RCA Board had evidently seen a need for a radical revision of strategy and management, for so long based on technological risk-taking. Burns had a technical background, but he was an outsider who had spent much of his career in management consulting and he had been hired at least in part to establish RCA firmly in the computer business. He did not have a great affinity for the Laboratories.

Burns proposed to define the role of research at RCA within the context of a strategic redefinition of RCA's business. He changed the leadership in the RCA Laboratories and involved the divisions directly in the evaluation of research activities.

81

Burns replaced Douglas Ewing, the current head of the Laboratories with James Hillier, who was viewed as a compromise candidate. Ewing's academic orientation had endeared him to the younger scientific group at the research center at the cost of disaffection among veteran problem-solvers and estrangement from much of the RCA organization. Hillier's status as a potential bridge builder between the Laboratories and the divisions stemmed from his experience as co-inventor and developer of the electron microscope while at the University of Toronto, as former research physicist at RCA's Camden and Princeton facilities, as former research director at Melpar, Inc., and then as Chief Engineer of RCA Industrial Electronic Products. He was familiar with both academic and industrial research environments.

At Burns's invitation, representatives of RCA's product divisions working with the top layers of the research management team, scrutinized and evaluated every research project in the RCA Laboratories, using newly established corporate priorities. These reflected Burns's intention to move RCA away from its traditional areas of radio-purpose electronics, now seen as mature and no longer able to yield licensing revenues, toward other commercial and industrial systems applications. For the Laboratories, the appraisal resulted in an emphasis on research relating to large-scale systems projects, and in particular data processing. All applications-oriented areas received encouragement, and more fundamental projects were instructed to form ties with more directed projects. Electronic device research, for example, was told to form closer ties with the computer research laboratory, which increased its staff from five to twenty-five to support RCA's entry into commercial data processing. In addition, RCA Laboratories organized a number of new projects to cooperate with advanced engineering work already proceeding in various product divisions. Joint projects commenced in nuclear energy, acoustics and audio, videotape for the home, and computer control of autos on the highways. At the same time, many small-scale theoretically oriented projects were dropped. To make the most of outside sources of revenue, more emphasis was placed on seeking government contract work.

82

Videoplayer research begins

The attempt to implement the new research thrust brought with it a number of practical problems. First, the move towards applications required a sudden and rapid augmentation by 10 percent of a research staff that had already become too large to manage comfortably. Not only was it necessary to absorb the twenty-two new researchers needed for computer work, with their supporting staffs, but researchers already on the staff had to be persuaded to shift from work they were doing to join the large projects of the divisions' choice. Moreover, the increase in government contract work placed heavy demands on administrative staff, substantially increasing overhead.

The divisions saw the new cooperative research efforts as an opportunity to cut back on the money they were spending in-house on advanced development engineering. The RCA Laboratories in turn did their best to resist this attempt to shift development costs borne by the divisions to their budget. Resistance among technical staff members to the new research directions was strong, and the research center was in danger of cropping most of its long-range work and losing some of its best scientists. Hillier warned that if the trend toward applications went too far, long-term research would cease to be done at RCA altogether.

The research reorientation movement turned out to be short-lived. About the time color television turned profitable John Burns left the company, and the research center's former head, Elmer Engstrom, became RCA president. The choice signalled a reversion to previous thinking, for as soon as he took over as president, Engstrom, with David Sarnoff's blessing, reaffirmed RCA's dedication to furthering its research into its core electronics technology. In his view, RCA had strengthened, beyond measure, its resources and capabilities for leadership in any direction that the science and the industry of electronics might take. During the five years of Engstrom's presidency, RCA remained in what might be called a strategic holding pattern, and research reverted to its former emphasis on long-range fundamentally oriented projects.

Fortuitous developments in the national environment for research, and in RCA's licensing operations, helped the research center to pursue its former course and to resist further

83

encroachments from the operating divisions. In 1957, Russia's launching of the Sputnik satellite opened the floodgates of government funding for U.S. industrial research, especially research that was related to the conquest of space, as almost all electronics research could be. The space age was hailed as a "new era in radio communications" in RCA's 1958 Annual Report and the corporation announced its intent to take a leadership role that matched its technological reputation. The old package licensing system, no longer legal for use domestically, developed new life, for it proved to be ideal for foreign licensees trying to catch up technologically. The Japanese and the Germans, in particular, saw technology as their route to economic prosperity after their successes in rebuilding their countries' infrastructures. David Sarnoff avidly promoted transfer of RCA's technology abroad through licensing and, in recognition of his technological aid to the Japanese electronics industry, he received the highest distinction ever bestowed by the Japanese government on a foreign businessman, the Order of the Rising Sun, Third Class.

Yet Hillier was apprehensive at management's reversion to the renewed all-electronics strategy. He saw the excesses of the Burns era as proof that RCA Laboratories would not be able to be all things to all people. The research center in his opinion needed a mission that would benefit the entire corporation but that would also take account of the realities of finite company resources and of the exploding electronics field. RCA might employ 300 scientists and engineers out of a total Laboratories staff of 1,000, but this was only 4 percent of RCA's total technical strength as a company, and the institution was only one among many competent electronic research laboratories in the world, accounting for only 0.2 percent of electronics research in the United States alone. It could not possibly hope to sustain a leadership position in all aspects of the field.

If top management chose not to focus RCA's corporate efforts into particular areas of electronics, Hillier concluded that the task of strategic planning would have to be done in the Laboratories. Perhaps hoping to stimulate further discussion and clarification from the top, Hillier published a list of strategic planning priorities in his 1963 Laboratory Annual

Report. The Laboratories, he wrote, saw RCA as participating in three classes of business – home entertainment; the supply of electronic apparatus and systems to economic and social systems outside RCA's usual realm, such as government and commercial markets; and the supply of components and information to the electronics industry complex. Only in the first area was RCA's commitment "total" in that "we will spare no effort or expense to maintain a favorable position or to react to a competitive threat." Primary efforts at innovation should therefore be concentrated in the entertainment electronics area. Other areas, such as technical support of government business, should be maintained and strengthened or, in the case of data processing, improved until they equal home entertainment in importance for RCA. RCA would continue to maintain a research program of sufficient breadth to provide support in the many areas where the company now had products, but it would not conduct specific applied research programs in supporting apparatus to complete systems unless RCA's future course was specifically spelled out to include products requiring this kind of applied activity.

A replacement for television

Hillier recognized the pressing need for long-range planning at RCA. Sarnoff had begun to talk in visionary terms about the coming information age, but the sad truth was that, in the wake of the exhausting battle for color television, he had traded his former insistence on self-obsolescence for wishful thinking. At the 1964 annual stockholders meeting he predicted that there would be ten more years of solid growth in color television before all black and white sets had been replaced. Hillier knew of more conservative estimates that predicted a decline in the primary market for television by 1970. For the RCA Laboratories this meant that the company would need an "act to follow" that was both as big as television, and as broad in scope. The only way for the Laboratories to be recognized as the continuing major source of RCA's long-range opportunities was for this crucial new product to be closely identified with it.

In Hillier's phrase, "the rest of the corporation would have to see the laboratory as a life raft not an albatross."[3]

Ample evidence suggested that it would not be enough to discover a powerful new technology and then reveal its exciting potential to the RCA product divisions. The research center had seen promising product technologies, such as transistor radios and liquid crystals, either meet with indifference or run into fatal difficulties when they left the Laboratories. Ironically, licensees had successfully launched major new businesses using RCA Laboratories' technology, for the investment climate at the time was conducive to high-technology products in general. The troubles of the infant RCA semiconductor business, which the latest reorganization had left to the jealous mercies of the Tube Division, had demonstrated the problem of technology implementation only too clearly. Signs that read "Stamp Out Transistors" could be seen in the division's production facilities, and RCA was already on its way to losing a leading position in semiconductors.

The two executives who shared formal responsibility for research and engineering at RCA, James Hillier and George Brown, corporate vice-president of research and engineering, diagnosed the technology transfer problem differently. Brown, whose work directing the Systems Research Laboratory in the early 1950s had contributed immeasurably to the development and ultimate commercialization of color television, believed that a product division would only adopt and promote a new product if it could take credit for the idea itself. In support of this philosophy, he sought to transfer new product technologies out of the RCA Laboratories at the earliest possible stage through the use of corporate seed money. The divisions received certain sums to develop new product ideas in their own advanced development groups.[4] On the other hand, after six years of disillusioning experience, Hillier had completely lost faith in the divisions' willingness to launch innovative products. Believing from his earlier experiences at Melpar and at RCA's Industrial Electronics business that communication was key to a coordinated R&D effort, he had used a number of different devices to try to create linkages between the research center and the various divisions. Annual technical reviews for representatives of the divisions and publications explained research activities. On the theory that people were the main carriers of ideas, he encouraged members of the research staff to visit the divisions. He established a program to allow divisional advanced development staff to bring their projects to Princeton for awhile to use the Laboratories' advanced equipment and benefit from their expertise. Finally, cooperative programs were set up that shifted researchers back and forth between product divisions and particular laboratories.

The program had its successes, but they were the exception. Dynagroove, a joint effort between RCA Records and Princeton's Acoustical Research Laboratory, produced a record with much improved fidelity, for instance. But in the end, Hillier and his colleagues concluded that, in general, the rest of RCA had so little interest in implementing their research findings that the Laboratories would have to assume the burdens of entrepreneurship and carry a product from idea generation at least through business evaluation. Privately, Hillier acknowledged that he no longer believed, as he once had, that the research staff was essentially responsive to divisional needs, given a clear definition of their problems. After years of what he described as "informal facilitative management," Hillier set out to adopt a more aggressive managerial approach, and to launch a reform movement, this time from within.

Attempt at reorganization of research

In 1964 Hillier began a two-year effort to restructure the RCA Laboratories and to reorient its research toward carrying out the entrepreneurial strategy he had devised. The mechanism he created to accomplish this purpose was the Interim Research Planning Committee (IRPCO). In hindsight, IRPCO was viewed by many of its participants as an abortive and costly exercise in organizational change, but seen from a still longer perspective, it was the turning point it was intended to be.

Hillier's plan, ironically, was a more focused version of the reorientation imposed by John Burns. He intended to transform the research center's university atmosphere into a more active, market-oriented environment. The two crucial and very sensitive pieces of the plan were first, to make the structure less discipline-oriented and more product-oriented by imposing a matrix organization, and secondly, to shift the final responsibility for resource allocation out of the hands of individual laboratory directors. Perhaps he suspected the unlikelihood of its working, but he proposed nevertheless to make his reforms without changing the composition of the research staff.

Hillier charged the IRPCO select committee, composed of current laboratory directors, with the task of classifying all research projects under way according to their potential relevance for identifiable end products that would ultimately be transferred to product divisions for development. The large number of projects that could not be related to end products were classified as "sustaining research." It would be up to the laboratory management to decide what the level of sustaining research should be at any given period. Among end-product projects, emphasis would be placed on a few high-priority research projects judged to be particularly useful to RCA. Each end-product research project would be specified in a line-item budget and would come under semiannual scrutiny by the senior laboratories management. The number of sustaining research projects, so attractive to researchers, would be reduced.

IRPCO was dominated by several problem-solving oriented veterans who were zealously outspoken advocates of reform. It plunged into its assignment, classifying projects, nominating project supervisors as matrix managers, and making preliminary recommendations for manpower allocation. Consistent with Hillier's earlier assessments, the two fields of applied research identified as having "the most impact on RCA's furture prosperity" were consumer electronics and electronic data-processing. In both areas IRPCO advocated that the number of researchers be substantially increased.

The IRPCO report split the Princeton research community along long-standing cultural lines. The scientists, so long in ascendancy at the Laboratories, viewed it as an attack on their fundamental research prerogatives and on their intellectual autonomy. The engineers and problem-solvers welcomed it as a long overdue attempt to restore essential discipline and looked forward to an increase in their resources. So threatening was the uproar to the stability of the laboratories that Hillier moved for compromise. The restructuring was adopted on a trial basis, but some of its chief proponents, who might have been expected to gain from the outcome, received staff assignments. One was appointed to head a new laboratory staff function, New Business and Research Evaluation, created to carry out market analysis of new product ideas originating in the research center.

Some of the key provisions of the IRPCO reform lapsed into disuse only two years later, when James Hillier moved on to succeed George Brown as RCA corporate vice-president Research and Engineering in 1968. William Webster, a moderate survivor of IRPCO, was named to head the Laboratories. Under his leadership, the organizational structure was modified to achieve the same basic objective. New laboratories were formed that had a more product-oriented mission, headed by directors who shared the applied philosophy. In place of the matrix, a new formal layer of laboratory management was set up between the directors and the head of the Laboratories to coordinate activities and to manage the relationships with the various divisions.

The only real attempt by the Laboratories to carry a product to full-scale commercialization was Homefax, a television-based facsimile system (precursor of modern videotext systems) for the home. Homefax was a 1960s product of the Acoustical and Electromechanical Research Laboratory, under the direction of RCA's noted videotape pioneer, Harry Olson. It had the enthusiastic support of Sarnoff and Engstrom, who saw Homefax as a corporate-sponsored innovation in the home information business that had all the earmarks of the kind of consumer systems product RCA had excelled in pioneering under Sarnoff's leadership. It entailed FCC standards approval and required coordination not only between different parts of RCA, but also with other television set producers.

The new New Business and Research Evaluation group took Homefax as its first project. When it had completed a business plan, a second group was formed at Princeton to set up the business. But industry response to the RCA Homefax announcement in 1967 was lukewarm, and the project soon lapsed into abeyance after the change in top management the following year.

Another project to receive formal approval during the period when the RCA Laboratories was becoming more product oriented was "high-density recording," a forerunner of several of the nonmagnetic videoplayer projects that were later pursued. This project began in the Systems Research Laboratory and continued under different names in the newly organized Consumer Electronics Laboratory, which combined researchers from Systems Research, Acoustical and Electromechanical Research, and Electronics Research. Later, under the name "prerecorded videoplayers," it served as an umbrella project for several different approaches to videorecording that began as small sustaining research projects during the early 1960s and found themselves in need of justification under the new planning system. Because some had originated in discipline-based work and some were problem-solving in their orientation from the start, a rivalry developed between the projects that reflected the continuing competition between research philosophies. For awhile, in the charged atmosphere of the post-IRPCO period, each individual project success seemed to vindicate one research philosophy or the other.

In their spring 1964 meeting, the laboratory directors concluded that "theoretical and experimental" work was needed on high-density recording as a start toward developing a "practical and low-cost videorecorder that would lead to a mass market." The videorecorder concept had a classic RCA systems appeal. As a possible consumer product, it had been around the RCA Laboratories in some form since the early 1950s. Thought of as a synthesis of television and recording, both entertainment areas in which RCA had a substantial business and research stake, the project was comprehensive enough technologically to provide an opportunity for several different groups in the Laboratories to work together toward a common goal. But however important the product might be to RCA, the technical solutions to achieving a low-cost and truly usable system were by no means obvious. Thinking back from a later vantage point, Eugene Keizer, one of the original researchers, recalled how it looked to those who began the project: "We were attempting to do the impossible."

Videoplayer antecedents

Three laboratories mounted high-density recording efforts. Two of them had long-standing experience with consumer products work: Acoustical and Electromechanical Research (A&ER) and Systems Research. Both had been preeminent in the research center until the shift in emphasis toward fundamental research during the early 1950s had made them less popular among incoming researchers. The preferred laboratories then were those that offered more of a university environment – a chance to do theoretical research with minimal direction from the top.

A&ER had its closest contacts with RCA's Broadcast Division in Camden, which produced radio and television studio equipment, and with the Records Division in Indianapolis. Its director during the 1950s and 1960s, Harry Olson, had been trying to develop a videorecorder for the consumer market for over a decade. An early consumer model was the "Hear–See" player. This was a smaller version of the first technical approach, known as "longitudinal scan" because it read magnetic tape lengthwise, that Olson had developed for the professional market, only to have it bested in 1956 by Ampex's recorder, which had what was known as a "transverse scan" approach because it read magnetic tape crosswise, making more economical use of the tape.

Members of Olson's group had experimented with both magnetic tape and magnetic disc approaches to videorecording during the late 1950s, but in either case there were obstacles to successful conclusions. Size was a problem that could not yet be solved. Prototype players were as tall as a man because of the enormous amount of tape that had to be stored on a reel. Transistors were in their commercial infancy, and only a few of the solid-state devices needed for appropriate circuitry were available at that time.

Another major obstacle was the prevailing attitude within

the RCA technical community, or at least in Princeton, that magnetic tape was a "spent technology." The use of electro-mechanical means to develop a consumer videorecorder was denounced by electronics specialists in the Laboratories as something between a "brute force" approach and a theoretical impossibility. Conventional techniques of magnetic recording were short by a factor of three or four of the necessary recording and pickup capacity, they believed, and there did not seem to be much room for improvement.

Members of the A&ER Laboratory first became interested in nonmagnetic approaches to videorecording when General Electric reported successful attempts to do nonmagnetic television recording using thermoplastic material in 1960. A&ER personnel responded with an intensive three-month survey of all existing forms of videorecording and playback. The report by technical staff members E. Ramberg and J. Woodward concluded that "the greatest information density achievable with presently known methods will be obtained using electron beams for recording and readout, and with a plastic dielectric as the recording medium." It anticipated many of the central issues that were to arise concerning the nonmagnetic video-player research. The relative merits of frame-by-frame (a format that read one image after another) versus serial signal (in which individual signals were picked up one after the other and then translated back into images) information format, a coated or uncoated medium, and the proprietary aspects of different recording methods were all matters that would be argued and reargued within the RCA technical community for more than fifteen years.

For several years after the GE announcement, nonmagnetic research was tabled in A&ER as its members supported applied magnetic videorecording work being done on government contract in Camden. Their work was directed at improving the picture quality obtainable from magnetic tape through better materials and improved coating techniques.

The Systems Research Laboratory, which housed work on information transmission and display, was best known for its work in support of color television under George Brown, who

92

had moved to Camden as chief engineer in 1957, when applied television work was deemphasized at the Princeton research center in favor of research supporting electronic data processing. Many systems researchers then transferred into computer support work, although a few researchers chose to continue their work on kinescopes and other television-related activities.

The third laboratory that contributed to early work on high-density recording was the Electronics Research Laboratory headed by William Webster. The Electronics Research Laboratory was device-oriented during the late 1950s and early 1960s, but Webster made efforts to broaden the group's focus by encouraging cooperative research with the Systems Research Laboratory. In 1959, as part of this effort, Webster assigned Thomas Stanley, a solid-state specialist who had just returned from a year's work on computer systems at Cambridge University, as a group head in the Electronics Research Laboratory, while also heading a group in systems research. The researchers that worked with him were called members of Section $13\frac{1}{2}$, a reference to their half-way position between SR's Section 13 and ER's Section 14. Their objective was to explore the limits of what could be done with integrated circuits.

Among other things, Stanley's group calculated the potential for storing and retrieving information from a vinyl disc using the form of information retrieval known as electrical capacitance. This approach picked up the relationship between signals recorded in grooves on a disc and an electrode riding on a stylus and translated the signals into pictures and sound. Stanley followed up on key technical insights of Webster and Olson to calculate the mathematical prediction for capacitive detection of video signals from an uncoated nonconductive vinyl disc.[5] The results were promising enough to convince several interested laboratory directors that the capacitance approach had economic potential. If video information could be stored on a cheap vinyl disc and retrieved by an inexpensive player, there might be an opportunity to develop the mass consumer videoplayer that Olson had been pursuing for years. Competing research priorities in the Systems Research Laboratory delayed further investigation of the subject until 1964.

Exploratory work begins

Several exploratory research projects related to the videoplayer concept began following the 1964 spring directors' meeting. All were intended to determine the potential of various storage media. One looked at magnetic tape and three looked at different nonmagnetic media. To pursue so many alternatives at this early stage was a substantial commitment of researcher time, but it did not involve heavy capital investment. Most of the work was done on paper or with experiments involving simple laboratory models made of readily available components or fragile experimental materials, such as balsa wood and soda straws. Work commenced with a brief obligatory review of previous laboratory efforts.

The A&ER researchers who had worked on the Hear–See player earlier started up a joint project with the advanced development group at Home Instruments in Indianapolis to reevaluate the magnetic approach in light of recent technological advances. Their main goal was to substitute transistors for other cumbersome circuitry. The head of the advanced development team in Indianapolis was a former member of the Systems Research Laboratory in Princeton; he evaluated the laboratory models for their product potential. The laboratory team came to the conclusion that magnetic tape held little potential for a major breakthrough, and the project transferred out to Indianapolis, where it was absorbed in a larger effort backed by some corporate seed money.

Magnetic videoplayer product development

Meantime, reports were circulating that other companies, Sony among them, were developing magnetic videorecorders for eventual use in the consumer market. Interest was aroused in several RCA product divisions and in 1965 Barton Kreuzer, then head of the RCA Professional Broadcast Division, convened a meeting of all RCA technical and product development personnel who had interest in magnetic videorecording. Representatives from the Princeton Laboratories went on record at

Videoplayer research begins

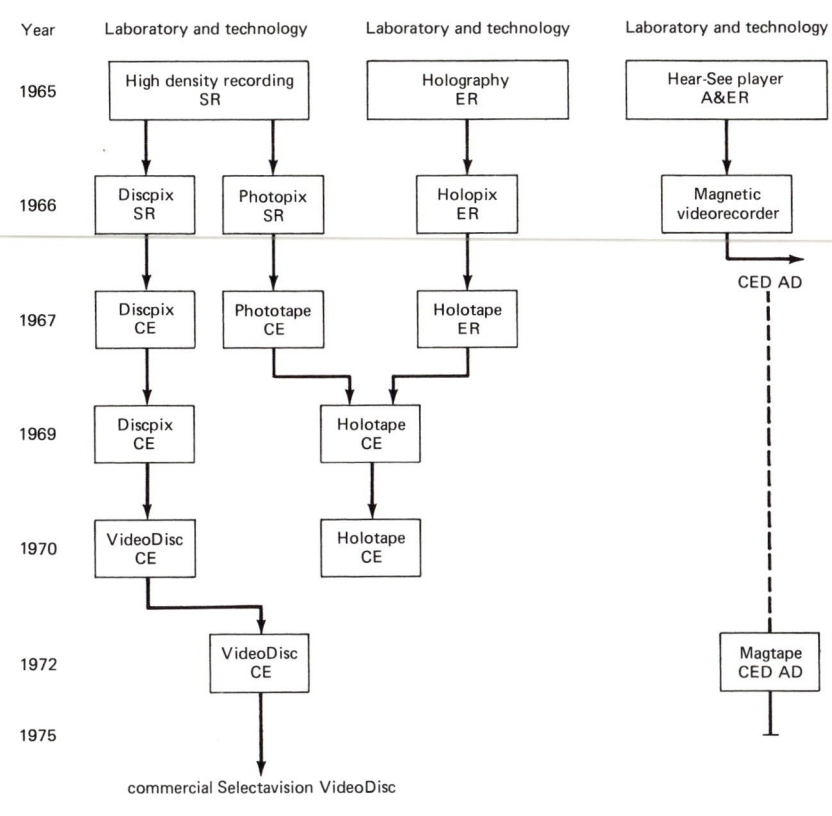

Year	Laboratory and technology		Laboratory and technology	Laboratory and technology
1965	High density recording SR		Holography ER	Hear-See player A&ER
1966	Discpix SR	Photopix SR	Holopix ER	Magnetic videorecorder
				CED AD
1967	Discpix CE	Phototape CE	Holotape ER	
1969	Discpix CE	Holotape CE		
1970	VideoDisc CE	Holotape CE		
1972	VideoDisc CE			Magtape CED AD
1975				

commercial Selectavision VideoDisc

Key
SR — systems research
ER — electronics research
A&ER — acoustical and
    electromechanical research
CE — consumer electronics laboratory
CED AD — Consumer Electronics Division
    advanced development

RCA videoplayer family tree.

the meeting as believing that magnetic tape would always be too expensive for a mass-market consumer product, but others disagreed.

A few months later Brown agreed to put seed money into corporate sponsorship of a magnetic videorecorder development program. Since the Professional Broadcast Division had no experience with consumer products, it was decided to locate the project in Indianapolis. Ray Warren, RCA's leading expert from Camden on magnetic tape technology went to Indianapolis to head the project that would also incorporate the Hear–See player work from Princeton. At the same time, Kreuzer moved to Indianapolis to head the Consumer Electronics Division.

Meanwhile, the nonmagnetic high-density recording project began in the Systems Research Laboratory under Eugene Keizer. The researchers working with him included pioneering television researchers, who conceived of the videoplayer end product as a television and phonograph hybrid. In their opinion, the disc should have the size, playing time, and ease of duplication comparable to conventional records. The player/recorder should be low cost and should produce pictures and sound through a standard television set. They concluded that it would therefore be necessary to pack 50 percent more information onto a disc than had ever been achieved through means known to the Laboratories. The first task, achieved within a few months, was to demonstrate that information elements smaller than a micron could be detected from a vinyl disc, as Stanley's calculations had suggested.

In its first year, the so-called Discpix project had the kind of difficulty that a directed project would be expected to have in the free research environment of the 1960s. The laboratory directors allocated manpower to it, but it was another matter to persuade researchers to stay with it when they did not find it exciting. For problem-solving researchers, the link between the theoretical work required and an achievable videoplayer seemed tenuous. Turnover was rapid, and the group consisted largely of beginning or temporary researchers who joined the project only until they found faster-moving or more stimulating work elsewhere. Under such circumstances progress was terribly slow, as each new team member had to learn the ropes.

The original workplan for Discpix was to analyze four main technical problems – resolution, signal-to-noise, control, and modulation – in terms of both theory and practice. Parallel teams looked at two different formats for storing information – serial signal picked up from the bottom of a groove, and frame-by-frame encoded and retrieved using an injection laser. In view of the slow progress, the laboratory directors urged that the effort concentrate on the capacitive approach (dealing with variations in capacitance – the relationship between charge and voltage of two adjacent electrical conductors), but researchers viewed this as the least interesting method and continued to work on multiple alternatives, including vidicon, laser and electrostatic pickups, and spiral, line-by-line, and frame-by-frame formats for information storage.

The first nonmagnetic approach to demonstrate feasibility was a photographic approach called Photopix. The approach used a vidicon (an electronic camera device) to retrieve tiny pictures deposited on the disc. This approach was finally rejected because both the vidicon and the photographic disc were too expensive for a mass market. The capacitive approach was the hardest from which to get tangible results because all of its elements were so interdependent, and each held major uncertainties. To test a pickup for the serial signals system, for instance, a new way first had to be found to produce test records.

The Discpix project finally achieved stability, and therefore a steady rate of progress, when it was joined by Jon Clemens, a newly hired electrical engineer from MIT who had previously worked on teaching machines for the blind. Clemens had earned a PhD, but like Keizer, he was a problem solver, and together the two men gave the project continuity. They were each to spend more than a decade on the Discpix, later Videodisc, project and they shared most of the patents arising from these projects after 1965.

After spending his first year defining the capacitance Discpix system characteristics, Clemens concluded that the system could not work as originally conceived, as sufficiently strong signal resolution could not be achieved on an uncoated disc. Clemens believed that playtime would be limited to ten minutes per side even when a vinyl disc was given a metallic coating. Moreover, since coating the disc would involve very expensive manufacturing processes, the findings seemed to invalidate the major economic advantages assumed for a capacitance disc.

In late 1966, after two years of effort, the capacitance system concept seemed to have neither of the two ingredients that made a project attractive from a research point of view – intrinsic scientific appeal or an obviously feasible end product. Moreover, the core idea on which the entire system hinged – Stanley's original calculations for a simple uncoated disc – had been at least partially discredited; this led to discord among the researchers who could not agree on the best approaches for other elements of the system. Nevertheless, it did have management backing within the RCA Laboratories. Stanley and Webster were its champions, and they were moving into positions in Laboratories management where they were able to keep the project alive. Webster became vice-president of materials and device research in 1966, and Stanley joined the New Business Evaluation staff. When Webster became head of the entire research center in 1968, Stanley took over the newly formed Consumer Electronics Laboratory. Had Stanley not been in a position to promote the capacitance approach, it is doubtful whether it would have survived the decade.

Holopix

While Keizer's team in Systems Research was pursuing Discpix, a completely different approach to the videoplayer concept was under investigation in Electronics Research. Holopix, which involved storage of holographic images or holograms (light interference patterns) on a vinyl disc, possessed much of the scientific appeal that capacitance lacked. It originated in work on two of the most interesting phenomena that were subjects of study in electronics research in the 1960s, lasers and holograms. RCA had been studying lasers of all kinds, injection, gas and crystal, for their potential in communications and recording for a number of years. RCA's Applied Research operation in Camden had devised a number of uses for lasers in practical devices for the military. At the same time, a two-man team in Princeton became interested in the phenomenon of holography, a new branch of the science of optics.

In the space of a year, this two-man Holopix team was able to demonstrate the feasibility of a "phase hologram" on a rotating disc which could be read using a pulsed laser and a vidicon. The promising aspect of this development was that the phase hologram could be produced by simple mechanical stamping, in the same manner that a disc could be produced. On the other hand, since neither the vidicon nor the laser had been commercially developed, major economic uncertainties remained.

When the Holopix project requested further funding in 1965 under the new planning system, the laboratory directors opposed it as impractical. But Henry Lewis, who had succeeded Webster as head of the Electronics Research Laboratory, backed the project and would not let it be moved too quickly into the newly reorganized Consumer Electronics Laboratory where it might be shut down. As a concession to the concerns about impracticality, however, he hired a director for the project from RCA's Applied Technologies Division in Camden, William Hannon, who had been involved with several recent government contracts on lasers and was known for an aggressive, results-oriented style.

Some directors charged that continued support of the holographic player project was nothing more than a blatant attempt to appease the disgruntled scientists. But Webster saw real merit in encouraging an applied team effort among researchers who had not generally experienced much of this. While he conceded that the likelihood of Holopix reaching the economic goals set for the videoplayer end product was small, he believed that much useful learning could be gained from it. He considered competition inside the Laboratories a spur to focus the disc project's efforts, as the Discpix and Holopix projects soon became rivals.

After a year of Hannon's energetic leadership, his team was able to demonstrate feasibility for a phase hologram-based system in which a ring of phased holograms was pressed onto the surface of a phonograph record, picked up by a laser and decoded by a vidicon. The images were extremely poor in quality but, as they were the first images demonstrated by either of the two rival systems, they produced much excitement in the Laboratories.

99

Under the new controls, all projects received more formal economic goals in 1966 than ever before. Discpix adopted a target selling price of $100 for the player and $3 for the disc, while comparable goals for Holopix were $300 to $500 and $5 to $10. Both projects planned to complete selection of their key components and demonstrate system feasibility by the end of 1967.

Outside and inside competition

In late 1966, the *New York Times* published a story that CBS was developing a new videoplayer. CBS denied the report, and RCA researchers considered the description of the system highly implausible. Nevertheless, such potential competition from CBS, of all companies, was not to be taken lightly. When further reports confirming the existence of CBS's Electronic Videorecorder (EVR) appeared in 1967, David Sarnoff himself raised an alarm. Hillier was quick to reassure the General, but he also took the precaution of having the CBS concept investigated in the research center. He commissioned Ray Kell, one of RCA's television research veterans, to pick up on some of the earlier work done on Photopix. The Phototape project, as it was now called, was an insurance project. Kell and a small team of researchers devoted a year of effort to the concept, enough to assess its economics and to put RCA in a position to follow closely on a CBS announcement if that proved desirable. When the year was up, Kell convinced Hillier and Webster that CBS's economic claims had to be based on erroneous assumptions.

Both Discpix and Holopix ran into delays in 1967. By mid-year the Holopix team had developed its system elements far enough to discover that the means they had to use to achieve high-quality holograms generated too much information for the disc they were using to accommodate unless the playtime were drastically limited. The team then began to experiment with a plastic loop as substitute medium. But if the new medium were to work, the entire system would have to be altered.

The Discpix team had an even more difficult problem selecting an acceptable recording technique for the capacitance system. They devoted almost all of 1967 to studying materials and equipment associated with a high-resolution recording method used to make test records. Then it was necessary to complete a full-sized test record with a pattern of submicron signals in very fine grooves in order to try out the pickup technique.

The electron-beam recording technique that the Discpix team first used to make test records was initially only intended to be a versatile research tool, not the final choice for recording salable discs, but this quite sophisticated recording method in fact became the chief organizing principle for the entire project for several years. The electron-beam recording method was used because it would do both FM and AM signal formats, and the team could not agree, on theoretical grounds alone, on which of these signal formats to select. Conventional electro-mechanical recording techniques used for recording simple audio masters might be adapted to record some test samples, but Discpix team members were convinced that these could never be improved to the point that they would achieve the degree of high resolution at the recording speed necessary to make masters economically. Some team members preferred an alternate, laser-based, high-resolution recording technique, and unfortunately one of them was the researcher whose mechanical skills were needed to make electron-beam technique feasible. But since the Laboratories already had a pocket of expertise in electronic-beam technology – existing electron-beam equipment and researchers familiar with its use for other applications – that technique prevailed. The team was able to work on adapting it for use even before its own custom-designed equipment arrived, and Hillier persuaded a former associate in electron microscopy to assist while the recording technique was under development.

The negative side of using either high-resolution technique was that both involved major capital investments, costly and time-consuming work in adapting the equipment, and highly trained technicians who were not readily available in most labor markets, even if they might be available around Princeton. In November the disc project leaders made a formal decision to concentrate on the capacitive system and to request a major capital appropriation for the electron-beam recording apparatus. The use of the electron-beam technique as a central part of the disc research program could not hurt the project's chances for support with Hillier and, more important, the presence of such leading-edge technology as part of the project made it much more attractive to researchers working with the project.

The Stanley–Tan Report

The widely publicized CBS announcement of its EVR system in August 1967 provided the opportunity to attract the attention of higher-level management to nonmagnetic videoplayer work under way at Princeton. Until then, no one outside the David Sarnoff Research Center was even aware that RCA was pursuing nonmagnetic videoplayer alternatives for the consumer market. Hillier agreed that Stanley should prepare a full report on prerecorded videoplayers that could be presented to David Sarnoff on his annual visit to the Laboratories in November 1967.

Stanley collaborated with Henry Tan, a technical staff member working on the Discpix project, on a comprehensive report.[6] He also held discussions with representatives of various parts of RCA that might be involved with such a project: RCA Sales, Home Instruments, NBC, and RCA Records. This first attempt to think through a consistent product idea from the point of view of the Laboratories focused on a player of prerecorded video entertainment material that had a strong audio bent and was geared for the mass consumer market both in programming and in pricing strategy. Depending on timing and the features that were ultimately considered desirable, either Discpix, Holopix, or both might be the systems developed. Decisive factors in the eventual choice of technology would be cash flow, the role that other RCA divisions might play, and the competitive response it seemed necessary to make to CBS.

Stanley and Tan made two key recommendations. First, a

full-fledged business task force needed to be formed to plan the project. Second, since programming was critical and would require as much lead time as hardware, immediate attention needed to be given to that subject. Neither was heeded at first; it was to be a long selling process.

The Stanley–Tan report produced no immediate response from its top management audience in late 1967. David Sarnoff was in failing health and a planned management change was imminent. On January 1, 1968, Robert Sarnoff replaced Engstrom as RCA's chief executive officer (CEO); and a new approach to product planning was one of his first avowed reforms.

Only a few years after its successful repulsion of divisional attacks on its autonomy, the Laboratories prepared to reenter the mainstream of corporate life in the mid 1960s. The decade of building block research was over, and the business of research was entering a new phase. But self-reformation was painful and after a period of low involvement it was not easy to get from the rest of the corporation the kind of long-term direction that would guarantee the Laboratories the type of strategic role it had had under David Sarnoff. Obliged to define its own mission, the Laboratories management recognized in videoplayers a new product focus that could propel the research center back into the corporate mainstream. The technology was chosen to exploit the research center's existing capabilities and to enhance its proprietary position in the long run. But by its two significant choices of product and technology, the Laboratories also inadvertently placed itself in direct competition with other parts of the corporation, equipped with their own product development capabilities and with their own ideas of what the market would accept.

5

Selectavision Holotape: RCA's professional innovation

RCA unveiled Selectavision Holotape, a direct descendant of the Holopix project, as the first of a succession of Selectavision videoplayers on September 30, 1969. Said to be the largest public event ever staged by the company for a new product demonstration, the unveiling took place in grand style under a large marquee erected on the grounds of the David Sarnoff Research Center. Members of the assembled press noted with interest that Robert Sarnoff himself, CEO of RCA since January 1968, played a central role in the proceedings and that he was accompanied by a group of senior RCA executives.

To RCA insiders, the press conference conveyed an important message. Nearly two years after his elevation to the top spot in the company, it was the first clear indication of Robert Sarnoff's own style of management, specifically in terms of innovation. The emphasis on planning, the priority given to marketing, the use of the venture group as an organizational device – all were new to RCA and were signs that the new RCA would be using modern professional management techniques to maintain its old position in the industry.

When he took over as RCA's CEO in January 1968, Robert Sarnoff had already recognized that television's prosperity of the late 1960s was temporary and that its current technology was maturing rapidly. RCA was having trouble maintaining market leadership in businesses it had pioneered and he blamed this in part on the RCA Laboratories. Sarnoff believed the divisions were right in complaining that the Laboratories held onto a new technology too long and tried to perfect it far beyond what the marketplace wanted or was willing to pay for. He felt that RCA's difficulties with developing and commercializing new technology-based products would make it hard for the company to move decisively to rejuvenate its core business when it needed to.

Having spent most of his career at NBC, Robert Sarnoff shared the view held by NBC employees that RCA was dominated by a "hardware mentality." The Laboratories was the tangible representative of this hardware mentality. Although Robert Sarnoff always maintained that his policies were designed not to undermine RCA's technological strength but to make it more effective, members of RCA's powerful technical community watched nervously as various components of the company's traditional technology-based strategy were called into question. The corporate image review that accompanied Robert Sarnoff's recasting of the corporate strategy symbolized the uncertain role of the corporate laboratories under the new regime. When Robert Sarnoff insisted that the entire worldwide RCA enterprise adopt RCA's new red acrylic systems logo, only the David Sarnoff Research Center was exempt from the change. In deference to David Sarnoff's intense dislike of the new trademark, the RCA Laboratories was allowed to keep the old sign that read "Radio Corporation of America." It seemed as if the Laboratories remained part of the father's domain, the last unbreachable bastion of the technocracy with which the son was obviously uncomfortable.

The three guiding tenets of the new RCA strategy that had particular meaning for the Laboratories were that RCA would improve its balance between manufacturing and service operations and toward the high-growth service segment, that it would expand its international marketing efforts, and that it would improve relations between the Laboratories and the rest of the company.[1] These guidelines suggested that RCA would begin to compete more aggressively in markets formerly left to its international licensees. The stress on better relations between Princeton and the divisions suggested that top management would be less partial to the Laboratories than before. And how could the Laboratories possibly contribute to the broad spectrum of RCA's businesses if the company diversified heavily into nonelectronics enterprises? For Robert Sarnoff the move toward diversification was a way of moderating the extreme peaks and valleys of the electronics business and a chance for lower-risk investment of RCA's returns, but for RCA's technical community it was a sign that the urgent commitment to technology as the major source of long-term opportunity was likely to diminish.

The implications of Robert Sarnoff's other departure from former RCA practice – the move to a strong corporate staff – were likewise ambiguous for the Laboratories. With the new emphasis on marketing, it would be the readiness of the market, and not the readiness of any particular technology, that would in theory determine when RCA would introduce a technological innovation. It would be the marketing staff that would decide when the market was ready. Chase Morsey, Robert Sarnoff's pivotal staff appointment in new product planning, came from Ford, a company renowned for its professional management, especially in the areas of marketing and finance, but not well known at that time for technological innovation.

Morsey soon became vice-president of operations staffs adding to his previous duties responsibilities for planning, manufacturing, services, materials, patents and licensing, and research and engineering. Hillier, who left the RCA Laboratories to replace Brown as head of Research and Engineering, was assigned to work closely with Morsey to develop new product concepts arising from the Laboratories and elsewhere into RCA businesses.

The RCA Laboratories, long frustrated with the indifference of the divisions to their new product proposals, was willing to give the new system a chance. An active corporate staff might provide an opportunity to gain top management attention and support. But the research center soon discovered that it was not exempt from the more onerous aspects of corporate intervention. Corporate headquarters expected to dictate which research projects should be emphasized, many times without reference to the stage the projects were in. The laboratories again came under pressure to devote more resources to short-term work, particularly to computer business technical support, as the new corporate staff launched its all-out drive to challenge IBM. By 1970, when computers had become a major RCA corporate focus, nearly one-half the Laboratories' manpower was dedicated to computer-support activities.

Within months of joining RCA, Morsey had put together an organization called Advanced Product Planning that worked out of his office in New York. Heading the group was William Enders, a former member of the Laboratories New Business Evaluation group, who had spent much of his previous RCA career handling government research administration for the Laboratories. Morsey had joined RCA just as the first declines in RCA's color television sales began to be evident and the company was caught in a pincer movement, with Japanese imports beginning to enter the low end of the market at the same time that RCA's strongest competitor, Zenith, was catching up with RCA in sales volume. Morsey's immediate priority was to find a product that might help television sales. The Laboratories' Homefax had been intended for such a purpose, but Morsey's investigations convinced him that it was unsuitable, and he cut off its corporate support. The technical side of the project seemed to have been adequately developed, but the business uncertainties and complexities in such a systems business did not augur well for speedy or high-volume market introduction.

Having rejected the Laboratories' candidate for a new consumer video product, Morsey appealed to the corporation at large. Responses came in from several quarters. The Consumer Electronics Division put forth its magnetic videotape recorder project, NBC proposed cable television, Electronic Components in Lancaster suggested its consumer color television camera, and Princeton tried again, this time offering its prerecorded videoplayer.

Morsey assigned Enders to carry out a general market study for each idea and to rank them according to consumer preference. Enders concluded that among the available alternatives, the greatest consumer appeal attached to the prerecorded videoplayer. Stanley, who was now directing the technical development program for both Discpix and Holopix (now called Holotape because it had adopted the new plastic loop in place of a disc), used the 1967 Stanley–Tan Report to convince

107

his former colleague, Enders, that prerecorded video had by far the lowest equipment cost of any of the products proposed. CBS's presence in the field was also a powerful argument, for videoplayer advocates could argue that competing technologies such as cable television would be superseded. Consumers would have better control over their own entertainment with videoplayers than with the cable systems then proposed.

Morsey accepted the Enders recommendation and alerted the heads of concerned RCA divisions that his staff would be contacting them for help. In the fall of 1968 these were Hillier as vice-president of Research and Engineering, Julian Goodman, president of NBC, and Delbert Mills, executive vice-president of the RCA Home Instruments Division (soon to change to Consumer Electronics). At the corporate level Enders organized a major business evaluation effort called prerecorded electronic video systems (PREVS). The business and technical programs concerned with videoplayers were to work together under its auspices to resolve three major issues: which of its three technical approaches (Discpix, Holotape, or Phototape) did the Laboratories want as its primary focus, how would the product compare with CBS's EVR in performance, cost and timing, and what could be done about compatibility and standardization?

Stanley did not choose to back just one approach. Instead, in a memorandum to Morsey in October 1968, he noted the strengths and weaknesses of all three approaches according to five criteria: technical risk, development time required, player cost, medium cost (disc versus tape), and advantage to RCA. Stanley's own personal preference, Discpix, was still so uncertain that he could hardly select it as the system to back. Yet if its serious problems with master fabrication in particular could be resolved, he believed that Discpix would be the overwhelming preference because of its low cost, expected shorter development time, and proprietary technology. Holotape and Phototape both had the disadvantage of using expensive components. For Holotape the technology would also be proprietary, but Stanley predicted that its product development cycle would be longer. Whether or not the disc system uncertainties could be resolved during the next few months, he recommended that both the Discpix and Holotape projects continue in parallel for a time, for Holotape would have second-order advantages, such as the ability to record, that might eventually permit it to supplant the disc product.

Stanley took a chance when he put an open discussion of the relative merits of the technical systems under consideration on paper at such an early stage in the development cycle. The Laboratories was in an awkward position: it wanted corporate commitment to its prerecorded video concept even though its preferred technical approach was far from being ready for the kind of action it was seeking. The hope was that giving Morsey more information, however uncertain, might forestall his acceptance of the contending magnetic videoplayer product backed by Home Instruments. By comparison, more was known about the magnetic videorecorder, because it was believed to be based on a technology so mature, as the Laboratories pointed out, that only minor potential existed for cost reduction.

Race with CBS

CBS helped secure corporate commitment to the Laboratories' prerecorded videoplayer concept when, in December 1968, following up on the August 1967 announcement of its EVR, its flamboyant research director, Peter Goldmark, fulfilled his promise to demonstrate a black and white version of EVR. He promised color in a year. Enders, who attended the demonstration, circulated a memorandum in RCA afterward that described CBS as having "an obvious total commitment to EVR as a major new business venture."

The CBS commitment impressed Morsey, and he prepared a list of strategic guidelines by which RCA was to outmaneuver its old rival. RCA would differentiate its product from EVR in several ways: where CBS proposed to enter the market by way of the institutional and education markets, RCA would go directly to consumers; RCA hardware and RCA software would both aim to be superior in performance to those of CBS;

109

and, most challenging of all, production should be planned for 1971, or earlier, if possible.

To those who had previously talked of 1976 as a realistic production date, Morsey's strategic directive was a rude shock. It was Morsey's conviction that stiff goals produced creative results and that working toward a challenging common goal would be one way of turning RCA's collection of semiautonomous divisions into a unified system. Unfamiliar with the research process, Morsey saw the outcome as primarily a matter of motivation. The Discpix effort should be pushed to demonstrate feasibility, he declared, and then "pushed still harder to completion." If Discpix did not prove technically feasible, then Phototape was the logical fall-back candidate. To Morsey in January 1969, as to everyone else, Holotape was still a distant second-generation approach.

PREVS business planning

PREVS business planning went into such high gear from January to March 1969, that it caused the technical program to bog down. Although the nontechnical parts of the study (program content, market research, and business study segments) could be handled by any number of staff members drawn from either corporate or divisional staffs, technical effort was dependent on one small group of people at the Laboratories to proceed with research and to provide information. Researchers were suddenly overwhelmed by a steady stream of visitors from all parts of RCA wanting demonstrations and technical data on which to base their evaluations.

Meetings between corporate staff members and the consumer division personnel revealed big differences in views of the consumer market. Preliminary studies, while drawing on information from some divisional personnel, had reflected almost exclusively the opinions of the Laboratories' evaluation staff. Divisional personnel put more emphasis on system features. Any consumer videoplayer RCA produced, they said, should include a minimum of eight system features including broadcast-quality color video, ten to thirty minutes playing time, ability to play on existing color sets, stereo sound, slow motion, stop motion, indexability, and remote control. The Laboratories had specified only the first five as desirable, and only Holotape included all eight among the technologies it was developing.

Business studies included seven major areas of analysis: design, manufacturing, marketing, scheduling, competitive analysis, finance, and organization. Each dealt with all reasonable product alternatives, and each was handled by the most likely organization within RCA to do the work in the end. Representatives from the research center met with Consumer Electronics Division personnel, for instance, to do the design and manufacturing analysis of each possible configuration. Marketing strategy was handled by a representative from RCA Records who planned strategies for product pricing, penetration, market share, advertising and publicity, and competitive posture. Scheduling was worked out by the divisions, and the corporate staff took responsibility for competitive analysis, with a review of all companies that had announced any intention to enter the consumer video market at some future time – CBS, IBM, Playtape, 3M, and CATV. In view of later developments, the complete absence of Japanese contenders was noteworthy. Only CBS received more than token consideration, for it was unquestionably the key competitor in RCA's view at the time. The corporate staff identified ways that RCA could differentiate itself from CBS: RCA would produce its own components, while CBS would license its to others; and RCA would come out with color immediately, whereas CBS had announced black and white first.

Talks between divisional and laboratories personnel uncovered an obvious source of conflict. Consumer Electronics preferred its own magnetic tape player and predicted that it would be far easier to develop in the time allotted than any of the Laboratories' alternatives. Even assuming that the Laboratories could choose immediately among its three options, only a very expensive crash development program would allow the divisions to produce a system by December 1971. Design approval in the usual way would require between one and two years' work by five to eight staff members, and a rough estimate would put the time from product engineering approval to mass production of 10,000 units per year at 120 weeks.

The Records Division also anticipated lengthy lead times, since all the options under consideration would involve new mastering processes. If Discpix were to demonstrate feasibility by December 1969 (an unlikely event, since the original electronic mastering equipment was still on order), the earliest market introduction would be mid-1973. Holotape would require cost reduction of two new components, which could not be hoped for before 1975. The chief limiting task would be to design tooling for the vidicon at Lancaster, which would require at least twelve months on a crash basis, and forty-one months normally. Preliminary estimates put development costs, regardless of system, at $800,000 in capital cost and $200,000 operating expenses.

The marketing staff conducted studies covering all proposed videoplayer concepts, ranging from small information-gathering discussion groups to a consumer survey reaching thousands of respondents. Enders' early efforts had already indicated that a third of the consumers polled would rent or buy a prerecorded videoplayer if it were available. More focused studies portrayed the likely consumer as a light television viewer who would be attracted to the system for the control it offered over program selection. Responses suggested that the consumer divisions might be partly right about features – results from more than 100 respondents showed a strong preference for tape over records because of its recording capability, but stop motion and freeze frame were viewed as not essential. Color too was desirable but not necessary. An initial program catalog would be adequate if it contained mostly entertainment programming (musicals, dramas, and sporting events). The cost of such an initial library was calculated to be $9 million.

The Sorenson Consulting Group, a private consultant hired to conduct a marketing strategy meeting at New York's University Club, brought together marketing experts from various RCA divisions. The consensus of the meeting was that a videoplayer was the kind of systems entertainment product that RCA was uniquely suited to produce. Participants also agreed that someone else would produce it if RCA did not, and that it would have a profound effect on several major RCA businesses, including television, phonograph and broadcasting. The group also recommended that the business be launched by a venture team independent of any of the major businesses.

In a summary report of all the marketing findings, the Sorenson Group stressed that the unique opportunity for RCA was to allow consumers control over their own programming.[2] This should differ from television programming in that it should be what Sorenson termed self-regenerating – a different experience each time it was played. Convenience would be important, and it should be possible to view an entire program on one disc. It was definitely the systems nature of the product that made it especially appropriate for RCA, and it could later be combined with other products from RCA divisions. Finally, it was essential that the price be low enough for the mass market.

High-level strategy

Certain questions could only be addressed by senior management. What levels of corporate commitment would be needed? What evidence might still be required to obtain such commitment? Who should make the commitments? What threshold level of technical risk should RCA take on? When should RCA publicly demonstrate or announce its system? To answer these questions, a high-level meeting convened at Rockefeller Center in late April 1969 consisting of Enders, Hillier, Stanley, Webster, Donald Savage representing RCA Records, and George Evanoff, a newly appointed corporate staff member who would shortly succeed Enders.

Discussion centered on the tricky problems of systems innovation and soon turned to the early days of color television. In view of the interdependence of videoplayer sales and program availability, disc sales would only take off when there was a substantial videoplayer population, and vice versa. With

113

RCA's many complementary divisions and large resources, the group saw the systems problem as potentially RCA's main competitive advantage, but this was only valid if the company organized itself properly. What form should the organization take? The alternatives were a lead division that would take the coordinating responsibility versus a venture group approach. Representatives of the Laboratories strongly favored the latter approach to ensure that no division would be able to strangle the new product program or, for that matter, substitute its own preferred technology before the product was safely launched.

Later conversation turned to timing. Should RCA attempt to capture the lead, or would it hang back and work on software, which was essentially nonexistent? Once again the logic of RCA's unique structure and capability was the determining factor. RCA was structured to lead, and this surely justified "the highest levels of effort," as the minutes noted afterward. Since Robert Sarnoff and his most senior managers were scheduled to meet in executive session in August, that meeting would provide an opportunity to seek Sarnoff's commitment to the videoplayer business. The earliest possible date that a public demonstration could be staged, it was agreed, was in seven months, in December 1969.

But Robert Sarnoff himself unwittingly knocked this carefully constructed new product planning apparatus into a cocked hat. In May 1969, RCA's color camera lost out to a rival Westinghouse model in a contest held to equip the Apollo 11 space capsule. Camera technology was one of the areas where RCA considered itself to be a technological leader, although this particular contest had not been viewed by those directly involved as either important or profitable. The defeat had symbolic content, however, for the Westinghouse equipment used color camera technology developed by CBS, a system derived from the CBS predecessor that RCA had defeated only after much difficulty back in the 1950s.

Robert Sarnoff first learned of the defeat while watching Johnny Carson's "Tonight Show" on NBC. The next morning he expressed his deep personal displeasure in a memorandum to Morsey, demanding to know what CBS would do next. It would be only a matter of time, he predicted, before CBS emerged with some further challenge to RCA's leadership. Morsey feared that CBS's demonstration of the color version of its EVR, planned for the end of the year, was precisely the kind of challenge to which the memo referred. Robert Sarnoff had not yet been formally told of the videoplayer plan, but the top management presentation planned for the August meeting would bring the program to his attention. Morsey decided to accelerate the public demonstration. The RCA videoplayer had to be shown in color before CBS came out with its next version of EVR. He directed the PREVS planning team to "start counting backwards" from a new press conference date of September 15, 1969.

A hastily reassembled PREVS strategy group at the end of May decided that it would be Holotape and not Discpix that would be shown. Phototape was closer than either of the others to being ready for demonstration, but it was too similar in technology to EVR to support the key message of the press conference – RCA's continued technological leadership. If a proprietary technology were needed, then Holotape was closest to being a complete system. It had shown pictures, and the parts of the system had been combined to the point of feasibility. One thing had to be clear, however. Webster, Stanley, and Hillier wanted it understood that Holotape's demonstration in no way changed their ultimate preference for the Discpix version of the videoplayer. The same meeting also agreed on the choice of a venture group whose tasks would be to plan the September press conference, to write a detailed business plan, to set up a program of software research, and to coordinate the multidivisional PREVS development program.

The Holotape research team at the Laboratories then began a three-month crash program, its objective being to achieve TV-quality video with sound better than television, all attractively packaged in a player using a convenient tape cassette. Members of the Phototape team contributed to the effort. When the system still lacked both sound and color with a few weeks to go, it was decided to concentrate on color for demonstration purposes.

Enders and Stanley collaborated on the formal PREVS presentation to Robert Sarnoff. The presentation had two separate versions, the first directed by the Laboratories staff, the second completely revised by the marketing staff at Morsey's direction. A comparison between the two brought out a few telling contrasts between the approaches of the two groups. The Laboratories version stressed the CBS threat and dwelt heavily on the three technical approaches that could be used to counter it. The marketing version, prepared by George Evanoff, stressed the need for such a product in RCA's market and the gap in RCA's projected growth that the videorecorder would fill. The researchers said what could be done in light of what they thought was possible; the revised version sketched out a plan in the form of "target" predictions and outlined how RCA, organized and directed by the venture team as the tool of the corporate marketing staff, could achieve the stated goals.

The differences in the two versions were substantive as well as stylistic, particularly in terms of timing, cost and organizational structure. Although the product concept remained unchanged with respect to function and consumer group served, and the final technical choices were still to be decided on the basis of retail price and features, the financial picture was quite different. The Laboratories presentation discussed maximum cash runoff of $60 million, while the marketing staff presentation asked approval for a $35 million investment. Where the first version had said that the lowest possible Holotape price would be $550, Morsey assigned it a "target price" of $450. Finally, where the researchers gave an introduction date of June 1973 for Discpix and June 1974 for Holotape, the marketing staff said the necessary date must be early 1972 and would require a "compression of the ideal." They told top management that the feasibility of the compressed schedule had not been checked with the divisions, but those who had studied the matter assumed that parallel activity on prototype development and product engineering could achieve the required date.

The proposed new venture group also took on a different slant from the Laboratories' original idea of it. Hillier had suggested that the venture group should work toward four objectives: a long-range business plan, expanded and refined market research, a fully developed program catalog, and a presentation of RCA's image, presumably in the press conference, that would counteract CBS's competitive stance. The marketing staff version charged the venture group with providing direction for development and product engineering activities, including "selection of the technical approach of the first generation PREVS and facilitating the transfer of applicable technology from the Laboratories to the product division."

The August executive meeting gave its approval for a September announcement, and Selectavision, as the new marketing staff called the concept, was on its way.

Holotape to the front

The choice of the Holotape version of the videoplayer for demonstration in September 1969 was a consequence of the unusually rapid progress that its research team had made during the spring of 1969. The shift from the disc format using holography, Holopix, to the tape, although it had required major changes in the interdependent components of the system, nevertheless gave the program a burst of momentum. The team was also able to use the CBS EVR system as a moving target now that the new tape approach made their product more like the EVR's frame-by-frame, film-based format.

The program's exposure to the scrutiny of the Consumer Electronics engineering group during the planning effort also contributed to the system's progress. The move from a disc to tape format made the product more forgiving in its production schedule than Discpix, and much more congenial from the standpoint of Rex Isom, chief engineer of the Records Division. Isom favored Holotape over Discpix for several reasons. He believed that the equipment needed for tape would be three to five times less expensive, and more readily available, so that it would not be necessary to commit to procuring equipment until mid-1970. There was more to Isom's judgment than simple pragmatism; his preference for the tape version was also a matter of personal experience, having spent most of his career working on magnetic tape products in RCA's government systems business in Camden. He saw real technical

117

promise in a tape product that was not magnetic but that had some of tape's advantages.

Meantime, planning for the demonstration was going ahead. Morsey, as he was not well acquainted with people in RCA, asked the personnel department to find a candidate with relevant experience to head the new venture group, someone whose status would demonstrate the seriousness of the company's commitment to the program. Robert Bitting, who was then working in planning and capital budgeting, combined early experience as a television engineer in the Camden plant with project management experience on two major government projects: the Ballistic Missile Early Warning System (BMEWS) and the Minuteman Missile program. More recently he had spent a year as a Sloan Fellow at the Massachusetts Institute of Technology's Sloan School, where he had taken an interest in science-based innovation at RCA. He had done his required paper on RCA's pioneering role in black and white television. The study had convinced him that the modern RCA needed to recapture the entrepreneurial vigor it had possessed under David Sarnoff. On the other hand, unlike many RCA veterans, Bitting was sympathetic to Robert Sarnoff's efforts to change the company and to give it more professional management. Morsey's belief that corporate headquarters could enforce much more effective use of RCA resources, particularly its technical capabilities, was one that Bitting shared.

Back in the Laboratories, success followed success for Holotape that spring. As so often happened, the team that was investigating novel problems found it easier to get help from the Laboratories support staff, who gave Holotape any time they could spare from their high-priority computer work. Small wonder that the Holotape team, headed by Bill Hannon, began its three-month crash program with momentum and with a sense that they could achieve the impossible if anyone could.

Despite high morale, the crash program was an exhausting experience for those involved. Toward the end, researchers were spending as close to twenty-four hours a day on the project as was humanly possible. Some members of the team complained that the circumstances were causing them to do a good deal of unnecessary work, work that would ultimately lead nowhere and that might even hamper the ultimate progress of the project once it was back on track. Certainly as the deadline approached, more and more decisions were made for the sake of expediency. Most of August was consumed in experiments devoted to choosing a color-encoding scheme, for the circuitry could not be completed without it. In the end the stripe color encoding system was selected because it was easily attained and not because it would be best for ultimate use. One team member commented wryly at the time that the results of all the intense effort was "a shotgun wedding of holotape and spatially encoded color television on film," a method close to the competing EVR system that derived its know-how from earlier Phototape achievements. Yet for many of the participants, often young researchers with no previous experience of such proceedings, the crash program was an exhilarating experience. Considering where they had begun, they accomplished an enormous amount of work in three months.

But members of the corporate marketing staff, who had had virtually no contact with the particulars of the technology before it was demonstrated and who were unfamiliar with the stages that research-based programs could be expected to go through, were to react differently. They would be shocked by the poor quality of the pictures, and some would even charge that they had been misled into believing that the system was more advanced than it was. Naturally the researchers would react with anger to such charges. Their pride in achievement would turn to chagrin at having exposed to public misunderstanding a system that they had known all along could not be ready in anything but a relative sense. Mutual recrimination would grow between corporate staff and laboratories, and the bad feeling would eventually produce a rift in relations.

Ironically, despite Holotape's obvious performance deficiencies, the marketing staff, in the act of formulating a business concept for the demonstration, had sold themselves on the system's virtues. Losing sight of the tenuous basis on which the product had been brought forward, and forgetting the clear statements of the Laboratories' management in May that Holotape was not its choice, they prepared to pursue the business development timetable set forth in the demonstration.

The September 30th press conference

Robert Sarnoff, who played a central role in the presentation, took pains to stress the ways in which this press conference differed from all of RCA's earlier "firsts," lest his presence mislead observers into thinking that he intended to follow his father's style of innovative leadership. "While RCA Selectavision Holotape," he noted, "might be the latest in a chain of notable technical achievements – television, videotape recording, computer memories – there was a profound difference this time in the circumstances which surrounded its debut." Selectavision was to be the first in a series of what Robert Sarnoff termed "market related research projects":

> For the first time in RCA history, this major breakthrough is accompanied by specific plans for its early introduction as a consumer product. For the first time, an RCA laboratory project has reached the demonstration stage with its own record of exhaustive market studies to define the nature and extent of the demand that can be expected. These studies have made clear not only the consumer desire for such a product but, more importantly, the willingness of consumers to buy it if the price is low enough.... Important as the product is, this aspect of its introduction has even broader significance as the first tangible demonstration of RCA's new marketing orientation.[3]

There were several important reasons for the unusually flamboyant style of the Selectavision press conference. In the first place, the new home videoplayer met both short-term and long-term needs for RCA and represented an important element of continuity, linking RCA's past role as technical leader with its intentions to be a shaper of the home communications center of the future. Selectavision was introduced as a radical enhancement for RCA's most important existing consumer product, color television. It was hoped that a product that would offer new uses for a color set would bolster sales for RCA's Consumer Electronics Division, which was for the first time encountering damaging competition in the marketplace. Later the product would be well positioned to serve as a follow-on product when the market for color television had been saturated.

A second reason for the display was the need for an answering gesture to the CBS initiative in introducing its EVR videoplayer. The CBS introduction had received much attention in the press and RCA needed to prevent EVR from picking up hardware licensees and software suppliers before RCA was ready to approach them on behalf of its own product. Finally, Robert Sarnoff's attendance at the event was a gesture to reassure investors. Holotape was displayed as proof that RCA's new top management was not planning, as recent diversification efforts might imply, to neglect RCA's core consumer electronics business.

The RCA speakers at the demonstration labeled Holotape a technological breakthrough – the first consumer application of lasers and holography – a story that delighted the press. One of the most impressive claims that RCA made for its player was the price of $450, strikingly low compared to the CBS EVR price of $750. The plastic tape RCA proposed to use for the recording medium was the same inexpensive plastic wrap used by supermarkets to package meat. It was said to be virtually indestructible. On such mundane material would be embossed space-age images, light-interference patterns called holograms that would reproduce moving pictures with the aid of a laser beam. The press kits distributed at the demonstration were made of the very same plastic wrap. The idea that exotic technology could be sold at a price low enough to appeal to a mass market naturally caught the attention of those present.

In a key presentation, Morsey, called Selectavision a "sure-fire formula," a marketer's dream. Holotape had replaced Homefax as RCA's candidate for the centerpiece of the Home Information Center, believed to be just around the corner in the 1960s. RCA envisioned the new media center in the home to be anchored firmly to television, not to the telephone or the computer as AT&T and IBM had proposed. With Selectavision, Morsey suggested, RCA was responding to a strong consumer need for "personalized television." The choice of the name obviously connoted consumers' personal control over the timing and selection of their own television programming.

Morsey stated RCA's intent to launch a multifaceted business. He predicted that Selectavision would one day be a billion-dollar industry with room for many hardware manufacturers and software suppliers. RCA's early announcement would, he said, give the rest of the industry a chance to make plans. Such a unique medium would surely spawn programming opportunities of all kinds, and he invited producers to contact RCA if they wished to partake of the multimillion dollar fund that RCA had set aside to acquire programs for the initial program catalog.

Morsey characterized RCA's plans for its new business in terms reminiscent of previous RCA television strategies. The company would approach the new market on a systems basis, taking advantage of technologies that had only emerged from its laboratories during the previous five years. The entire corporation, he promised, was committed to develop and entrepreneur its product "as a tightly structured marketing technical and economic system." To bring this about, a new organizational mechanism, a corporate venture group, had been formed.

From the standpoint of technical performance the Holotape demonstration did not bear very close examination. The picture scarcely qualified as the "better than television quality" described in the brochure. The holograms produced a weird unfocused effect, distorted even further by static in the picture. Color was barely detectable, and the means to produce sound from the tape had to be simulated.

A stranger to the world of consumer electronics might have noted a little irony in Robert Sarnoff's assurances that his company would never again repeat the mistakes of color television. No one who covered the event recalled in print RCA's earliest demonstration of color television before the FCC, which had signalled the beginning of a very long and tortuous road to actual market introduction. Later, the comparison would be made quite often. Perhaps the spectators, accustomed to the conventions of an industry that frequently showed products in their earliest working stages, took the observed state of the product for granted.

Repercussions of the presentation

Designed to achieve public objectives, the press conference affected the substance of the technical program in important ways. Holotape researchers were encouraged by the enthusiastic public response their system got, and they reaped countless tangible benefits for their project. Even though Webster and Stanley remained adamant that no firm decision had been made on videoplayer technology, it was impossible to translate technical impartiality into evenhanded support. Whatever its preferences, the Laboratories management team could not fail to play ball with New York – the project's budget depended on orders from New York, and it needed top priority treatment from support services at the Laboratories like the model shop whose responses could dramatically speed or retard progress. It became easier for the Holotape group to recruit new researchers, for the project promised not only technical excitement but prominence in the field of applied optics.

Discouraged by the attention that the rival Holotape team was getting, the Discpix researchers sank into the doldrums. The electron-beam apparatus was still not producing good test masters. The Records Division, on which they depended for pressing their test records, was giving preferential treatment to Holotape. Don McCoy, who was promoted to replace Stanley as director of the Consumer Electronics Laboratory, where both teams were working, found himself in a frustrating position. Morale was so low among the Discpix team members that he had to give them a series of pep talks, urging them to consider demonstration of pictures a top priority. Yet McCoy became convinced, as he familiarized himself with the new business plan, that Selectavision Holotape would never attain the economic targets it was shooting for.

Eventually the Holotape team encountered the negative side of their increased visibility as work was constantly disrupted by requests from corporate staff members bringing outside visitors for demonstrations. The researchers had to retrace their steps to undo many of the technical expediencies that they had adopted, a time-consuming process with no results to show. Meanwhile, the corporate staff was following Morsey's injunction to push the project hard, insisting on quick specification and documentation of the project so that work could proceed elsewhere. The schedule that the venture group had adopted in September 1969 called for work to proceed in parallel in four separate locations. RCA Laboratories was responsible for selecting suitable systems for color encoding and sound, Records was to begin work on the method of tape replication, Consumer Electronics was to put together an engineering prototype, and the Electronic Components Division was to design and begin cost reduction procedures on two critical components, the laser and the vidicon. All divisions prepared to follow orders and transferred personnel to the Holotape effort. In the case of Consumer Electronics, this meant diverting people from the magnetic tape project headed by Ray Warren, but he continued to work on his pet project on a bootleg basis, even after the project had formally been stopped.

Preparing for the future product

The Selectavision venture group was still very much in the process of formation in the late fall and winter of 1969. Yet it was this team that had to deal with the conflicts that surfaced around Selectavision in the aftermath of the press conference. Bitting assembled his six-man Video Playback Systems Team, as it was formally known, very gradually. He had to find people to fill the functions of marketing, finance and administration, public relations, program services, and product engineering who could work together as a team.

Filling the program services slot proved the most difficult, as NBC employees, among whom Bitting hoped to find a suitable candidate, were generally unwilling to transfer to RCA. Although Records provided good advice, a venture group member from the Records Division was considered to have too limited a perspective to deal with programming for a visual medium. While the slot remained vacant, Bitting shouldered some of the duties himself.

Since the lack of an expert made it difficult to tackle the problem of finding good programming sources, the group spent most of its early efforts trying to manage according to the "compressed" schedule RCA needed to capture the lead from CBS. Bitting understood it to be his job to remove the key business and technical decisions out of the political arena at the divisional level to RCA headquarters, where they could be considered from an overall corporate perspective. This brought him into direct conflict with Webster and Stanley at the Laboratories who, in all planning meetings had never conceded that the venture group's powers should have anything to do with making technical decisions. They had no intention of relinquishing control over these matters to Bitting.

When Bitting in early 1970 tried to pin down the specifications of the Holotape system, he found few, if any, of the publicly announced procedures consistent with what was actually going on. Not having been a party to the spring strategy sessions, he assumed that Selectavision Holotape was a working consensus backed by strong top management support. He discovered that it had in fact been a flimsy truce, settled solely for the purpose of the public demonstration. His attempts at intervention in technical matters met with sharp rebuff from the Laboratories. In response to his urgings to deploy all available manpower on resolving the few remaining issues, Stanley, now staff vice-president at Princeton, informed Bitting that he had completely missed the basic issue. The Laboratories' top priority was not to complete Holotape as such, but to meet or do better than the stipulated targets of $400 player cost, $10 program cost, and two years to introduction. In short, the basic issue was still the choice of the optimum technology. "I'll be damned if I'll be stampeded by our show," Stanley noted with exasperation in his files. He told Bitting that he would be welcome to join the Laboratories' council of directors at their next meeting, but decisions would be made by them, and he would be treated as one among equals.

When Henry Ball, the design engineering expert, took up his post on the venture group in February 1970, he soon grasped the real state of affairs. His first attempt to list key specifications to be used as a common basis for discussion in the first of his monthly coordination meetings in New York uncovered a major misunderstanding between the Laboratories staff and the marketing staff. Holotape research was effectively in a state of paralysis brought on by premature exposure and subsequent unrelenting pressure from the outside to freeze and transfer specifications. Ball saw no alternative but to break the logjam by declaring the question of specifications reopened.

Research progress resumed immediately, with major improvements occurring in rapid succession, but valuable months had been lost in the name of compression. The divisions, working with the preliminary information they had received, had time to expose the flaws in the conception. Already committed to preferred projects of their own, they were in a mood to make the most out of every inconsistency or inaccuracy, and to show that the technology they were receiving was unworkable. As a result, just a few months delay turned out to be costly for the hopes of the Holotape team. Moreover, the competitive picture was changing dramatically during the first half of 1970. When the competitors' responses to CBS and RCA were all on the table, two important facts stood out. Most of the responses were magnetic systems, and CBS no longer looked like the competitor to watch. It appeared that what the Laboratories management had been saying all along was justified.

All this paled in significance, however, in the face of other events. The economy suffered a recession that resulted in a severe business downturn for the consumer electronics industry as a whole. And along with that bad news came unmistakable signs that RCA's computer business, which was supposed to have turned a corner, badly needed attention.

Holotape was an "RCA first" in management terms as well as in technical terms. It was the first attempt by a new top management to conduct innovation "by the book," and it came after a period when RCA had not pursued innovation in its core business for some time. The Selectavision project's use of systematic planning and goal setting and its venture team structure, market research, and focused resources were in vogue at the time in management circles, but they could not make up for the fact that many of the managers outside the research organization who directed and coordinated the Selectavision effort lacked experience with science-based innovation. Coming out of government systems within RCA, and the extremely stable, low-technology, auto industry of the 1960s, they did not appreciate the nature of the technical uncertainties they faced.

Holotape proved to be only the first of several Selectavision videoplayer projects that RCA pursued over the next decade. Many other companies joined RCA in the pursuit, for the need for innovation was even greater in the consumer electronics industry at large than it was at RCA. The problem was how to organize to meet the need in an industry that was becoming more fragmented domestically and more fiercely competitive internationally.

6

Everything ventured

The enthusiasm for videocassette systems, as they came to be called by 1970, was less a matter of technology in a state of readiness than a reflection of the desperate need of the consumer electronics industry, which was in an economic downturn such as it had not experienced for over a decade. The press stimulated interest into something approaching frenzy, calling the videocassette a major opportunity for hardware manufacturers and entertainment producers alike, and predicting that it would have an immediate and stunning impact on life in America. Peter Gruber, vice-president of Columbia Pictures, echoed the general air of wishful thinking when he wrote an article entitled "The New Ball Game." In a passage that was widely quoted at the time he said:

> The impending cartridge revolution will have an enormous impact on the motion picture industry as well as every other American institution – music, theatre, publishing, politics, sex, journalism, religion and big business. Financial empires will rise and fall; the 'home entertainment center' will become the backbone of the national economy, surpassing the automobile in production.[1]

Signs of a new industry taking shape were ubiquitous during the winter and spring following RCA's Selectavision press conference. Companies that had followed CBS's pioneering videocassette announcement with little more than idle interest took RCA's Holotape demonstration as a signal that the "videocassette revolution," had indeed begun. Not to be left behind, other electronics companies in Europe and Japan, as well as in the United States, responded with videoplayer announcements of their own. Some systems were said to be intended immediately for the consumer market; others like

128

CBS's EVR or Sony's Umatic, slated for the institutional segment, were seen as stepping stones to the larger consumer market. While most companies were aiming at their own domestic markets initially, a few of the Japanese companies, especially Sony, looked as if they might quite soon become competitors in the U.S. market.

It soon became apparent to industry analysts that the video-player industry was likely to consist of two types of competing technologies. In general, magnetic tape systems appeared to be destined for the low-volume segment of the market that could afford to pay around $1,000 for a player and anywhere from $20 to $50 for blank and prerecorded tapes. Disc player systems would be considerably less expensive (because of the more favorable economics of disc replication), but the range of prices discussed was wide and less specific.

Magnetic tape reconsidered

At first a stream of announcements of magnetic tape systems, all incompatible with each other, and all priced well above RCA's Selectavision Holotape figure of $450, supported the early judgment of the RCA marketing staff that magnetic tape would be no threat. The high tape cost and severe standardization problems were seen as chronic conditions that magnetic tape products would never escape. In the collective view of RCA's marketing specialists, companies that proposed to sell such products were doing so only because they lacked options.

An announcement from Sony in mid-1970 caused RCA's Selectavision venture group considerable unease for Sony, unencumbered in Japan by the types of laws that prohibited collusion between competitors in the United States, had persuaded seven other Japanese companies that had previously announced their own videotape machines to adopt the Sony format. The agreement put RCA in a wholly new competitive position, as it seemed likely that this cartel arrangement would permit lower development and production costs. Sony, in fact, had announced its player as a product able to compete with RCA's Holotape playback system.

129

"Sony's videotape achievements make them, and their seven co-signers, our most formidable competition," Ball warned Bitting in April 1970. He predicted that a videocassette player would reach the market in one to two years. This was much earlier than Holotape, after its recent technical reappraisal and resulting schedule adjustment, could possibly appear. There was a real danger that Sony and RCA would fight it out in the marketplace and that neither would be likely to win.

The advanced development group at the Consumer Electronics Division had maintained all along that a magnetic tape videoplayer, not Holotape, would be the next new product and it compiled a detailed study of magnetic tape economics that challenged previous assessments put forth by the RCA Laboratories. Sony's claims that it could sell prerecorded one-hour tapes for $20 tended to bolster the Consumer Electronics Division case, and Enders, still head of Advanced Product Planning on RCA's corporate marketing staff, reevaluated the case for a magnetic tape recorder and launched a program to develop a business concept for a magnetic tape product for RCA. His conclusions, based on limited market research, were that both record-playback and home movies through television (which involved a consumer television camera hooked to a videorecorder) were concepts that had potential for RCA.

Enders's conclusions were not welcomed by the Laboratories' management. Webster openly challenged the validity of the Consumer Electronics Division study and opponents charged bitterly that he had tried to keep its conclusions from reaching higher levels in RCA. He feared that any consideration of other new product alternatives would divert efforts from taking their Selectavision product to market in a timely manner.

Ball entered the fray in late spring 1970, when he undertook a four-month study of magnetic videoplayer systems on behalf of the Selectavision venture group. His study, "A Report on the State of the Art for the Consumer Market," concluded that no magnetic tape player yet in existence held a significant edge in performance terms, nor were there important distinctions as to degree of technical difficulty or hardware cost. The one area in which there appeared to be significant differences was in tape usage, which determined the cost per hour of the tape.

Those who were projecting much lower costs were using a way of storing information on magnetic tape called a "skipped field" approach to minimize tape usage. There was still room in the industry, Ball believed, for significant improvements in player hardware, specifically in tape interchangeability and player reliability.

Technical experts from all three interested parts of RCA – the Laboratories, Consumer Electronics Division, and the Venture Group – were spending substantial amounts of time monitoring developments in the industry and attending competitors' demonstrations in Europe and Japan. In the summer of 1970, after a Philips demonstration of its videocassette system, Ray Warren, who was RCA's leading magnetic tape expert and a member of the Consumer Electronics Division's advanced development team, worked on extending and modifying his own tape system in response to what he had seen. He informed the Selectavision Venture Group that he had an approach that would be superior to the Philips system. Although it would contain fewer elements with RCA patents than his previous approach, he believed it would have manufacturing cost advantages.

Warren's approach appealed to Ball because it addressed hardware improvements which he believed the Japanese had not so far tackled. Japanese advances in consumer videotape recorder technology represented substantial improvements in standardization of tape formats and information encoding. They had also perfected new techniques for economical replication of prerecorded tapes. But equipment costs remained high because of the precision manufacturing required for tape transport mechanisms. It was this cost factor that was causing all hardware producers to emphasize playback of prerecorded material, for producing machines that recorded well enough to permit other machines of the same format to play back their material required very exacting design and manufacturing tolerances.

Warren's central idea to reduce player manufacturing cost was in-cartridge scanning, which involved a four-headed scanning system inside a single, precision, mechanical assembly called the scanner module. By eliminating the threading

131

mechanism from the rest of the player, it located all the precision manufacturing in one module, the tape transport mechanism (TTM), that could be manufactured separately, using numerically controlled equipment for the required precision machining. The rest of the player would be easy to assemble, and the equipment would be easy to maintain and operate.

Convinced that RCA needed a magnetic videocassette recorder, the RCA venture group adopted Warren's proposal as its candidate, calling it Selectavision Magtape. Ball was persuaded that Warren's system compared favorably with the others he had studied, and the team funded Warren and his small group at the modest rate of $500,000 to complete an operational Magtape prototype by mid-1971.

One of the arguments that the Laboratories had consistently used in the past against a magnetic tape system was that Indianapolis lacked the manufacturing capability in complex and precision assembly that would be required to make it. To meet this objection, the venture group looked for an outside manufacturer. In 1971, they signed an agreement with Bell & Howell to produce the complex TTM and scanner module at the heart of Warren's system. Bell & Howell agreed to begin with a pilot run for field testing in 1972.

Holotape revival

The Holotape research team had spent the entire 1969–70 winter following the Selectavision press conference trapped by the decisions it had been forced to make in order to have a product ready for the September press conference. Henry Ball's willingness to "unfreeze" the product specifications (the measurements that determined what the product would be and how it would perform) liberated the researchers in the spring of 1970 to pursue continued improvement in the product. The team added new members and resumed a brisk pace of achievement. The researchers began to investigate alternative forms of hologram format that were designed to improve the picture by eliminating some of the sources of "noise" (extraneous matter that is picked up as information by the player and appears as static). They also tried out new sound systems.

Within months, the research group had demonstrated a new set of advances. Improvements in generating holograms, improved optical elements, and clean-room production techniques all helped reduce the "noise" in the picture. The team discovered a means of producing sound that could be recorded in an embossed groove on the edge of the tape and could be replicated at the same temperatures and pressures as the embossed holograms themselves. By manipulating redundant holograms, the team also found ingenious ways to circumvent some of the other picture quality problems. Each performance improvement unfortunately also added to the cost of the system.

Meanwhile, product division engineers at the Consumer Electronics Division who had been pulled off other projects in order to work on Holotape, found major difficulties with the techniques that the Holotape research team had devised for tape replication. To make a master for replicating tapes, a plastic tape coated with photoresistant material was encoded by recording onto it the series of light interference patterns, or holograms. The tape then went through a chemical wash and nickel plating. To reproduce the pattern from this master onto other tapes, each clear vinyl strip had to be run the entire length of the master. This process took close to "real time," the actual amount of time it took to play the program at normal speed. It meant that each hour of programming tape required almost a full hour to replicate, an impossibly expensive operation.

Don McCoy, head of Princeton's Consumer Electronics Laboratory, estimated in early 1971 that the Holotape player price originally set at $450 had climbed to the neighborhood of $750. The Holotape team disputed this figure vigorously, but even as they worked to address the excess cost problem, the ground eroded from under them in the materials area. To produce acceptable quality images, fundamental developments were needed in photoresistant materials, and grave uncertainties also arose concerning the appropriateness of the "simple vinyl meatwrap" used for the basic tape. The material proved much too unstable to replicate in large quantities, and chemical companies that supplied other plastics were unwilling to make up small quantities of other material formulations for test purposes unless they were guaranteed a substantial market for high volumes afterward.

Holotape might still have retained its support at RCA headquarters had CBS's EVR remained the front runner in the prerecorded video race. But in 1970 word leaked out that CBS's project had also run into snags. EVR looked less and less attractive compared to other products that were being announced. It would cost as much as a magnetic tape system, but would lack recording capability. Since the RCA Laboratories' management had never believed that CBS had an economical product to begin with, the news of the EVR demise only served to undermine further the Holotape effort.

Meanwhile, another competitive development occurred in the spring of 1970 that breathed new life into the Laboratories' languishing disc effort. A European joint venture between Telefunken and Decca, called Teldec, announced that it was developing its own version of what it termed a videodisc product.

VideoDisc becomes feasible

Teldec's announcement had a striking effect on thinking about videoplayers at all levels of the RCA organization. Its product was based on an electromechanical approach to high-density recording and pickup, essentially an improvement of conventional audio recording technology. The player used simple needle-in-the-groove methods to produce black and white pictures from flexible plastic foil discs, each with five minutes of play time. Hardware prices at $200 to $250 and programming prices at $6.50 per half hour were the lowest so far quoted for any videoplayer. Even though the demonstration in Berlin was hardly more than a laboratory prototype with little in the way of serious business planning, the system was estimated to be ready for market as early as the second half of 1972. No plans

134

had been made to market the player in the United States, but Teldec declared itself willing to license the technology abroad.

Although the RCA Discpix research team judged the Teldec approach to be substantially inferior to its own concept in playing time and in picture quality, it had some advantageous features. Its thin, plastic foil disc was easy to package and to transport, and its light weight eliminated the need for a sophisticated turntable. The Teldec disc spun on a spindle at 1,500 rpm over a stationary platter, and its stylus moved by means of a simple pulley-and-cord arrangement, guided by fine grooves in the disc. Teldec's system promised to be sturdy, reliable, and, above all, easy to manufacture, with a disc that was cheap and simple to distribute.

For the Discpix team, the mere existence of Teldec was a tremendous boost to morale. For the first time they had a moving target comparable to the one that the Holotape effort had had in CBS's EVR. Teldec eliminated a huge amount of the uncertainty they had faced and focused their goals. They devised a plan to demonstrate real pictures of their own by summer's end, they laid aside their disputes over whether to use an AM or FM signal format, and they persuaded the people at Indianapolis to speed up production of test records that had been holding up their progress. The Discpix team also reorganized, taking on a project manager whose style and manner resembled that of Holotape's dynamic leader, Hannon. Keizer, who had previously borne all the administrative burden, concentrated on technical leadership. The team working with Keizer and Clemens was soon joined by other researchers. Within three months of encountering their first real rival, the Discpix team demonstrated their first black and white pictures. The system still lacked both sound and color, and the image was barely decipherable, but the capacitance pickup system had produced more than just test patterns.

But Teldec was also a threat. Worried that the venture group, and perhaps even the advanced development groups in the RCA consumer divisions might consider licensing Teldec technology as a basis for a first-generation RCA videoplayer, the Discpix (now called Videodisc) research team redoubled its efforts.

Selectavision becomes a family

The venture group was becoming simultaneously disenchanted with Holotape and aware of other attractive technical alternatives toward the end of 1970. As a consequence, they proposed a revision in RCA's videoplayer strategy for the following year. With RCA's unique ability to participate in any or all of the technical approaches currently vying for videoplayer leadership, and with routine market research continuing to reflect strong consumer interest in some form of videoplayer, they proposed to keep the technical options open. Their assessment of the options suggested that a successful Holotape program would be the most profitable and magnetic tape the least profitable and the closest to being achieved, while a videodisc might or might not be profitable, depending on competition from other disc formats.

In the end they recommended a strategy that played down Holotape and pushed ahead parallel efforts. It called for swift introduction of an RCA magnetic tape product, accelerated disc research, and selective development of a small but exciting core catalog of programs. Meanwhile, RCA's financial staff was pressing for curtailed product development and abandonment of a leadership position in new products for consumer electronics. The Laboratories argued for focus on one system, the Videodisc. The Consumer Electronics Division, which had to produce the system, still preferred its own Magtape as the focal product.

RCA's worsening financial picture notwithstanding, videoplayers received $2.2 million in corporate support for 1971, of which the Consumer Electronics Division received $1.2 million to divide among its several projects; RCA Records $650,000 to divide as well, though the largest share was for Videodisc; with Holotape research and laser development at Lancaster cut to the bone. The Laboratories' management protested the corporate resources diverted to tape and made it known that they would expect to call on Ray Warren and his team members any time after the tape system prototype was finished to do development work for the Videodisc at the Consumer Electronics Division.

The new, higher priority status for Videodisc research took time to translate into an increased level of effort. Gradually the team grew from thirty to fifty members, new equipment was ordered, some with substantial lead times (elapsed time between order and delivery), additional space was procured in the Laboratories, and recruiting proceeded for skilled technicians in such highly specialized fields as vacuum equipment, optical equipment, and electron-beam equipment.

April 1971 brought the long-awaited delivery of the scanning electron microscope capable of recording a full-length disc. Its initial mastering speed was 250 times "real-time," meaning that it took more than a week of work to record a ten-minute program. The arrival of this critical piece of equipment prompted a new list of Selectavision Videodisc milestones (performance goals to be achieved). The team set up three goals: to plan and describe the entire system, resolving all critical issues such as modulation choice of AM versus FM, system trade-offs, and channel evaluation; to assemble a working model using working components and circuitry; and to improve operation of the scanning electron microscope to accommodate full-size records at speeds of 10 rpm.

Now it was the Videodisc team's turn to pay the price of high visibility. Their research activities were constantly interrupted by mandatory progress demonstrations for members of the venture group or other visitors. Each time Teldec gave a demonstration, RCA found it necessary to replicate the results in order to keep up confidence in RCA's videoplayer research. At mid-year 1971, for example, Teldec demonstrated an improved color version of its videodisc system for potential licensees in New York. The demonstration was anxiously attended by members of the RCA Videodisc team, for Clemens and others perceived Teldec's ability to show color as the principal threat to the RCA program. For the venture group, eager to market an RCA product, the attraction of the Teldec system continued to be that it appeared close to being marketable, and contained fewer of the frustrating research problems that turned all scheduling into guesswork. Ball described Teledec as a system that had already undergone a number of engineering refinements, while the RCA Videodisc was still a set of defined research problems awaiting a solution.

The RCA research team responded by replicating Teldec's color system in their own player, proving not only that they were able to produce color themselves, but that the Teldec choice was inappropriate for RCA's system. Indeed, because Teldec's Tripal (line-sequential) color had its origins in the European television standard rather than in the American standard, it displayed unacceptable horizontal lines across the picture. Only after spending some three months preparing demonstrations for Webster and for the venture group could the Videodisc team turn to developing its own approach, using a different method of storing color information called a buried subcarrier.

In the meantime, Magtape came back on the scene. In April 1971, under pressure to justify its existence and to show RCA dealers and the industry that RCA was still innovating, the venture group issued a start-up plan for Magtape. Billed as a primary maneuver, internally it was regarded as a holding strategy. Magtape's major attraction was that it would provide RCA dealers with the full line of RCA television-related products they wanted, a way to supplement anemic television sales. Erroneously it was believed that Magtape, unlike the research-based systems under development in the Laboratories, did not contain major areas of uncertainty. Moreover, its record-off-the-air feature made it less dependent on software than playback systems were, at a time when investment in expensive and uncertain programming was becoming less and less appealing.

The plan was to market both equipment and programs for Selectavision Magtape by early 1973 at the latest.[2] A price of $600, to be announced in mid-1971, if possible, would give RCA the opportunity to take a commanding leadership position, if not a very profitable one. In actuality, the Magtape system demonstration did not take place until March of 1972, and then it was low key, for overtures to other domestic companies failed to attract support for the magnetic tape recording format that RCA was proposing the industry adopt as a standard.

Selectavision programming

Every study of videoplayers, every market survey, and every discussion of the videocassette revolution, laid heavy emphasis on the importance of programming to business success. The case for programming as a vital concern was grounded in RCA experience, for it was widely believed that the scarcity of color programming had been the greatest obstacle to the spread of color television during the 1950s. Oldtimers remembered that it had taken artists like Milton Berle to create real and lasting enthusiasm even for black and white television. They said that in the long run, programming, and not hardware, would be the generator of videoplayer profits. Prerecorded systems in particular were viewed as the classic "razor blade" business, in the sense that repeated purchases of software would continue and grow when demand for players had moved into a replacement mode, just as the real money in razors was in the replacement blades, not the handles. Because they could record their own programming, magnetic tape players might be different in this respect, but no one in the early 1970s suggested selling Magtape hardware alone.

In addition to being a vital part of the videoplayer system, programming, like all entertainment software, was a source of major risk for all who became involved with it. Despite RCA's claims to have unique advantages in programming because of its complete business system approach, the company's resources were not as readily adaptable to the development of a new visual medium as a superficial look might have suggested. Two RCA organizations had programming expertise in the early 1970s: NBC and RCA Records. Both were in transition. Like other major networks, NBC had been mainly a distributor, not a producer, of programming since the 1950s. Antitrust activity initiated by the Nixon administration in the late 1960s and early 1970s was enforcing this arrangement by compelling all networks to give up whatever program production activities they might still have. RCA's always cautious relationship with NBC became a rigid arms-length setup during this period.

The case of RCA Records was different, and in the early days of videoplayer program development, RCA Records took an active part. The Laboratories had viewed long-play records as the closest analogy to videoplayer programming because of the expected similarities in economics and in consumer demand, and had used the expertise of the Records Division in early assembly of sample program catalogs. For the Records people, the new medium amounted to an illustrated version of sound. A rock concert or an evening at symphony was the type of big event they envisioned for videoplayers.

When Selectavision took over programming and looked to hire its own programming coordinator, the tilt toward the Records Division halted abruptly. Until the summer of 1970, Bitting covered the programming responsibilities himself while trying to find a suitable specialist. It soon became apparent that the entertainment business was no place for novices. It was a business in which large sums of money were risked on hunches, where knowing people was all-important, and where a large-scale deal could be concluded on the basis of a handshake. When overtures to NBC failed to turn up any prospects, Bitting's boss, Morsey, consulted Robert Sarnoff and his immediate staff for suggestions.

The name that turned up was that of Thomas McDermott, a veteran of the television business. McDermott had co-founded with Dick Powell and others, a company called Four Star International, a leading distributor of domestic and foreign television shows. McDermott viewed RCA's announced intention to be a central player in the videocassette industry as a chance for him to pioneer in yet another media revolution, this time with the resources of a large company behind him. Resources aside, McDermott was not attracted by the large corporate environment. Temperamentally an entrepreneur, he was suspicious of corporate ways and openly hostile to what he called RCA's "hardware mentality." During the several years he worked for RCA, he frequently reminded his associates of the terms under which he had agreed to serve. These were that he report only to senior management, which in practice meant

Morsey; that he travel first class; and that he base his operation in Los Angeles. Since his tenure at RCA coincided with a period of corporate austerity, his terms often made him inaccessible to those who wanted to consult him.

In effect, McDermott's appointment considerably reduced the scope of the venture group's influence over the entire Selectavision program. McDermott was never part of the Selectavision venture group; his efforts proceeded in parallel. He joined RCA at the level of staff vice-president, a notch higher than Bitting's position. The venture group all received promotions at the time of McDermott's arrival, but they already lacked decision-making authority over most of the basic technical choices and then ceased to have any authority over programming policy.

Assuming that big corporations had big pockets, McDermott did not negotiate up front with RCA's senior management any commitment to the budget he would have at his disposal. He was confident that "Bobby" – Robert Sarnoff – knew the business and therefore was aware of the magnitude of investment required to finance a library of newly created programs. Since this had been one of the key points made in the Selectavision press conference in late 1969, McDermott further assumed that strategy still obtained.

McDermott understood his mission to be building from scratch an RCA programming business for Selectavision. Bringing with him a team of former associates from the world of television production and distribution, he deliberately did not consult other programming experts at NBC or Records and ignored earlier programming studies. An error that he was later to regret was that for some months he did not examine at firsthand the hardware for which his programming was being prepared; technical matters should be left to experts.

Speed was McDermott's first priority. His sense of urgency stemmed from the tight Selectavision timetable, requiring introduction in eighteen months, and from his belief that timing would be crucial in the current state of the entertainment world as he knew it. McDermott sensed a temporary atmosphere of high excitement in late 1970, created by a recent rash of videoplayer announcements. For a short time, he believed, the situation would be fluid, but then the old interests would reestablish control and begin to shape the emerging industry according to their own purposes.

Having weathered one major transition in the entertainment world in the course of his own career, McDermott anticipated that trouble would soon erupt on several fronts. The networks and the film companies, who between them controlled most of the existing production facilities in New York and Hollywood and employed much of the creative and technical talent, were both inclined to view videoplayers as a threat to their established businesses. If consumers could purchase programming of their choice to watch at home, they might watch less network programming, and they might cease going to movie theaters. Furthermore, the film companies controlled almost all of the existing material in their film libraries. Organized labor had already seized on the new videocassette systems as a major opportunity to negotiate better terms. The Screen Actors Guild, the Writers Guild, and the several production unions had proclaimed their collective intention to make substantial demands in the next round of collective bargaining.

Variety, the entertainment industry's influential journal, carried McDermott's first public pronouncement about the shape of RCA's programming strategy in October 1970. The amount of money mentioned that RCA intended to invest for new program production was $50 million.[3] In *Variety's* language, RCA was "planning extensive programming in every area, with particular accent on kid-vid, cultural such as ballet and opera, Legit (Legitimate Theatre), sports, animated and pop singers." McDermott explained that his Special Programs activity at RCA would finance production for independents and creative individuals while doing limited amounts of production itself. Perhaps in an effort to call the bluff of the major studios, McDermott denied having any interest in buying film backlogs from them, and he said RCA itself would not produce movies until 1975 or 1976. As the name Selectavision implied, the chief initial commitment was to offer programming that the public could not otherwise have.

Only when he returned from his first trip overseas on RCA's behalf in late 1970 did McDermott discover that his operating

142

assumptions were invalid. Neither Selectavision technology nor RCA's financial condition were what he had assumed them to be. McDermott quickly adjusted his plan. If RCA's technical leadership were no longer assured, it would be harder to gain commitment from programming sources, but he devised a strategy to get around the obstacles, such as multiple technical standards, that he foresaw might pose problems. The result was an "all-systems" programming strategy.

McDermott's all-systems programming strategy would enable RCA to aim for dominance as a program supplier to the entire videocassette industry. By acquiring and producing programs on a worldwide basis, RCA could avoid the expenses and problems posed by U.S. unions. McDermott urged that RCA take the lead in negotiating with unions to avoid mistakes made in early television where, he said, negotiations made by radio interests had sacrificed television interests to protect radio. RCA could make high profits by setting up a distribution business of its own to supply all domestic companies and by doing worldwide distribution on a co-venture basis.

In view of RCA's financial constraints, McDermott proposed to begin his operation in a way that would minimize up-front investment by distributing programs to other media until videocassette systems were available. In this way, the business could be self-supporting. An example of the type of offering he had in mind was a production of Dylan Thomas's *Under Milkwood* featuring Elizabeth Taylor and Peter O'Toole, whose costs of $600,000 would be covered even before it was used for RCA videocassettes. Asked to estimate the financial implications of the strategy he proposed, McDermott calculated that the initial Selectavision catalog of fifty new and fifty acquired programs would cost under $10 million. Additional programs introduced over the following three years would add up to just over $5 million if RCA were to handle distribution. It could expect distribution profits of 47 percent of the gross added to the 15 percent producers' margin.

In 1971 McDermott received permission to spend $500,000 on acquisition and product development. He negotiated with Henry Moore and Arnold Palmer to make how-to films, and he looked into acquiring film libraries such as the Walter Reade

143

documentaries and the Charlie Chaplin films. When it came to closing the deals, however, his requests for money were denied. Wiring from Europe in the summer of 1971 for the $500,000 he needed to finance RCA's joint participation in a deal to acquire the entire library of Charlie Chaplin films, he was told that Morsey's office refused to authorize the purchase. Unaware that RCA was on the brink of a serious financial crisis with the impending computer write-off, McDermott concluded that RCA's corporate hierarchy was too cautious to engage in any aggressive programming activity, even when a handsome payoff was virtually guaranteed.

Back in the States, McDermott learned that his entire front-end budget had disappeared with the general cost reduction that followed the computer write-off. Proposals to begin programming distribution by supplying only existing programs in existing markets, stressing short-term profitability, were vetoed by RCA's legal department in mid-1972. New FCC regulations barred all television networks from engaging in syndication or from acquiring either financial or proprietary rights in programs of which they were not sole producers, and RCA's conservative chief counsel interpreted the regulations as applying to RCA as owner of a network. From then on McDermott's entrepreneurial activities were effectively foreclosed, and his staff had to confine itself to a limited program to support Selectavision Magtape alone. He was told to acquire the kinds of programming that would make Magtape attractive to uncommitted manufacturers and mass merchandisers. In effect, Magtape would be a limited laboratory for Selectavision VideoDisc programming when it materialized.

Family breakup

The computer withdrawal caused a devastating decline in morale at the Laboratories. For a time it brought all progress nearly to a standstill. Inasmuch as 40 percent of the Laboratories had contributed to the support of RCA's computer business in the last years before the withdrawal, it was no surprise that an immediate 10 percent was chopped from the

Laboratories' budget. Faced with the task of laying off a substantial portion of the research staff, Webster was observed to age visibly in the space of a few months. He made two critical decisions: he would spread the dismissals throughout the Laboratories rather than simply severing those allocated to computer work and he would eliminate parallel projects first.

Where possible, personnel were shifted to advanced development groups in the divisions. At the same time, the Holotape project was notified that its budget would cease after June 1972. Holographic applications might continue to be pursued at the Laboratories for licensing purposes or supported by government funding, but the Holotape project would cease to be part of the corporate Selectavision budget. By such means, a 10 percent budget cut was translated into a 6 to 7 percent cut in staff.

The computer write-off also focused unfavorable attention on the venture group and its style of operation, which had already attracted criticism. The group had spent much of its time preparing detailed reports and entertaining industry representatives and potential licensees. It had also made major trips to Germany (Telefunken), Vienna (Philips), Cannes, and Japan and had given worldwide briefings to RCA divisions. Although it had been formed as a coordinating device, organizational unity had not been achieved. Bitting's staff and McDermott's staff were requesting 1972 budgets totaling nearly $1.5 million.

With pressure mounting to cut corporate staff activities, the Selectavision business development team received orders in December 1971 to transfer its operations in January to the Consumer Electronics Division. Bitting would continue to head Selectavision Business Development, but he would report to Barton Kreuzer in Indianapolis. McDermott's Selectavision Special Programs Group would remain in New York.

The timing of the move, which would have taken place in any case with Magtape commercialization, came as a surprise to venture group members. Geographical separation from top management seemed yet another erosion of its ability to influence what was going on. As soon as possible after the group reassembled in Indianapolis, it pressed ahead

145

with the Magtape demonstration, committing RCA to a late-1973 introduction. Kreuzer, executive vice-president and head of the Consumer Electronics Division, was present and so was Donald Frey, chairman of Bell & Howell, RCA's partner in the enterprise.

The Magtape system had three different functions: it would play prerecorded tapes; it would record up to one hour off the air; and with an auxiliary camera, currently black and white but with color promised, it would record and play back home movies. No specific price was mentioned, but it was promised at a price lower than any competing videorecorder player to date announced. The team was by then working with an $800 figure. Two manufacturers had signed up to produce machines based on RCA's standard, Bell & Howell and Magnavox.

The main competitive target for Magtape in 1972 was Avco's Cartrivision system. As the only cartridge television system currently available in the U.S. market, Cartrivision combined a television and a camera with its player. RCA's planners believed that a stand-alone version of the system could be a significant competitor at the predicted price of $1,350. On the other hand, Avco's system influenced Magtape in two ways. Its programming distribution strategy through rental convinced the Selectavision team that it would not be able to sell a player without some available programming, probably also through rental. Avco's full system approach reinforced RCA's idea of selling Magtape with camera.

The Selectavision team gained valuable market information from watching Avco's system in the market during 1972. Consumer acceptance was discouraging, for it sold only half the expected 20,000 units. Whether this was a response to videoplayers in general or to the Avco combination system was not clear, but Avco postponed its original plan to sell a stand-alone version. Other failures occurred in the industry at the same time. CBS took a $10 million write-off of its EVR in December. It discontinued production of cassettes, stranding its partner, Motorola, which had manufactured players. Marketing experts in RCA's Consumer Electronics Division viewed the other failures as an opportunity for RCA, but the venture group was inclined toward pessimism.

Everything ventured

The Magtape program was not going well; part of the reason was its complexities. Magtape had been configured as a multipurpose system in part to involve as much of the organization as possible, to keep the Selectavision operation going, and to serve as a test activity for McDermott's Special Programs activity. The auxiliary camera was to give RCA's Lancaster Components Division a much-needed product. Unfortunately, the multipurpose concept also increased the organizational and technical problems of the program. The requirement to play prerecorded programming, for instance, necessitated higher precision in manufacturing than if the player only accommodated specially recorded tapes.

To coordinate among several geographically dispersed divisions would have been difficult under the best of circumstances. From Indianapolis, it was particularly hard. The venture group adjusted slowly to its new surroundings, while the Consumer Electronics Division tried to find ways to make better use of an unwelcome addition to its overhead budget. Not long after the group arrived, some members were dispersed into other activities. In March 1973, Bitting left RCA altogether, and the Selectavision venture group ceased to exist.

7

All in the family

Members of the press who picked up on the release from RCA's press office in October 1974 were disarmed by what they read. William Hittinger, executive vice-president in charge of all RCA's electronics businesses, announced that RCA was setting aside its plans to market its consumer videotape recording system called Magtape. Hittinger's candor about the new product was rare enough in consumer electronics circles to prompt at least one journalist to call his statement a "show of extraordinary frankness." He explained simply that RCA had been unable to achieve the necessary performance level at the required level of cost to allow the Magtape system to be a profitable venture for the company.

Hittinger by no means welcomed the task of scuttling the Magtape. Indeed, he had encouraged Roy Pollack, his successor at the Consumer Electronics Division, to keep the project alive on divisional funds for a year after corporate funding was withdrawn. But his announcement was a concession to the hard realities of corporate existence. Resources were limited and Robert Sarnoff had made up his mind to back VideoDisc, a product he believed was more compatible with RCA's mass market aims. Ostensibly ruled out because of rising component costs and schedule delays, Magtape had really fallen victim to other factors, including the lack of support at top management levels, general disillusionment with the prospects for magnetic videoplayers after recent failures among early entries in the cassette player industry, and active opposition from the RCA Laboratories that had wanted an all-out focused effort to be directed at its favorite project – VideoDisc.

During the mid-1970s, RCA's decision not to stick with

Magtape was received by the press and the industry as a healthy focusing of the company's effort on a product with higher potential. Only later, when it would become apparent that RCA's decision had in effect determined that no American company would be able to compete with the Japanese in manufacturing videotape recorders, would the press, in its customary fickle way, ask how such a thing could have happened. How could RCA, the American consumer electronics industry's traditional pioneer, fail to produce a magnetic tape player of its own making?

Magtape aground

Although it surprised the media, the demise of Magtape was not sudden. The Bell & Howell arrangement, required for the precision manufacture of the Magtape TTM, was fraught with difficulty from the start. RCA's attempts to transfer its Magtape technology to the engineers at Bell & Howell never succeeded. Bell & Howell fell behind schedule and blamed its lack of progress on what it said were RCA's incomplete, poorly documented, and essentially unworkable designs. Ray Warren and his team invented their way out of every problem, but that led to endless engineering changes for Bell & Howell's process engineers.

William Hittinger who had succeeded Kreuzer as head of the Consumer Electronics Division, decided with Gordon Bricker, who succeeded Bitting as head of the Magtape program in the spring of 1973, to bring the manufacturing of the TTM back in-house. Anxious to establish that any failure on its part to fulfill the contract was RCA's fault, Bell & Howell lodged a complaint with RCA's top management. Rumor had it that, in fact, much of the problem stemmed from a change of heart by Bell & Howell's chairman, Donald Frey, who had reportedly seen a demonstration of the new Philips videocassette system and wanted to license it instead. A conversation between the several executives involved more or less confirmed the rumor, for Frey observed that Philips' Vienna facility was already producing its magnetic videocassette recorders (VCRs) at the

149

rate of 30,000 units per year and the operation "had the smell of profitability."[1]

Anthony Conrad, RCA's president and chief operating officer (COO), and Hittinger asked Hillier, as RCA's chief technical officer, to evaluate both the Magtape program and its prospects in light of recent consumer videoplayer failures in the marketplace. Avco had just become the latest casualty by taking a $1 million write-off for its Cartrivision in July 1973.

Hillier's negative opinion of Magtape was well-known, so it was not surprising when his August 1973 report expressed grave doubts about some of its technical aspects and recommended that it be discontinued. Hillier said that neither RCA's engineers nor those of Bell & Howell had the necessary consumer product experience. He thought RCA should license magnetic tape technology from another company and then conduct a design program that would gradually increase RCA's portion of the technology.

Corporate backing for Magtape, never strong at the highest levels, eroded rapidly. Robert Sarnoff and Conrad directed Hittinger to complete the Bell & Howell pilot, end the connection, and prepare a comprehensive review of Magtape. Noting the changed environment for magnetic tape products, the Selectavision status report indicated that the Magtape strategy would have to be revised. Even if RCA could manufacture its own player, it would have to sell it at $995, and without prerecorded programming. If the Consumer Electronics Division wanted the product, it would have to sponsor and finance it itself.

Robert Sarnoff chooses sides

Meanwhile the Videodisc project at the RCA Laboratories had been moving at a rapid pace, suggesting a possible 1973 introduction date. All parts of the system had been combined at the end of 1971; during 1972 the research team had turned out experimental discs whose picture quality and recording time were steadily improving. Disc #234, produced in September 1972, which contained an episode from the "Get Smart" television series, was judged to be the first quality color disc that incorporated all the research team's preferred approaches. Admittedly it had many serious defects and played only ten minutes per side, but it was demonstrated with great excitement to the entire Laboratories' community at a monthly colloquium session. With such exposure, the outside world was bound to hear that RCA was actively pursuing a videodisc system.

There were, however, frequent reports of other disc competitors besides Teldec. The most highly respected in a technical sense was Philips where, in September 1972, Ball and McCoy witnessed a demonstration of an optical videodisc system developed in Philips' Eindhoven corporate research facility. It involved real-time television signal recording, using a laser to pick up information from a disc, with a thirty-five- to forty-five-minute playback capability. The player also used a laser for reflective light information recovery from a twelve-inch disc turning at 1,500 rpm. It appeared that Philips had not then decided on a replication method, for the demonstration disc was glass rather than vinyl.

RCA's 1972 disc system compared unfavorably with the Philips system both in length of playtime and in signal quality. Ball suggested that RCA's team would do well to consider Philips' comparatively simple recording procedure, which was based on a thin photoresist and a laser, much less complicated than RCA's scanning electron-beam technique. Philips' color encoding also looked promising. On the other hand, Ball doubted the Philips claim that it could produce a $10 laser, he saw difficulties with manufacturing a warp-free disc, and he thought RCA's simpler player using a groove system was a distinct advantage. Ball thought the Philips system an unlikely candidate for a consumer market, but ideal for broadcast and cable television.

Other forms of optical disc technology soon turned up at Thomson in France and at MCA in California. Teams of RCA technical experts visited each demonstration, gathering all the information they could get from visual observation and from question-and-answer sessions. Meanwhile, a large technical team from RCA's Videodisc research group exchanged in-

151

formation with Teldec representatives at Telefunken's Berlin manufacturing facility. The Teldec videodisc was said to be in the preproduction stage and its playing time had increased to ten minutes.

After months of information gathering, RCA experts concluded that, except for Teldec, which they did not view as a threat, they were in the lead even though their planned introduction date had slid to 1974. Optical systems were considered to be well out of mass-market price range in any case. The competitive review helped in the critical process of defining for RCA's Videodisc team their system's specifications as well as the amount of research they had left to do.

The gap between the status of the system in November 1972, and the goals they defined was summarized in a few key measurements:

> Goal for playtime, 30 minutes: 20 minutes achieved
> Goal for luminance bandwidth, 3 MHz: 2.5 MHz achieved
> Goal for Chroma bandwidth, 15 MHz: 15 MHz achieved
> Goal for signal-to-noise ratio, 40 db: 36 db achieved
> Goal of four stereo channels: one achieved
> Goal for disc life, 100 plays: 500 plays achieved
> Goal for stylus life, 200 hours: 50–100 hours achieved

Indianapolis gets into the act

Soon after the disc system first showed feasibility at the Laboratories in the early 1970s, the research team had involved the advanced development groups at the Consumer Electronics Division and the Records Division, as they needed the complementary skills of the divisional engineers to turn their concepts into prototype players and discs for demonstration purposes. The first player built by the design engineers at the Consumer Electronics Division was an engineering model intended to replace the laboratory prototype that had been pieced together from soda straws and other mock-up materials. It was estimated to cost about $1,500 to manufacture. Knowing that it would be the player group's responsibility to turn this model into a piece of equipment that could be manufactured for less than $150, Roland Rhodes, long-time head of the Consumer Electronics Division's advanced development group and an alumnus of the Princeton Laboratories, raised concerns that the division might be saddled with a technology of questionable feasibility.

Eugene Keizer and Kenneth Lockhart, directors of the player research team in Princeton and the player engineering team at the Consumer Electronics Division, worked hard to establish rapport. Lockhart made monthly trips to Princeton and Keizer encouraged his people to go to Indianapolis, and slowly the barriers came down. Although the Laboratories researchers had placed a high priority on economics, they were mostly unfamiliar with manufacturing realities. Their interactions with Indianapolis provided their first opportunity to understand the manufacturing consequences of their design choices. For the first time, they had to take into account the views of divisional engineers on such technical issues as AM versus FM signal format and constant groove velocity versus constant rpm, previously debated only inside the Laboratories.

Fortunately, the most sophisticated aspects of the player, such as the stylus and the high speed turntable, were design problems rather than manufacturing ones. In general, the Consumer Electronics Division development team and their research counterparts saw eye to eye on the merits of the capacitance approach. Its requirement for a simple player was a reasonable proposition for manufacturing, and the player engineering group found it much preferable to the Holotape design.

A much less cordial relationship existed between the advanced development team at the Records Division and its research counterpart. The research solution of locating the most sophisticated technology in the mastering process might make strategic sense in that it created technical barriers for would-be competitors. Nevertheless, it caused endless problems for the disc manufacturing people. Divisional engineers expressed their opposition to the combination of electron-beam recording and capacitive pickup from the start. They did not believe that the electron-beam recording apparatus could be made to work reliably in their production environment or that

153

it would be possible to mass-produce coated discs of high uniform quality. They also believed that the disc technology that RCA proposed to use would discourage potential licensees from adopting the RCA videoplayer technology.

As soon as he learned of the electron-beam mastering approach, Al Stancel, manager of Recording Engineering at the Records Division, determined to find an alternative method. When Teldec demonstrated its use of improved conventional techniques, electromechanical recording and pressure pickup, he urged the Laboratories to adopt those methods instead. He bolstered his opinions with frequent references to an engineer with whom he was in touch at Matsushita, who was said to be already at work replicating the Teldec approach. Stancel sent a lengthy memo to his own chief engineer, Rex Isom, in which he predicted that the scanning electron beam would never achieve a commercial level of resolution.

To appease the critics, the Princeton team took a fresh look at electromechanical and pressure pickup alternatives. They rejected them when their calculations proved to their satisfaction that electromechanical recording was not feasible for the recording of information elements of the small size required for Videodisc. Yet Stancel persisted. In the winter of 1971–72 Stancel jumped at the chance to hire Jerry Halter, a research engineer from the Laboratories whose electromechanical mastering project had been eliminated in the recent Laboratories budget cuts. With the full support of Isom, Stancel gave the three men working with Halter the goal of achieving an electromechanical recording process that would match or exceed the precision and recording rates achieved by Princeton's electron-beam method. Webster and others on the Princeton technical staff opposed Halter's activities on the grounds that parallel efforts would dilute the primary drive of achieving real-time recording with the advanced technique, but they failed to convince Isom and Stancel, neither of whom had high regard for the Laboratories and its approaches.

By this time, the Laboratories commitment to the electron-beam method of recording was very strong. The techniques associated with the use of the electron beam were generating many provocative research questions in materials and process

154

research, areas that were known to have wide applicability and that provided satisfying work for some of the Laboratories' most able people. Many of these had previously been involved in the computer effort, and Videodisc had made it possible to retain them on the technical staff. The proprietary advantage that the electron-beam technique afforded was also an important matter to the Laboratories staff.

A second source of conflict with the Records Division was the coated disc. The Laboratories' design called for three different coatings to be applied in microscopic thicknesses – a conductive metal layer, a plastic film that kept the stylus from making contact with the metal and shorting out, and an oil coating for surface lubrication. The Records Division was given the task of selecting the best materials for the purpose and of finding ways to apply the coats thinly and evenly. Experiments were conducted with aluminum, gold, and ultimately copper. Each coating had different properties and all were difficult to apply by hand in dust-free circumstances. Recording specialists soon concluded that it would take a wholly automated process, in a clean-room environment, to produce mass-production quantities properly. Naturally, the pressure pickup that worked with an uncoated disc seemed infinitely preferable to them.

The third major problem was to find a suitable stylus design to be used in the pickup assembly, and to devise processes by which it could be manufactured. To avoid having to use a costly diamond stylus, the research team specified sapphire, but new ways were needed to work commercial sapphire material. This investigation was contracted to Arthur D. Little. Meantime, the Records Division contracted work from Matsushita, which was already involved in videoplayer work of its own, to design and develop a pressure pickup mechanism and needle. They agreed that Matsushita would retain proprietary rights to any developments it originated. The assignment was expected to take six months and ended up lasting two years, partly because of delays at RCA in producing good test records and partly because the deal had not been negotiated between the two companies at high level. A formal joint development effort between the two companies never materialized, but the arrangement kept Stancel informed about Matsushita's assess-

155

ment of RCA's system in terms of the competition and kept Matsushita apprised of the developments occurring at RCA. Ironically, it also gave Matsushita early exposure to RCA's capacitance approach which, through its Japan Victor subsidiary, it ultimately adopted and modified.

The Records Division's parallel development program on electromechanical recording made remarkable progress during 1972, even though it was hampered by lack of manpower and equipment delays. By late 1972, it demonstrated an electromechanically recorded disc playing color at 450 rpm and recording at 4,000 grooves per inch. It was approximately three months behind the Laboratories' team and moving at about the same rate. In 1973 Halter's effort received a larger budget, better tooling, and additional equipment.

Buoyed by what appeared to be a manageable set of problems left to tackle, the Laboratories' management mounted a year-end 1972 review of the project for Robert Sarnoff and Conrad. Sarnoff rarely visited the Laboratories and had previously showed no interest in learning more about the disc project, but Hillier persuaded him to attend the review. He was visibly impressed by what he saw at the meeting held in his father's old dining room at the Laboratories. He appeared especially attracted by the favorable economics that Webster and Hillier outlined, and encouraged Webster to go "at flank speed" to achieve full product status for the VideoDisc as soon as possible.

Whatever the contrary beliefs of some of his staff members and line subordinates, Robert Sarnoff held to the notion that RCA should remain a pioneer in technology. The company needed a solid period of technical leadership in which to establish market dominance and take advantage of its complete system structure, and the demise of the computer business had left Robert Sarnoff without a growth business that he personally could sponsor. Under the circumstances, the next likely candidate was a videoplayer. But Holotape had proved a disappointment, and Magtape lacked the two essential ingredients of mass-market economics and proprietary technology that he believed RCA needed in a new product. Now Video-Disc seemed to hold out the kind of strategic opportunity for planned innovation that he had described as his philosophy three years earlier at the Selectavision press conference. He wanted the Laboratories to develop its VideoDisc to a state of readiness so that it could be kept on the shelf until the marketing and planning staff could certify that the market was also ready.

Sarnoff gave formal orders to the Videodisc program to proceed on three assumptions: (1) that there would be a mass consumer market for videodiscs that could be developed soon and rapidly, (2) that it would be desirable for RCA to enter the market as soon as possible, and (3) that RCA's capacitance pickup technology was the best videoplayer technology with which to develop the market. At a follow-up demonstration for Sarnoff and Conrad in April 1973, the research team showed its first, full-length, color disc, Disc #308. It still had numerous defects and would only play on one side, but playtime was a full twenty minutes and the color was good. It convinced Conrad and Sarnoff to make a commitment to Videodisc, giving the program the support it needed at the level necessary to move into the final stages for a product introduction in mid-1975. The next step would be to set up a new Selectavision organization and prepare for formal transfer of the technology from Princeton to Indianapolis. In focusing corporate support on Videodisc, this move cut off further corporate funding for Magtape.

Organization for transfer

The conditions for technology transfer at the receiving end of the process were not ideal. No organizational mechanism existed to carry out the transfer, there were no standard procedures to follow, and the consumer divisions were anything but receptive to the product. The Consumer Electronics Division in particular was preoccupied with its own serious problems, for only four years after being overwhelmed by demand for color televisions, it was confronting a declining market share and a pressing need to redesign and re-engineer its own product.

157

Meanwhile, the development group in the Records Division continued to be concerned that it would be held responsible for bringing to fruition a technology that it had openly opposed for years. As far back as 1969, when the original planning had taken place, Isom as chief engineer at the Records Division had warned that should the disc product be adopted, it would be the most difficult of all to transfer from Princeton to Indianapolis. The processes were unfamiliar, the equipment required extraordinary lead times, and the product division disagreed with the Laboratories' product design and production philosophy. Without an effective organization to arbitrate the different views there was little likelihood of speedy project implementation.

In fact, the hand over of disc technology from Laboratories to divisions had been going on informally for many years. The divisions had worked on pieces of the project on a purchase order basis and the earliest planning efforts had involved consultations concerning cost estimates and schedules. The divisions had also advised on player and player component design, and on test record fabrication procedures. But in all previous contacts, the Laboratories had control over the technology; a formal transfer of technology was certain to change the balance of control to some extent.

The Laboratories' management had to engage in a good deal of negotiation and compromise to get the Videodisc transfer started. Regardless of the commitment at the top to the project, Webster and Hillier had a difficult task arranging to implant their product in the divisions in the face of much indifference and some active opposition. For more than a year, the Consumer Electronics Division continued to develop its own video product on its own money. There was no question where its priorities lay in the deployment of expert manpower.

It was the Consumer Electronics Division's desperate need for a major effort on color television that gave the Laboratories its most useful entree. Under Hittinger's leadership, the division mounted a program called Colortrak to redesign RCA color receivers as solid-state equipment. The program needed technical expertise that the Laboratories could provide, and that highly successful experience helped to smooth relations between the two organizations. Hillier and Webster sent McCoy, for the past four years head of the Consumer Electronics Laboratory at Princeton, to Indianapolis with a dual mission. He was to advise the Colortrak program on colorimetry and he was to set up, supervise, and coordinate the new Selectavision program. Hittinger agreed to accept McCoy into his organization only because of his value to the Colortrak program.

McCoy faced a diplomatic maze and an organizational nightmare. To prepare for Videodisc transfer he had to set up an organization with management personnel drawn from the two divisions that would be involved; he had to plan for and hire the manpower; and he had to order the equipment and establish procedures for start-up. All this had to be accomplished from within a highly convoluted reporting relationship. Despite his urgings that one person should be given ultimate responsibility and authority for the entire Videodisc program, McCoy was coordinating not from the top, but from somewhere in the middle. He reported three ways, to the heads of the two consumer divisions, and to a Selectavision business coordinator in New York.

McCoy's reports back to the Laboratories about what he found in Indianapolis were discouraging. The dissolution of the former Selectavision team had left key personnel not speaking to each other. Reporting lines were long, and no one person had authority over all parties and organizations concerned. McCoy recommended that a minimum of twenty-eight new people were needed, increasing the development team to seventy. He estimated that it would take at least six months to remedy the program's deficiencies in mechanical and electrical engineers with appropriate experience. Finally, he reported that no lead division arrangement was possible, since neither division was willing to take on total financial administration for the corporate project. McCoy had spent his entire career at the Laboratories where bureaucratic controls and procedures were deliberately kept to a minimum. For him the complexities of coordinating between two different divisions, each with its own budgeting and resource allocation procedures, was particularly frustrating.

159

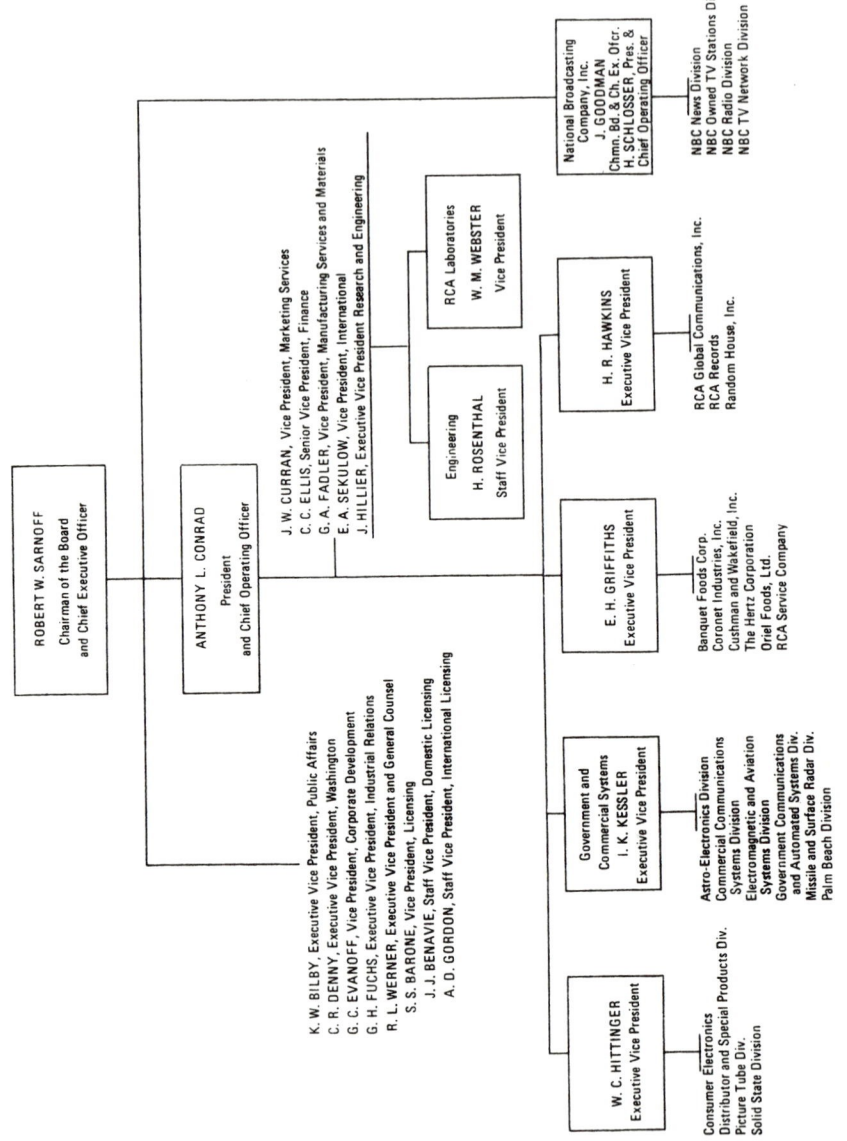

All in the family

From 1973 to 1975, the program struggled along in its divided state. Divisional personnel complained loudly of its "many-headed character." At the same time they took advantage of the organizational ambiguity to promote their own courses of action. While the negative effects of the setup – conflict, redundant effort, needless delay, and wasted resources – were obvious, there was an unappreciated benefit. A few technical alternatives kept going that would never have survived in a more orderly world, and those technical alternatives were eventually to come to the aid of the Videodisc program.

Unwelcome competition

It soon turned out RCA's technical teams had underestimated their competitors, for not long after RCA's internal commitment was made, Philips launched a "wait for us" campaign that astounded the industry. Representatives of RCA's corporate Research and Engineering and Laboratories staffs came away from a new Philips demonstration at the Berlin Radio and Television show in 1973 convinced that the Philips' system was superior to RCA's both in features and in performance. Moreover Philips announced plans to market its product simultaneously in Europe and the United States in 1975.

N.V. Philips was a much more serious threat than Teldec had been, for it was one of the handful of organizations in the world that RCA's Laboratories recognized as its technical equal. Unlike Teldec, which had reinforced RCA's technical preconceptions, Philips called them into question. Word soon got around that MCA's effort was also proceeding apace, but it was the Philips' program that RCA regarded as its key competition from the time that optical systems first became serious contenders.

The Philips' system achieved its superior picture quality, equal playtime, and superior color by rotating its disc at 1,500 rpm, three times the speed of the current RCA model. Since only one picture frame appeared per rotation, the Philips player had the ability to "freeze a frame," and it incorporated a timer and search capabilities. RCA had none of these features.

161

RCA and the VideoDisc

Moreover, the Philips' optical system involved no contact between disc and player, so that it could emphasize product reliability and indestructibility. These qualities had not been high on RCA's priority list when its product was in its early phases, but the American consumer movement was beginning to have its impact on U.S. businesses, and recent testing had showed that RCA's product was vulnerable in precisely these areas.

When RCA's top management learned of the Philips system and its virtues, its April 1973 commitment evaporated. RCA had an inferior product that would appear with little if any advantage in time. In an effort to regain top management commitment, the Videodisc program mounted an intense campaign to achieve an ambitious set of goals for improved playtime and quality.

Two months of concerted effort in the fall of 1973 by RCA R&D teams at all three locations produced a two-sided disc playing thirty minutes per side. A coating of copper improved picture quality, and recording speed had improved to twenty times real time. In addition, a search mechanism had been developed, and there were improvements in the electronics to compensate for minor disc defects. All witnesses agreed that this version had Philips beat. Yet as Roland Rhodes, heading the Consumer Electronics Division's advanced development group, wrote to McCoy, cautious realism was in order. "As is typical of demonstrations," he wrote, "what was shown represented substantially the best we can do at present, and although it was quite good, the task of converting a demonstration achievement to a consumer product remains."

The December 1973 demonstration had succeeded in restoring Videodisc's development status with top management, but the reaction to Philips had cost the program more than six months delay. The earliest possible introduction had to be set back to late 1976.

Choosing a process

Despite the longstanding assumption that disc technology was advantageous because of the similarities between the processes used to manufacture its components and those used for other RCA products, divisional engineers quickly concluded that conventional record production processes would be entirely unsuitable for Videodisc. This was partly because it had been decided to treat the product as a mass-market item from the start, for this implied achieving high-volume production rates and high yields almost immediately. Accuracy of molding and freedom from impurities and defects would be orders of magnitude greater than anything used for normal record production, and this appeared to eliminate the usual compression molding and labor intensive materials handling. Process engineers decided on injection molding for more accurate dimensions, automated transfer equipment to avoid operator handling, and clean-room production that would eliminate contamination from airborne particles.

Major uncertainties were associated with procurement of the proposed process equipment. Ready-made equipment of this type was not available, and engineers had to locate and work with new suppliers who would make custom equipment. Within months after McCoy's arrival in the spring of 1973, process engineers had negotiated preliminary purchase agreements with the Husky Company of Canada for the injection molding equipment, and with the Airco Technical Company of Canada for the automated vacuum coater and transport equipment that was dubbed the "autocoater." Initial purchases would be used for a pilot line. As for any custom equipment of a developmental nature, delivery times were long, costs were high, and there was no way of knowing for sure that such special items as the autocoater would work until they were actually installed on the production floor. Serious questions concerning the ultimate capacity of the process, the yields, the throughput, and the maintenance time could only be answered when the equipment could be tested in operation. Even more difficult, the final quality of discs produced by the system would only be known when the entire integrated system was in place, when discs had been exposed to varying use conditions, and when appropriate test methods had been devised.

The mid-1973 program delay, occurring at a critical point in the procurement cycle, extended delivery times and increased

163

costs even further than might have been expected. The electron-beam mastering equipment had been delivered, but the 1973 hiatus delayed its debugging program, and the earliest date that the production process could be defined and specified moved to December 1974.

Time and again the need to demonstrate interrupted an orderly and thorough engineering development schedule. To regain top management support at the end of 1973, for instance, demonstration quality discs had to be made, removing some of the equipment from regular use. In some cases, as for licensing demonstrations, the Laboratory team had to involve itself in actual production of masters. It was, in fact, in the Laboratories that the first electron-beam recorder capable of producing saleable-quality masters in real time was assembled in 1974, a piece of equipment that comprised an ultrastable frame, a new high-speed turntable, and specially designed optical equipment.

Confusion at the top

Some of the delays and disruptions that the Videodisc program had to endure were caused by confusion at the top of the organization. Leadership problems at RCA in the early 1970s were evident to even the casual observer. Robert Sarnoff had retained his post as CEO after the computer debacle, but the divestiture moves and the organizational reshuffling that ensued had devastating effects in all sorts of ways. RCA dealers complained that they no longer had a full line of products to carry and that they no longer knew whom to contact. Executives found it impossible to establish a coherent course of action because Robert Sarnoff was making such frequent changes in both his strategy and his organization.

The Videodisc program survived this period because of the dogged persistence of the corporation's two senior technical executives, Hillier, corporate head of Research and Engineering, and Webster, head of the Laboratories. From his vantage point at corporate headquarters, Hillier made it his business to keep pressing the program's cause with Robert Sarnoff, and to defend it against the threats that seemed to lurk in every corner of the RCA organization. Meanwhile, Webster did his best to shield his technical staff from the upheavals in the rest of the corporation, to keep up morale, and to preserve his budgetary stability.

Left to the official corporate Selectavision organization, the program would not have fared so well. James Johnson, the member of the corporate marketing staff who took over Selectavision coordination, ran a very low-profile activity. In mid-1973 he initiated monthly coordination meetings that brought together participants from all locations to define and resolve key issues concerning schedules, plans, and management problems. But when the Philips' threat put the program in doubt, Johnson first put a hold on all capital outlays and then resigned from the company. Another Selectavision program head, George Evanoff, then had to learn the ropes.

Evanoff conducted the first major strategy review for prerecorded videoplayers that RCA had had since the late 1960s in the spring of 1974, and suspended further capital outlays for a crucial additional six months. Evanoff's report concentrated on updating the assessment of the marketing opportunity for both discs and players. On the basis of new market research, he concluded that disc systems could achieve a penetration of 45 percent of the total market, compared to perhaps 15 percent for magnetic tape systems. He also asserted that RCA had significant timing advantages over the Philips' system.

Evanoff found that RCA had spent $55 million in operating money and $5.4 million in capital investment on all Selectavision systems. Of this, perhaps half had gone to Videodisc, mostly at the Laboratories. In his ten-year financial projection Evanoff predicted that the Videodisc business would reach profitability in the fourth year with an internal rate of return of 20 percent over twelve years. He projected the peak cash run-off, on a cumulative basis, at $58 million, occurring in 1980. Most important, he predicted that Videodisc would fill a strategic gap of 2.5 percentage points toward RCA's goal of 10 percent growth per year.

Besides financial projections, Evanoff concentrated on programming. New market research had shown that customers would be receptive to existing programming. Costly and risky new programming generated especially for Selectavision would not be necessary at the beginning. But the big problem would be distribution. To provide customers with the variety they wanted would entail a tremendous inventory exposure for any distribution system. The number of titles could expand to thousands within a few years.

Evanoff's report on the technical status of the program gave little fresh detail, but relied on the collective judgment of the line organization involved in product development and the corporate staff departments of Research and Engineering and Manufacturing and Materials. It concluded that "reasonable confidence exists that the open technical problems will be solved satisfactorily during the scheduled development program; major inventions or new technologies are not required."

Compared with all its competitors, Evanoff reasoned, RCA still had its characteristic systems advantage. It was the sole competitor that already possessed all the internal capabilities required to field a complete videodisc system in the United States. Of six key factors considered necessary – U.S. player manufacturing, player distribution, player component sources, disc manufacturing, programming source, and disc distribution – RCA lacked only the programming source in-house. The next best endowed competitor, MCA, lacked three of the six components of the business package.

Evanoff's report came to the conclusion that RCA should concentrate on Videodisc for the consumer market and enter the market aggressively if the current assumptions spelled out by Robert Sarnoff in 1973 continued to hold. If it was judged necessary also to have a magnetic tape system for the "specialty segment," RCA should adopt the best one available and concentrate its own funds on Videodisc. In what was to be his most important recommendation, Evanoff went on to say that both the Videodisc hardware and software operations should be "independent line entities reporting directly at the RCA executive vice-president level."[2]

Several weeks later, Videodisc's internal competition was swept away. In early June 1974, an RCA technical team composed of Henry Ball, Gordon Bricker, Tom Stanley, and

All in the family

Ray Warren visited Sony, where they witnessed a showing of its new SLX magnetic tape equipment, which invalidated once and for all RCA's previous magnetic tape strategy. This second-generation product for consumer use, based on the successful Sony institutional player, the Umatic, had significant improvements in tape economics. More striking, it elevated off-the-air recording, termed its "time-shift" capability, which had not before been touted as a major value, to its principal consumer attraction. Even the members of the Consumer Electronics Division Magtape team had to admit that this was enough to put the last nail in Magtape's coffin.

167

8

VideoDisc in the public eye

RCA exposed its version of a working videodisc system to members of the press on March 19, 1975. The "invitations-only" demonstration took place at RCA's Rockefeller Center headquarters in a new facility fitted out especially to be a "permanent" demonstration facility. The chief demonstrator was Richard Sonnenfeldt, recently appointed staff vice-president for VideoDisc operations. The event followed by only four days the videodisc demonstration staged by Philips and MCA at the elegant Cotillion Room of the Pierre Hotel. Obviously Robert Sarnoff's planned strategy for Selectavision VideoDisc – to complete the research program in time to hold the product on the shelf awaiting market readiness – had gone awry.

The Philips–MCA announcement threatened one of RCA's most important competitive advantages, more important than the pioneering image that the CBS EVR had called into question. With the entry of Philips and MCA and their optical disc system, RCA could no longer claim to be the sole "system producer" of entertainment electronic systems in the domestic market. Another contender now claimed the capability to resolve the traditional problems posed by the marketing interdependence of hardware and software. The new competitive maneuver raised a crucial question. Would RCA manage to adapt to the new competitive reality in time, while still keeping within the cost limitations essential to its VideoDisc strategy?

RCA had delayed public demonstration as long as possible. Two previous Selectavision announcements – Holotape and Magtape – had come to nothing and the VideoDisc program management took care to avoid premature publicity. Apart from obligatory showings to potential domestic and foreign licensees in late 1974, no one outside RCA had viewed Video-Disc, even though formal technology transfer from laboratories to divisions had been going on for two years. The Philips–MCA showing forced RCA's hand, but precautions were still taken to reveal the system only to a selected audience.

Sonnenfeldt's presentation was low-key and matter of fact, a noticeable contrast to the style of earlier RCA videoplayer events. His message was a modest but compelling story about the RCA system's design advantages over its rival. "Our philosophy," he said, in a pointed attempt to deflate the Philips' claim to superiority based on exotic laser technology, "is to put a simple, low-cost, easily serviced player in the home and to keep the space age technology in the factory."

The manner of the presentation was disarming, all the more persuasive in that it admitted certain drawbacks and openly acknowledged that much remained to be done before the intended market introduction in mid- to late 1976:

The RCA capacitance system is simpler in design and easier to build, but its stylus and disc wear out. All of the player's components are off-the-shelf items, except for the stylus and one or two other parts. The player will be easier to put together than a TV set once the assembly line has been debugged.[1]

The low-profile approach, so uncharacteristic of RCA, gained general approval for RCA's product. McCoy, who was heading the technical effort out of Indianapolis, reported to Sonnenfeldt that RCA's refusal to tout its system openly until the company was absolutely committed had helped to repair RCA's somewhat damaged credibility with potential licensees. Likewise, representatives of the press believed the announcement, despite their memories of recent RCA misfires.

Press coverage during the next few months generally favored RCA over Philips–MCA, and published reports gave RCA as much as a year's lead over Philips in reaching the market with its product. Observers questioned the practicality of Philips' plan to use lasers in a player designed for the home, and they were particularly skeptical of the contention that lasers could be mass produced. Potential licensees were quoted as saying that the Philips' approach was too complex and too costly. Even RCA's grand old rival, Peter Goldmark of CBS, said that while both systems were good, he would take RCA's, if forced to choose between them, "because of the two-sided record and the technology which is more conventional and which I believe will be more reliable."[2] On the other hand, proponents of the Philips system argued that Philips' technology was preferable because of its greater potential for added features such as stop action and indexing. Zenith's vice-president for Research, Robert Adler, for instance, was quoted as saying, "It would be a pity if we had to standardize now on a system that does not do all these things."[3]

Inside RCA a disturbing realization was dawning. Ever so gradually, the media were drawing the two companies into a contest not of their own making. Despite the very different views that RCA and Philips had of the markets they wanted to serve, the press, intentionally or unintentionally, was creating a head-to-head battle like that of RCA and CBS back in the 1950s. Philips executives vainly asserted that their vital interest was a new communications medium and not the mass market. "If we had wanted only an entertainment system, we would have picked a far simpler system," argued William Zeiss, head of Philips' worldwide videodisc program.[4] His statement was virtually ignored by the press in their efforts to dramatize the competition.

In time, the reality moved closer to the press scenario. The "Expensive Race to be First," as *Business Week* dubbed the competition, was wholly different for RCA from the comfortable technological leadership to which Robert Sarnoff had committed his company in 1973.[5] The publicity exposed both companies to intense public scrutiny at a time when numerous business and technical uncertainties remained to be resolved. Neither could refuse to respond to the image created for it, and some decisions were bound to be materially affected by the public competition. Ironically, RCA's contest with Philips remained a favorite press item long after Philips ceased to be RCA's foremost competitor, diverting attention from the far more serious battle that was shaping behind the scenes with potential Japanese competitors.

Attempts to coordinate

For RCA, the Philips–MCA contest had redeeming features. It convinced Robert Sarnoff to appoint someone to coordinate the program full-time and also helped focus RCA's development efforts on the critical path to market. The presence of a single, respected competitor lent urgency to RCA's effort to cut through the internal disorder that had impeded earlier Selectavision efforts. The person chosen to take over VideoDisc operations, Richard Sonnenfeldt, previously staff vice-president, New Business Programs, had two vital qualifications: he had "start-up" experience (putting new products into production), and he had an exceptionally tough reputation. Starting as an RCA television engineer, he had risen through the engineering ranks, collecting patents along the way. During the late 1950s, he had managed RCA's industrial computers business as a protégé of the short-lived RCA president, John Burns. When Burns left RCA, Sonnenfeldt went to head a division of the Foxboro Company, and later served as CEO of Digitronics, a small data communications company affiliated with Philips. After nearly ten years away, he returned to RCA in time to be one of the chief RCA staff people to recommend that RCA withdraw from the computer business.

Sonnenfeldt assumed his new duties in stages. For the first six months of 1975 only the operating side of the VideoDisc program came under his control – business planning was run by John Biewener, product management by Gordon Bricker, and engineering and manufacturing by Don McCoy. That summer he took on the task of merging divisional and corporate staff activities, and he also took over George Evanoff's marketing and planning functions. Sarnoff and Conrad, in a major planning session of July 1975, set the intended date of market introduction a scant two years away.

The first issue for Sonnenfeldt to resolve was whether VideoDisc technology was really in a state of readiness for transfer. The documents at his disposal were ambiguous. They indicated that the technology was under control, but with reservations. A report from Hillier found "no serious showstoppers and no open research questions" in the VideoDisc

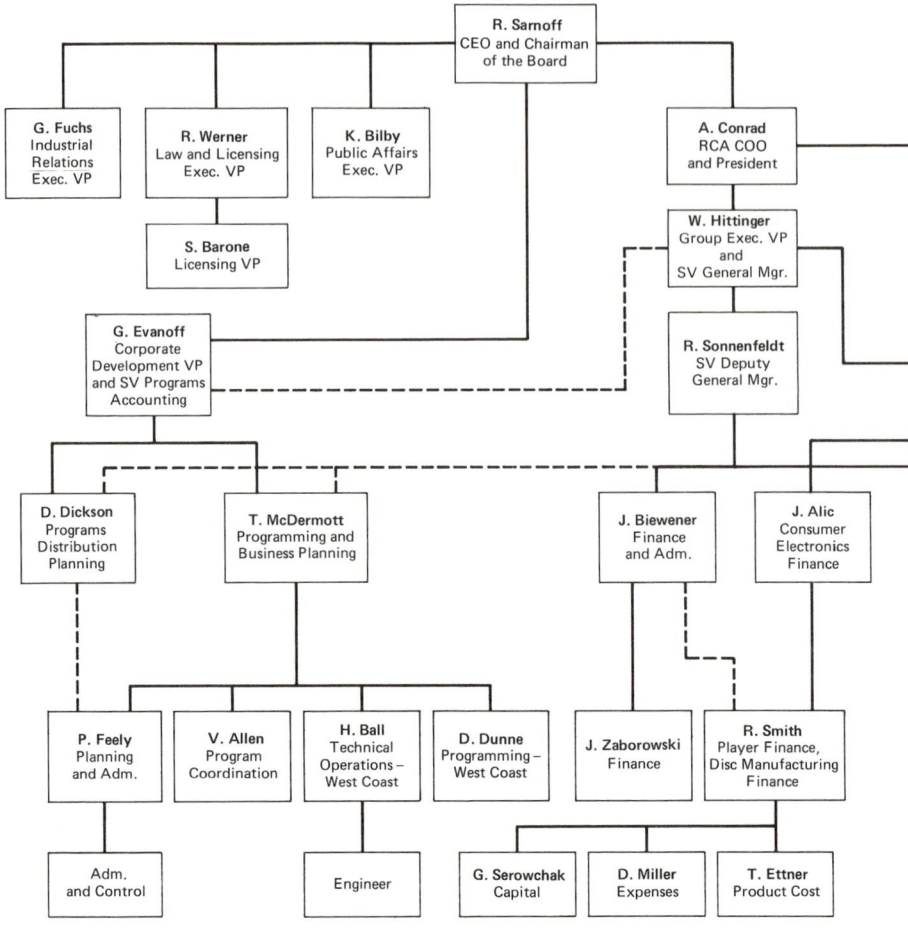

RCA Selectavision program organization, May 1975.

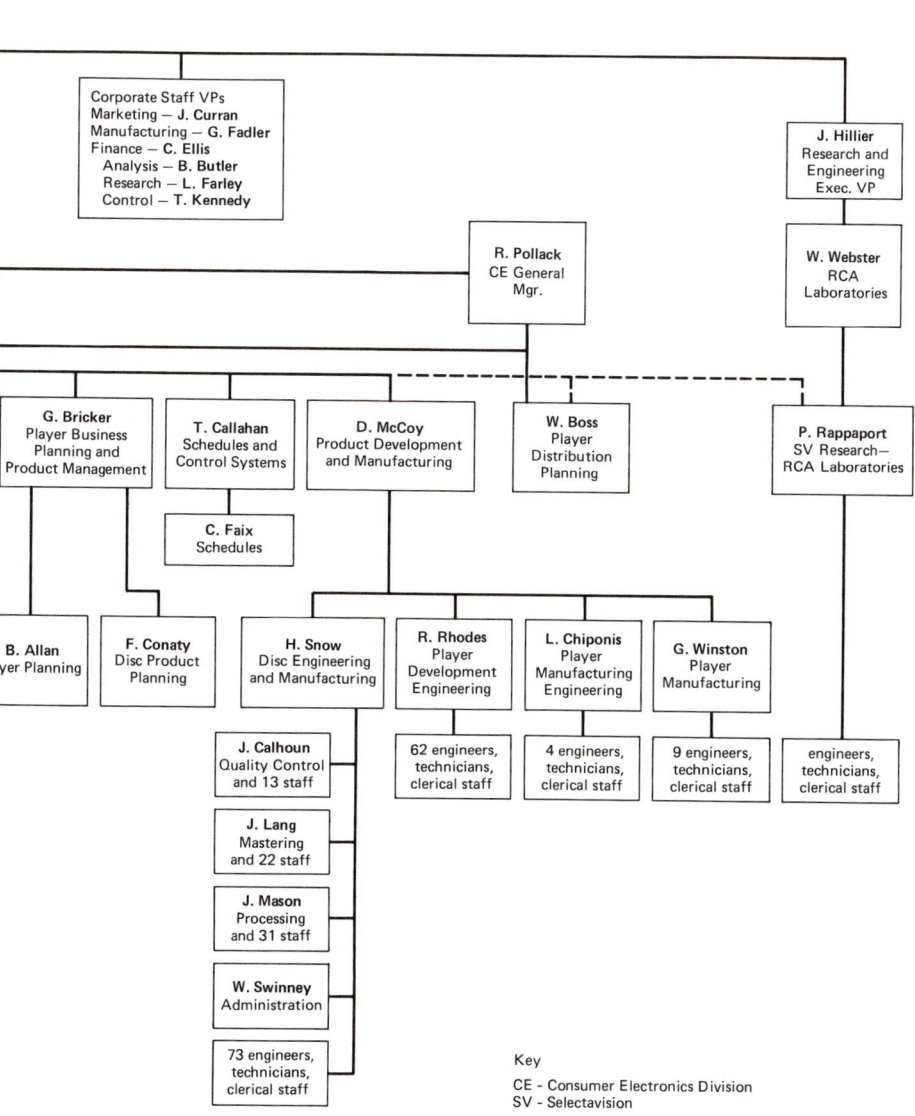

Corporate Staff VPs
Marketing — **J. Curran**
Manufacturing — **G. Fadler**
Finance — **C. Ellis**
Analysis — **B. Butler**
Research — **L. Farley**
Control — **T. Kennedy**

J. Hillier
Research and
Engineering
Exec. VP

R. Pollack
CE General
Mgr.

W. Webster
RCA
Laboratories

G. Bricker
Player Business
Planning and
Product Management

T. Callahan
Schedules and
Control Systems

D. McCoy
Product Development
and Manufacturing

W. Boss
Player
Distribution
Planning

P. Rappaport
SV Research—
RCA Laboratories

C. Faix
Schedules

B. Allan
yer Planning

F. Conaty
Disc Product
Planning

H. Snow
Disc Engineering
and Manufacturing

R. Rhodes
Player
Development
Engineering

L. Chiponis
Player
Manufacturing
Engineering

G. Winston
Player
Manufacturing

J. Calhoun
Quality Control
and 13 staff

62 engineers,
technicians,
clerical staff

4 engineers,
technicians,
clerical staff

9 engineers,
technicians,
clerical staff

engineers,
technicians,
clerical staff

J. Lang
Mastering
and 22 staff

J. Mason
Processing
and 31 staff

W. Swinney
Administration

73 engineers,
technicians,
clerical staff

Key

CE - Consumer Electronics Division
SV - Selectavision

program, but at the same time pointed to areas that his research and engineering staff, in a report of late 1974, had identified as in chronic danger. In Hillier's view not enough planning had been done for manufacturing and service. McCoy's pilot program needed to be enlarged, he said, and he thought that, for insurance against potential competitive developments, parallel programs should continue in both optical and pressure pickups. Hillier's study concluded on an upbeat note indicating that the house of research was in order and that the remainder of the program was the responsibility of the divisions and the new product operation. If appropriate production processes could be devised, a high degree of confidence was justified. Since the divisions had what he judged to be relevant manufacturing experience, this should pose no problem.

Dissenting voices unconnected to the Laboratories suggested that Hillier was being naive about the relevance of RCA's previous manufacturing experience. Commenting on the 1974 report by Evanoff and his staff, one R&E staff member warned that too much reasoning was being done by vague analogy and rules of thumb. Disc yields, for example, were projected to be at 95 percent after only a few years of production because that was RCA's experience with audio disc technology. But audio disc technology was mature and stable; videodisc technology was likely to remain in flux for some time. So far very few hard data pertaining to disc yields were available, and testing procedures had yet to be devised to produce better data. Other reports were filtering back from RCA's licensing demonstrations in Japan to Sonnenfeldt, which, if accurate, contradicted Hillier's assessment, for they contained evidence that the program had fundamental technical problems.

Licensing demonstrations

Throughout 1974, the RCA licensing department had pleaded to hold VideoDisc demonstrations for potential Japanese licensees. RCA contacts inside Japanese consumer electronics companies warned that Philips was courting their respective top managements. For the technical people at several leading Japanese companies, there seemed a real danger that a long and fruitful set of relationships with RCA personnel might be disrupted or foreclosed if RCA did not soon present its system for equal consideration.

Despite the urgency of the situation, it took months for RCA personnel to mount full-scale demonstrations in Japan. The logistical problems of transporting a large number of prototype players and other paraphernalia associated with major demonstrations were enormous. For the program personnel, the chief difficulty was producing working prototype players and quality discs. The pilot player assembly program was just starting up in the fall of 1974 and the task of supplying seventy good stylus arms and cartridges for Japan was a serious diversion from the main objective of preparing for a 1975 field test. The latter would require 400 good stylus arms and more than 200 cartridges, and the pilot assembly was already behind this schedule, owing to parts shortages.

The road show to Japan left in November 1974, headed by McCoy and accompanied by members of the RCA licensing staff. In a two-week period the team presented seventeen formal demonstrations to some 800 people representing 120 different Japanese hardware and software companies. The RCA licensing people came away with the impression that the trip had accomplished its primary goal, to show the Japanese that RCA had the simplest and lowest-cost player design concept. But there were also reports that demonstrations had left the impression in Japan that RCA's system was inferior to the Philips system in performance.

RCA offered extraordinarily generous terms to potential licensees to try out the capacitance system for themselves. They could purchase a trial package of engineering model drawings, sample discs, and a prototype player for $3,000, and six Japanese companies took advantage of this offer. Feedback from Matsushita indicated reservations about the high cost of RCA's mastering system and suggested that RCA consider locating a disc reproduction facility in Japan. Nevertheless, Matsushita was believed to be committed to the videodisc concept. It was one of the first Japanese companies to be

Eugene O. Keizer, head of Video-Systems Research at the RCA Laboratories, displays a 1975 version of the VideoDisc.

involved with the work, and it was working on its own versions of the RCA technology.

For some at RCA, the Japan trip had been an unpleasant eye opener. The RCA technical team was used to the vagaries of prototype demonstrations; they had been demonstrating the system in the Laboratories all year long and they knew how hard it was to put together a prototype player and disc combination that would yield acceptable performance. But the RCA executives who accompanied the trip and who had not attended previous demonstrations raised alarms. Tom McDermott, whose bias against hardware and hardware people was well known, as was his gift for colorful exaggeration, returned to tell staff members in New York that fifty stylii had broken in the course of demonstration, and that 300 discs had been required to show a few segments of demonstrable quality. Further inquiry confirmed McDermott's account. Gordon Bricker, of Sonnenfeldt's staff, found that stylii were lasting an average of 50 to 100 hours, with stylus tracking a contributing problem. In a January 1975 memorandum, Bricker argued that it would be premature to specify any system parameters for the VideoDisc because there were too many matters that required further research.

McCoy, in a separate report to his divisional boss, Roy Pollack, acknowledged that a number of technical problems with the discs had surfaced on the trip to Japan. Principal areas for concern were locked grooves; dropouts (spots on the discs where information had disappeared) or defects; and an unexpected sensitivity to climatic conditions, such as temperature variation and humidity, that produced a mysterious condition known as "video virus" in which moist dust particles collected in grooves and blocked the advancing stylus in its track.

At the beginning of 1975, Sonnenfeldt asked McCoy and Biewener, who were responsible for technical and business planning of the VideoDisc program, to identify the major issues they believed warranted immediate attention. Their responses showed that an effort to merge the two parts of the program was long overdue, for each man pointed to serious obstacles to progress falling in the other's domain. For instance, McCoy was preparing to ask the RCA Board for a $5 million appropriation to support a major investment in VideoDisc production equipment, but he could not prepare a credible justification without a revised business plan by Biewener to replace the Evanoff plan, rendered obsolete by the Philips–MCA entry into the market. McCoy said the plan should focus on the roll-out strategy, licensing support samples, technical aid support for licensing, player model diversification, and software to support the major field test, now scheduled for October 1975. Most important of all, he said, was that the target price of $400, sacred since the days of Holotape, was no longer obtainable with the current player design. He wanted to know what trade-offs he should make. Should he sacrifice features or allow the price to rise? Moreover, a limited field test was about to take place, in early 1975, in which ten players would be placed in the homes of RCA executives. McCoy wanted to know what to use as a yardstick by which to judge the results of this test. He saw this question as especially critical for product handling.

Biewener had his own list of program concerns, or "potential showstoppers." As far as he could see only two parts of the program, player design and facilities arrangements, were free of these potentially lethal problems. Organization and staffing, programming distribution, product definition (dimensions and materials), real-time recording, licensing partners, and programming availability, in his opinion, all had serious, unresolved questions.

Almost everyone involved with VideoDisc had complained about demonstration difficulties, and the way that requirements for demonstration interfered with the progress of the program. Sonnenfeldt responded by moving the demonstration facilities to Rockefeller Center. It was his intent to set up what amounted to his own test facility, a place where he could see for himself what state the technology was in without intervention of any interested party supplied by the technical side of the project. The corporate facility not only made it possible to insulate the program from outside pressures, it made the Sonnenfeldt operation the single conduit for VideoDisc information to the outside world and Sonnenfeldt himself the main channel between the program and top management. With a single stroke, he did what Bitting had been unable to do – to take over the Laboratories' role as chief program advocate and evaluator.

Sonnenfeldt's rationale was obvious. He believed that leaving the Laboratories as chief spokesman had unnecessarily politicized the program and thus had disrupted technical progress. Hillier and Webster had been under such pressure to promote VideoDisc that they had had little time for leading an effort to resolve the remaining technical issues. Sonnenfeldt also believed that they had glossed over problems out of fear that the least sign of a snag might prompt Robert Sarnoff to terminate the program. Sonnenfeldt's approach to top management was different, and from the Laboratories' perspective it was not necessarily an improvement. He presented himself not as an advocate but as a neutral mediator, ready to terminate the program himself if progress were not forthcoming. This approach made the Laboratories nervous at first, but it gradually succeeded where Bitting had failed, to gain the Laboratories' cooperation.

Sonnenfeldt saw the task of managing the relationship between the Laboratories and the divisions as a matter of resolving whether the technology was indeed ready to be transferred and how the transfer procedure should work. VideoDisc was a technology more unconventional than any the Laboratories had developed in the area of consumer electronics since television and new procedures were required.

> When I came everything was based on existence theorems. Nobody in Princeton had manufacturing experience and there was nobody in Indianapolis who had experience with technology transfer. I was the man in the middle who wanted to realize the technology's potential. But it seemed clear there was serious work to do that required science.[6]

After the successful March 1975 press conference, Sonnenfeldt followed up the concerns raised by his subordinates on the project, McCoy and Biewener. His June report to Conrad, then COO, was aimed, he said, "at bringing the project down to earth, smoking out all the business issues, and finding out what promises had already been made to licensees." A new start-up date of November 1976 was set, with full production to begin the following month. The timing depended on having a comprehensive business plan ready by August 1975, covering the roll-out (or pattern of product introduction to dealers) plan, anticipated production volumes, and demand expected for players and discs. The formal equipment authorization would be based on the findings of the limited pilot program then under way in Indianapolis.

What he saw in Indianapolis confirmed Sonnenfeldt's impression that the usual pattern of technology transfer from Princeton to Indianapolis, which Hillier had assumed in his fall 1974 report, would not work for VideoDisc. Indianapolis lacked the necessary personnel with experience in transferring technology, and it lacked the necessary skills in the technologies that the program was using, especially electron beam mastering and vacuum-coating techniques. Only the Laboratories could compensate for these deficiencies. As Sonnenfeldt put it later, the Laboratories would not be allowed "to hand over their pearls and expect the divisions to make necklaces out of them." Moreover, he insisted that the Laboratories take a central role in product development, a proposition viewed in Princeton with mixed feelings.

It was a measure of the importance the Laboratory management attached to VideoDisc that it accepted the new role Sonnenfeldt proposed. Laboratory personnel were unaccustomed to the painstaking and tedious routine associated with pilot programs. They were not attracted by Sonnenfeldt's management approach – a rigorous routine of statistical testing, weekly reports, and frequent meetings between members of all parts of the technical program.[7] Hardest to bear, it involved regular and often extended trips between Princeton and Indianapolis.

The Laboratories might have found good reasons for opposing the new regime, reasons grounded solidly in its understanding of its mission within RCA. As the recent effort on the computer program had demonstrated, technical staff who were tied up in the development program could not contribute to longer-term work, such as next-generation developments on the videodisc system, or to other Laboratories' projects. On the other hand, a clear advantage of continued participation was the chance to continue to have influence over the program's main technical decisions, and to ensure that proprietary processes developed at Princeton would continue to be used. The formal agreement was that McCoy would serve as the program's chief technical officer reporting to Sonnenfeldt, and that McCoy would have functional authority over everyone serving the project in a technical capacity. The Laboratories ended up supporting this arrangement in full.

New competitors

Within a month of the March 1975 prototype demonstrations by Philips–MCA and RCA, the first videodisc system appeared in the marketplace. Teldec, the joint venture between Telefunken and Decca announced in 1970, offered its player and disc system for sale in Germany. The final product was little changed from its earliest demonstrated version. Its discs were still limited to fifteen minutes of playing time each, and it was offered with a very small selection of programming material, which RCA planners viewed as a critical defect in the system. Teldec did poorly on the market and was withdrawn in just over a year, but some of the lessons from this brief offering were surprising. For instance, buyers purchased far more discs per player than Teldec's planners had expected. This led RCA to worry even more about the range of programming required for VideoDisc.

A second new videoplayer product market introduction, unlike Teldec, did not sink without a trace. The Sony Betamax, introduced in the summer of 1975, was viewed at first as another learning opportunity, but it soon developed into a serious threat for RCA's VideoDisc program. Opinion was evenly divided at RCA between those who saw Betamax as direct competition for VideoDisc and those who maintained that the two products were so different that they complemented each other. The latter view stemmed in part from the price differential between the two products, which was widely expected in RCA and the industry at large, to hold constant. Few believed that Sony would be able to reduce its price from the $1,300 figure at which Betamax was introduced. The RCA Laboratories' position was still that magnetic tape held little potential for cost reduction, and sales volume for all videotape recorders was expected to be too low to realize significant manufacturing economies.[8] Nevertheless, Sony was viewed as a formidable opponent, whose color television sales had been having a visible, though not necessarily large, impact on the market that RCA had once dominated. Few inside RCA were inclined in 1975 to ignore the possibility that Sony might be a serious threat in the videoplayer market as well.

The shakeup of top management at RCA in late 1975 posed a different kind of threat to the VideoDisc program. On the one hand, Anthony Conrad's promotion to succeed Robert Sarnoff seemed to augur very little disruption, for he had been a friend to VideoDisc and was committed to maintaining stability in general. Indeed his elevation nullified a recent reorganization that Sarnoff had decided, but not implemented. Edgar Griffiths, however, Conrad's direct subordinate in charge of RCA's electronics businesses, was emphatically not a friend from the technical community's perspective. Above all not a risk taker, in unguarded moments Griffiths was inclined to refer to the VideoDisc program as "Sarnoff's turkey." Early in 1976 he persuaded Conrad to consider seriously the premises on which the VideoDisc business strategy were based.

What Griffiths questioned was in fact the basic assumption that RCA benefited most from a position of technological leadership. He attached paramount importance to the bottom line, and argued that the company's traditional strategy was doomed to unprofitability, for after introducing new technologies in its core businesses, it had consistently failed to insure continued dominance of the market. Zenith's successful pursuit of a "follower" strategy suggested to him that the profitable approach to technology was to leave leadership to others. Griffiths persuaded Conrad to ask Sonnenfeldt to put down on paper the advantages of pursuing technological pioneering.[9]

Sonnenfeldt's report put heavy emphasis on historical precedent and compared RCA's color television experience with that of Zenith. It was true that Zenith's well-organized and well-executed marketing effort begun in 1969 had enabled it to take over the leading market share in color television from RCA. RCA's share of the market had fallen from 33 percent in 1965 to 23 percent in 1969. But, he noted, RCA had already handsomely recouped its investment by that time, netting a $391 million return between 1960 and 1969 on an investment of $100 million made between 1946 and 1959. Returns included profits from color sets and tubes as well as from NBC, Broadcast Equipment, Service and others. Furthermore, the company had realized licensing profits of $70 million from 1965 to 1969, rising to levels that had totaled over $250 million in the next five years, despite substantial reductions in licensing fees for color. In comparison, Zenith had made a profit of less than $300 million during the comparable period.

Would Selectavision have the same problems as color television in the early stages of market introduction, as some had suggested? Sonnenfeldt argued that there were enormous differences between Selectavision and color television, which he enumerated in a point-by-point comparison. Selectavision would not have to supplant an existing product, it would not be a threat to dealers' current sales, and it would have a generous supply of programming. Moreover, there were strong indications that consumers were interested in such a product. Market research showed that 8.3 percent of all homes with television were interested, five percentage points more than the Selectavision business plan assumed as a baseline. The timing was right, as consumer electronics was by then a mature product line, and there was large potential demand for videoplayers. Consumers would only have to purchase one to two hours of Selectavision programming per week to make the product a success.

Would RCA be better off following than leading? Sonnenfeldt dismissed this question as moot; there was no company to follow. No one else was then using capacitance so it was unlikely that a videoplayer using that system would appear on the market before 1980. With regard to systems using other technologies, the Philips' system was 50 to 100 percent more expensive than RCA's and thus not destined for the mass market.

There were three alternatives: RCA could lead with the capacitance system in May 1977 (the date to which the schedule had then slipped), it could "follow" Matsushita by producing a pressure pickup system, or it could stop work on the product altogether. A leadership strategy, Sonnenfeldt estimated, would yield profits through 1985 of $225 million after tax, rising to $400 million if licensing was included. A follower strategy might yield between $25 million and $50 million in 1981. RCA's investment in Selectavision totaled $18 million after tax, plus an additional $4 million by the Laboratories.

Sonnenfeldt recommended that the program be continued until the mid-1976 technical checkpoint, the next major milestone, and then either supported aggressively or terminated. Stopping the program, although cheaper, would forgo future new business income and curtail licensing income which depended on new products. Despite Griffiths' preference for withdrawal, Conrad chose to follow Sonnenfeldt's suggestion.

Indianapolis pilot

The two different parts of the development program located in Indianapolis, player and disc, were encountering very different degrees of success. The player program, whose components, as Sonnenfeldt had told the press in March 1975, were largely off-the-shelf items, was proceeding close to schedule; the disc program was running into all the problems that might be expected of a "space-age technology." In preparation for the full-scale Selectavision field test, set for June, the pilot assembly plant at RCA's Rockville Road plant turned out the first engineering models. Some 200 players were scheduled for distribution to the Licensing Division for demonstrations, to player engineering for further advanced design work, and to RCA executives for home trial.

Informal preliminary tests preceded the full-scale field test. Early models were given to RCA employees in Indianapolis to try out during January and February, and it was found that more improvements would still have to be made before June. Player problems were confined to the sapphire stylii, which broke frequently, but there were many complaints about the discs, which were very vulnerable even with the most careful handling. Users also complained that programming was so limited their families treated the systems as little more than curiosities. Players were reported to have received an average of thirteen hours of playtime over two weeks, and the long-suffering families could hardly be expected to use them more without more varied and entertaining programming.

The Selectavision management concluded from these trials that discs could not be tested adequately until they were produced by specialized equpment. In one sense this conclusion validated what the Laboratories regarded as a prime advantage of Selectavision: the autocoater process would be an important barrier to entry by others into the disc business and therefore an RCA strategic advantage. If RCA had so much difficulty with its coating process, a follower would have trouble replicating it. The company could count on dominating the disc business for a long time, or could decide to license the disc-making process for substantial sums. Licensing fees could include lump-sum charges up front for a three-year mastering package (which covered making the master disc alone) or a five-year replication package (which covered mass-producing discs). Replication could bring in royalties of between 10 cents and 15 cents per disc, with a minimum volume of 150,000 discs per licensee. As much as $50 million could be hoped for in licensing fees alone.

The autocoater arrived in Indianapolis early in 1976, and according to plan, autocoater-made discs would be ready for the June field test. Saleable disc production would have to begin in November 1976 for product introduction to take place in mid-1977, and the plant would have to be up to full rate within a month of the starting date. In the beginning, three Husky presses, with a capacity to produce 4,000 discs per day at start-up, would feed the autocoater, which had a coating capacity of 5,200 discs per day. Yield after coating loss was initially expected to be around 83 percent. In time, an autocoater would require four presses, and gradual yield improvement would produce 6,000 good discs per day, or just under three million discs per year in 1978. With gradual additions of autocoaters and presses, it was hoped to produce 38 million discs per year by 1983 – the seventh year of production.

As soon as equipment began to arrive it became clear that this schedule was optimistic. The autocoater was difficult to assemble, and although RCA engineers worked closely with equipment suppliers, it was mid-1976 before they could produce discs of any quality. It was impossible to devise a computerized testing program for discs without automated discs of testable quality. Initial production results proved to be discouraging, nowhere near the 83 percent good yield that had been planned. But the greatest problem was that autocoated discs deteriorated almost as badly as their handmade predecessors. The oil coating migrated on the surface of the disc, leaving parts of the metal coating exposed and collecting in a thickened layer elsewhere. Any handling by human hands seriously damaged the disc's surfaces. And when the testing program was finally devised it showed up problems with the mastering technique. The electron beam was not producing flawless masters but created its own noise on the disc surface. Materials specialists at the Laboratories were called on for further work to produce oil coatings that would not migrate and that would be less sensitive to handling, and electron-beam-resist compounds to produce more consistent masters.

Meanwhile, the Laboratories, personnel were adjusting with difficulty to the work routines that Sonnenfeldt had imposed on them. The monotonous pace of improvement required by the new statistical methods might be common to continuous process industries, but most electronics professionals at RCA would prefer to invest in new solutions rather than test and isolate problems in existing systems. New solutions could yield new patents – and publishable papers – while mere improvements on old ones held few rewards. Due to the pressure of time, Sonnenfeldt felt that he had to ask the Laboratories to continue to carry out the necessary testing programs, but he hoped in time to build a more appropriate support staff in Indianapolis, where technicians could be in close contact with the process, and the culture was more conducive to the new methods and procedures that had to be used.

Disc-production delays caused revisions in the schedule even before the formal 1976 technical milestone review. The first autocoater line would not be able to begin regular production until October 1977, and then only at a rate of seventy-five discs per hour, which implied product introduction of mid-1978 at the earliest. But despite earlier uncertainties, Conrad agreed to continue the program on the grounds that the

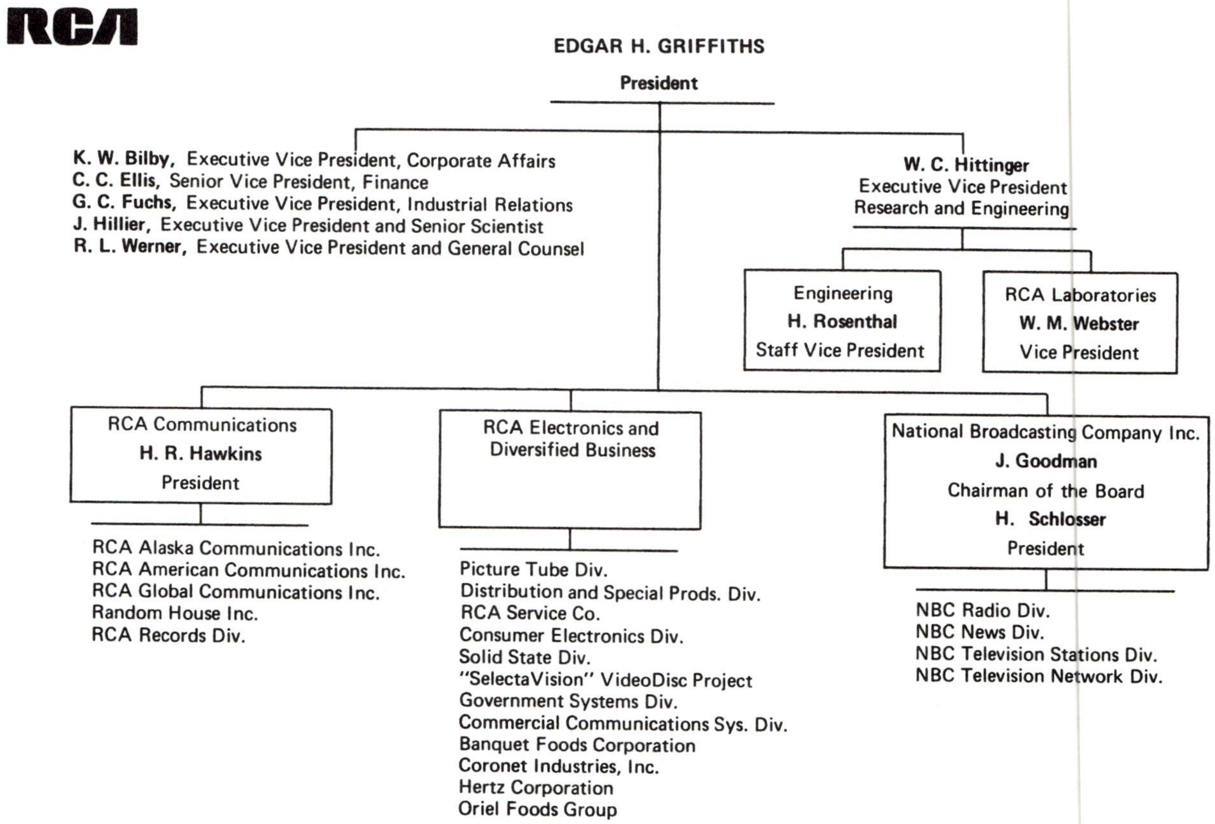

EDGAR H. GRIFFITHS
President

K. W. Bilby, Executive Vice President, Corporate Affairs
C. C. Ellis, Senior Vice President, Finance
G. C. Fuchs, Executive Vice President, Industrial Relations
J. Hillier, Executive Vice President and Senior Scientist
R. L. Werner, Executive Vice President and General Counsel

W. C. Hittinger
Executive Vice President
Research and Engineering

RCA Laboratories
W. M. Webster
Vice President

Engineering
H. Rosenthal
Staff Vice President

National Broadcasting Company Inc.
J. Goodman
Chairman of the Board
H. Schlosser
President

NBC Radio Div.
NBC News Div.
NBC Television Stations Div.
NBC Television Network Div.

RCA Electronics and
Diversified Business

Picture Tube Div.
Distribution and Special Prods. Div.
RCA Service Co.
Consumer Electronics Div.
Solid State Div.
"SelectaVision" VideoDisc Project
Government Systems Div.
Commercial Communications Sys. Div.
Banquet Foods Corporation
Coronet Industries, Inc.
Hertz Corporation
Oriel Foods Group

RCA Communications
H. R. Hawkins
President

RCA Alaska Communications Inc.
RCA American Communications Inc.
RCA Global Communications Inc.
Random House Inc.
RCA Records Div.

RCA corporate organization chart, September 1976.

187

technical effort had made enormous strides, and that new work methods were bearing fruit. The Laboratories' management had kept its pledge of full support for the divisions in Indianapolis. Underscoring his commitment to VideoDisc, Conrad told RCA's shareholders at their August 1976 meeting that RCA would proceed with VideoDisc introduction in 1978, contingent on expected technical progress.

New management again

This reprieve was short-lived, however, for Conrad's unexpected departure in September 1976, put the entire program in doubt. His successor, Edgar Griffiths, appeared at first to be pursuing the course concerning VideoDisc that he had long advocated. He moved aside Hillier, VideoDisc's most vocal advocate at headquarters, replacing him as head of Research and Engineering with William Hittinger, former head of RCA's combined electronics businesses, who in turn was replaced by Roy Pollack, a reputed opponent of VideoDisc. At the very least, the choice of Hittinger, a former operating executive, to head Research and Engineering, signaled a change in the relationship of Princeton with the rest of the RCA technical community.

In a move that was likely to spell further trouble for Video-Disc, Griffiths ordered RCA's market research staff to prepare a report comparing the prospects for VideoDisc with Sony's Betamax, which had been enthusiastically received in the marketplace since its introduction. The Japanese threat had finally been recognized. Japanese television companies had made impressive gains in U.S. markets in 1976 on several fronts. They had made sudden and devastating inroads into the color television market, jumping from 17 percent to 38 percent of the market in one year. While smaller television producers had suffered most of the losses in American market share, RCA could hardly ignore the likely threat to its core business by the Japanese. Zenith was no longer the competitor to be feared.

The market research comparing consumer response to

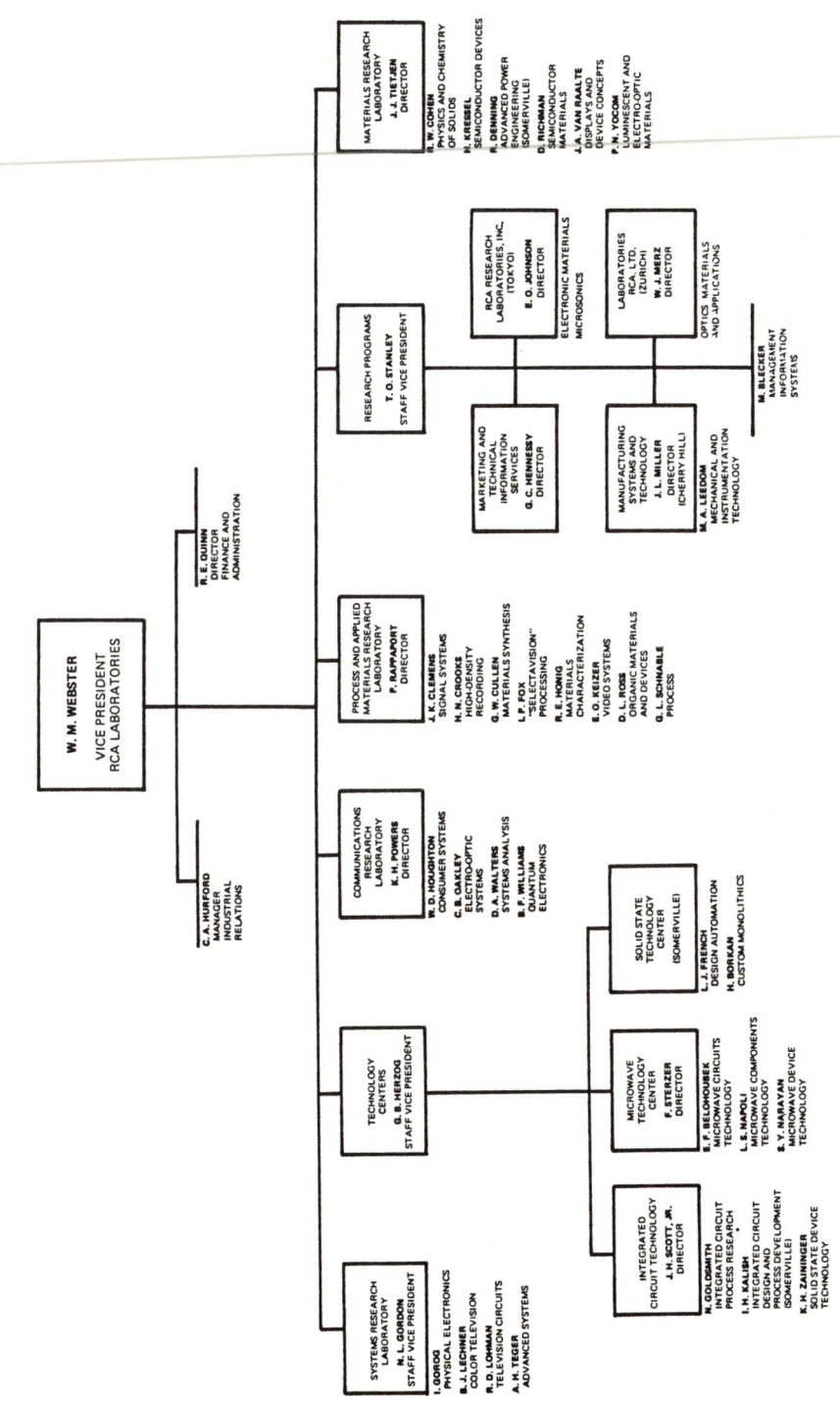

RCA Laboratories organization chart, October 1976.

189

Sony's Betamax, already in the market, with RCA's proposed VideoDisc product was inconclusive as to the relative appeal of the two different product concepts – recording versus only playback – but it left very little doubt as to the importance of price. The survey found substantial interest in video systems, and a theoretical preference for Betamax, with its reusable tapes and features of being able to watch one program while recording another, and to record while not at home. But when cost came into it, the survey found a decisive preference. At prices of $300 for the RCA system and $700 for the Betamax, 35 percent of the consumers polled expressed interest in Video-Disc. At higher prices of $500 and $1,000 respectively, the amount of consumer interest in VideoDisc dropped to less than 20 percent. The report strongly recommended that the RCA player be priced at less than $400.

Sonnenfeldt's staff viewed the market report as a panic reaction to Sony's Betamax promotion. They doubted that Sony would ever achieve a $700 price tag, and they pointed out that Sony would never use market research on new products as a basis for making a decision to launch. But Griffiths saw the report as a reason to initiate yet another full-scale review by his financial staff, an independent group not involved with Video-Disc. All key RCA managers who were either involved with the VideoDisc program, or whose businesses might be affected by VideoDisc in the future, were asked what the effect would be if RCA were to close down the VideoDisc program altogether.[10]

The first manager to respond was Kenneth Bilby, head of Corporate Affairs and guardian of RCA's public image. He left no doubt that he considered VideoDisc to be critical to RCA's image. The company's recent history, he argued, would magnify the significance of any course of action the corporation took – success would reinforce RCA's traditional role as a technology leader and would demonstrate the marketing skills of the new management. A failure after introduction, accompanied by the inevitable substantial write-off, would reinforce the effect of RCA's computer failure, still vivid in the public memory. At the same time, Bilby felt that to abandon Video-Disc altogether at that point would continue the indecisive stop–start pattern of the earlier Selectavision products. Management could portray the move as decisive cost cutting, but many would view it as short-sighted. Even to put the program on a back burner would be unfortunate, given Conrad's positive statements to RCA shareholders only a few months earlier. It would be better, even if the program was scheduled for closing, to play the role that Zenith had assumed with television sets, and wait to see if someone else failed with the product first. He noted that the VideoDisc program, in part owing to Sonnenfeldt's promotional abilities, had received an unusual amount of publicity during the past two years. "The press continues to focus its magnifying glass on us," Bilby cautioned. "To put it mildly, there is no place to hide."

Roy Pollack took a firm stand against the program. He saw VideoDisc in its present form as a very high-risk product for RCA and recommended that the program be discontinued and the project redirected to the Laboratories where the technology could be improved. He acknowledged that timing would be crucial if VideoDisc were to compete against magnetic tape products already coming to market, for the latter would soon be too entrenched to compete with. But a speedy introduction with a compressed development cycle would be enormously costly, for his own organization in particular. At a time when Consumer Electronics was already having to make substantial investments in its basic color television manufacturing capability to compete with the Japanese, it was not something RCA could afford to do. In any case, Pollack questioned the VideoDisc's competitive potential in terms of either the Sony or the Philips alternatives. In his view, the first had clearly superior production capabilities and the second, better features than the RCA product. But as RCA dealers were asking what RCA would have to counter the Sony Betamax, Pollack thought it would be unwise to shut down VideoDisc altogether until a substitute product was available. He supported an idea that had been proposed by Hittinger, to deal with that difficulty by negotiating with the two Japanese producers of videoplayers, Sony and Matsushita, and to license one of their technologies. He viewed the health of the entire consumer electronics business as too fragile to risk financing a new product at that time.

191

Sonnenfeldt's staff argued that Pollack's view was parochial in that it focused entirely on the effect of the program on Consumer Electronics. It ignored the question of licensing revenues forgone if RCA did not introduce a proprietary videoplayer. What Pollack had said would apply to any new product, they maintained. The central advantage of VideoDisc over magnetic tape was that RCA could retain the disc part of the business, which would remain a good business even if it eventually lost the player business. The staff estimated that disc profits would be four to six times player profits by 1985, seven years after start-up.

VideoDisc supporters based their arguments on cost and timing. From an overall company perspective, it would be more costly to shut down the program than to keep it going, they said. To lose the important technical talent that had been assembled for the project might even make it impossible to follow someone else's system, should that turn out to be the ultimate decision. The Research and Engineering staff stressed that timing was indeed of the essence and argued that VideoDisc should be introduced as soon as possible. A number of improvements were already in the planning stages but, as with color television, they could better be added later when the product was already on the market and RCA's standard had been firmly established. The main thing was not to allow videotape recorders to be in the market alone for too long.

The Licensing Department pleaded the VideoDisc case with the most passion, for Stephen Barone, its head, believed that RCA's technical image was at stake with VideoDisc. Companies did not license a product merely to acquire a particular technology, he argued, but because they wished to keep open a continuing source of leading technology in the future. "In recent years," he wrote in his response, "our technical image has been somewhat tarnished. We have gone out of one electronics business after another, from computers to audio." Success in a high-technology business would arrest this decline.

Licensing was also concerned about previous commitments made to companies it had already signed up, six in Japan and one in Britain. These had purchased players and had been led to believe that if they developed the players, RCA would provide mastering and replication. Japanese licensees had urged RCA to set up disc manufacturing facilities in Japan. Barone believed that Japan would be the place where the standards battle would be decided, and the royalties involved would be substantial. If VideoDisc succeeded it would return $100 million in license fees, most of it in years six through nine. But even if the product failed in the market, the company would still have a good licensing income. Failure to go on with the program might not only forfeit VideoDisc royalties, it might jeopardize much more if Japanese licensees decided not to renew their agreements on other lines in 1977. Barone added:

We announced Selectavision I (Holotape) and we didn't deliver; we announced Selectavision II (Magtape) and we didn't deliver; if we don't deliver on Selectavision III (VideoDisc) it could be strike three and out insofar as our technical image is concerned.[11]

Sonnenfeldt went right to the heart of the fear of Japanese competition when he made his case to Griffiths. As one who had spent the most impressionable part of his career at RCA in the early days of color television, he was fiercely loyal to the idea of RCA as America's leading consumer electronics company, and he felt that it was up to RCA to lead the American consumer electronics industry in a long overdue counterattack against the Japanese high-tech offensive. Sony's Betamax entry was not, in his opinion, the threat on which to focus. The real worry was that the Japanese companies would go after the mass-market videoplayer now that they had had ample opportunity to work with RCA's prototypes for a while. He predicted that Sony would sell only about 50,000 to 100,000 Betamax units per year to a highly selective market, and this might provide useful market research for RCA. Since Betamax and VideoDisc were designed for different markets he thought Betamax would be "on balance a help." Neither was Philips a strong contender for the market RCA was seeking.

The important point was to use VideoDisc to foil Japanese designs on the heart of RCA's preferred mass market, Sonnenfeldt asserted, and the VideoDisc strategy was planned with such a purpose in mind. Player production was to be automated from the start, and there were plans to automate the stylus and cartridge production. But the linchpin of the entire strategy was RCA's proprietary disc. RCA would introduce its product in a territory-by-territory roll-out, and only Selectavision dealers would have discs during the introductory period. The Japanese would have to follow in a territory-by-territory pattern as well.

When all comments from both sides were in, Sonnenfeldt summed up the case for VideoDisc by covering his opponents' most damaging points. He maintained that the project was, in general, in a state of technical readiness to support an April 1978 introduction. The pilot program had performed 5,000 tests on more than 1,600 discs with cumulative test acceptance of 79 percent. The need for technical improvements was not a reason to delay, for these were already under way. A sleeve or "caddy" had been designed to improve the ability of the system's discs to withstand normal handling, and recent work showed that a diamond stylus to replace the fragile sapphire stylus and a two-hour disc to give competitive playing time were feasible. These improvements would provide for competitive upgrading after the product had been introduced to the market. The long playtime would give RCA a decisive advantage over Philips, which could offer only one hour in its multifeature format.

The program's planners worked out a gradual and flexible introduction strategy for both hardware and software that would alleviate any potential VideoDisc risks to Consumer Electronics interests. A gradual roll-out of players suggested that only 10,000 players would be in the field during the first year, a manageable number to service or upgrade, or replace, if need be. If the launch did happen in early 1978, the Japanese onslaught would only come when RCA was ready for it, at the point when the product was breaking even. To minimize risk for the programming side, an area in which risks could be large, RCA would use a flexible approach, only selling programs acquired from others. As for market research, Sonnenfeldt was able to point to the highly regarded Frost & Sullivan service, which had just released a report on videoplayers. It predicted that videodisc sales would top videotape recorder sales from 1981 on.

194

Armed with the review results, Griffiths assembled the seventeen managers involved in one room. Apparently convinced that VideoDisc would have little support outside RCA's technical community, he chose to take a vote on the question of withdrawal. The result: one vote in favor of withdrawal, five abstentions, and eleven votes for continuing the program. Since this was not a sufficiently solid base for a new executive to take the radical decision to withdraw from the program, Griffiths agreed to continue it at least until the spring 1977 checkpoint. As a compromise measure it was decided that RCA would negotiate with Sony and Matsushita for a videotape recorder that it could market through its own dealer network as soon as possible.

9

RCA's "Manhattan Project"

Early in 1979, a statement from the office of RCA's chairman startled the press. Edgar Griffiths, in an apparent abrupt about-face, announced that RCA would rush VideoDisc to the market as quickly as possible. Although the schedule would not be given out until later in the year, the likely product development time would be eighteen months to two years.

Griffiths had been under pressure to make a final decision on VideoDisc ever since assuming RCA's top slot in 1976. But in July 1977 he acted instead to delay the start-up for an indefinite period, until specified problems had been solved. RCA discontinued the preproduction work for players and discs, dismantled the pilot plant in Indianapolis, and sent the project back to the Laboratories for further work. The media viewed this as a thinly disguised withdrawal from the program. Even insiders doubted that VideoDisc would ever return to high gear after the dispersal of 150 experienced project personnel in Indianapolis, and many senior technical managers either moved to different jobs or left the company altogether.

Much of the year 1978, when Griffiths was to have announced a final decision, came and went in silence. The trade concluded that this was RCA's way of folding its tents quietly after the VideoDisc race on which the company had bet a large amount of investment.[1] Presumably the chairman was unwilling to jeopardize the steady growth in quarterly earnings that had won him points with Wall Street. Griffiths was fond of pointing out that at RCA simply going ahead with a new product introduction was following the path of least resistance. "What has bedeviled this company for years," he told one reporter, "is the feeling that we had to have something new

196

and different all the time, and we had to go from one technical accomplishment to the other, never mastering the prior one and never realizing a proper return on the bottom line."[2]

What, or who, finally convinced Griffiths to take the step he seemed so reluctant to take was a matter for spirited conjecture around 30 Rockefeller Center. Some observers believed that as a result of his efforts to reassure the RCA Laboratories that he was not antitechnology, Griffiths had become a convert to their program. Others noted that Griffiths' hesitancy to bring technology-based products to market was the one critical note sounded in a generally favorable piece published in *Fortune*'s 1978 New Year's Eve issue. "Like his predecessors," the article remarked, "Griffiths is having trouble translating research into producible and marketable products."[3] In all likelihood, the article was only the capstone on a number of developments over the past two years that had convinced Griffiths that VideoDisc had to go forward.

Behind the scenes

The late 1976 financial staff review in response to the Sony threat and the managerial referendum that had followed on its heels had strengthened Sonnenfeldt's influence over the technical side of the VideoDisc program. This was partly because he had abandoned his neutral stance, and had come out squarely on the side of VideoDisc. At the same time, Griffiths' doubts about VideoDisc were no longer formless objections to the errors of his predecessors, or to the merits of RCA's traditional pioneering strategy, but centered on specific problems.

Sonnenfeldt had no trouble convincing those responsible for further improvements that the program would terminate unless they met the technical targets he had established. He needed the leverage, for whatever his optimistic assessments to those conducting the review, technical readiness was still an open question in early 1977. Test results of new discs were better, but in-home trials continued to reveal serious problems with discs in use. The oil migration problem had been solved, but the disc coating was still vulnerable to damage. Discs scratched easily, and all surface flaws had noticeable effects on the pictures a disc produced. Furthermore, new defects showed up that factory test programs had not revealed, prompting serious questions about the validity of test results overall.

While Sonnenfeldt pressed the materials research groups at Princeton to strive for improvements, he was also encouraging Indianapolis to develop their technical alternatives. The electron-beam mastering method, the sapphire stylus, and the vacuum-coating techniques were fraught with uncertainty and still required further fundamental advances in materials technologies.

The problems associated with manufacturing high quality multicoated discs consistently and in large quantities, proved to be much more demanding than anticipated. The disc made on the pilot production line required three microscopically thin coatings to be deposited by the autocoater at the rate of 720 to 1,000 discs per hour. Each coating material used had to meet both the demands of the product and of the production process. Although it conformed to the product's specifications for wear, adherence, cohesive strength, conformity, compatibility with the sapphire stylus, and the like, a coating material that did not work in the autocoater was useless. And all materials had to be stable and able to resist unfavorable environmental conditions. All of this took time to discover, but the more that was learned about the problems the more difficult they became.[4]

Progress was made, and the April 1977 checkpoint was a qualified success. Improvements were incorporated into an upgraded version of the product and a demonstration for GE went well, holding out the possibility that American companies might begin to line up behind RCA and adopt its disc format as standard. The VideoDisc staff then mounted more demonstrations in Japan, hoping to gain firm commitments to RCA's standard from a few of the most influential Japanese companies. On this trip some key Japanese observers expressed open admiration, admitting that during the previous demonstrations they had found Philips' technology more impressive, but that their concerns about VideoDisc performance were now dispelled.

Then, just as the program seemed to be on the verge of a standards breakthrough, RCA discovered a new competitor. A VideoDisc demonstration for a group of technical experts from the Japan Victor Corporation led to a surprise counterinvitation. JVC's researchers divulged that they had a project under way that they had not even revealed to the R&D group at their parent company, Matsushita. "To our complete surprise," noted Sonnenfeldt afterward, "the development the JVC research group had to demonstrate was an uncoated nonconductive disc that was produced by means of a high-quality, optical mastering method."[5] The disc was theoretically simpler and designed to be played at 900 rpm, a less demanding speed than that of the RCA product.

The JVC revelation invalidated at a stroke most major premises of RCA's VideoDisc strategy, based on its proprietary disc. If and when JVC announced its disc publicly, and Sonnenfeldt had little doubt that the Matsushita team would adopt the JVC alternative, RCA could no longer claim technical superiority for the mass market on the basis of simplicity and cost. Its coated disc was more difficult to produce, so that JVC's production cost could be expected to be less. JVC was using some RCA disc technology, but the licensing prospects were minor, for Sonnenfeldt could see that, working together, Matsushita and JVC could bring a videodisc to market without further reference to RCA technology.

RCA's one remaining advantage was timing. The Japanese companies had not yet started commercial development on their product. They were unaware of the problems involved in disc manufacture. All RCA efforts at testing and developing production know-how showed that production readiness was not a trivial advantage. If the VideoDisc program could achieve its schedule and be in the market at the desired price level two years before the Japanese system, there was still the hope that the RCA standard would prevail. But time was plainly running out.

Pressure builds

Although tremendous progress had been made by the April 1977 review, it was obvious that the program had slipped onto a course which would overrun its latest time and money targets. The earliest possible introduction date, without benefit of safety margin, had moved to October 1978, and inflation had nudged the player price above the sacred $500 threshold. The disc-coating process was proving to be more expensive than anticipated, and production costs for a two-hour disc, originally projected at $4, appeared to be closer to $5. The handling problems had been solved with the caddy, but this was an unexpected additional cost. The cost figures would still allow RCA to come in under Philips, but Sonnenfeldt had decided that the only way to compete with the new Japanese threat was to redesign the VideoDisc system to meet a radically redefined set of performance and cost targets.

Disc quality and ease of manufacture were to be the main focus of the redesign. The top priority was to find a method of replication that would more closely approximate conventional methods of record manufacturing, as JVC had done. The second priority was disc quality that was error free for the viewer; this meant solving such problems as locked groove clearance and disc scoring. Another major goal was improvement of the mastering technique, for current yields of good-quality masters were on the order of one out of twenty. Up until then, attention had centered primarily on achieving real-time recording, and master yields had not been addressed.

For Sonnenfeldt, the overriding necessity was that the program had to achieve technical independence of the laboratory for the remainder of the development phase. The direct involvement of laboratory researchers in process definition and operations testing at Indianapolis had been a short-term expediency satisfactory to no one. A major source of schedule uncertainty was that process development was still hobbled by open research questions, and process designers had to be free to choose solutions without regard to RCA's proprietary position. Particularly disturbing was the fact that exhaustive research efforts in the semiconductor field had demonstrated that, to meet the new goals, RCA's electron-beam recording technique would have to achieve defect standards that surpassed any so far achieved in the related area of semiconductor mask making. Only the alternatives advocated by the Consumer Electronics Division, electromechanical recording and a diamond stylus, were able to meet the new goals without further research.

It was hard to get the project team at Indianapolis, and some of the supporting researchers at the Laboratories, to agree to abandon the methods they had been developing. To lose out to "brute-force" methods – improvements on mature technologies achieved by trial and error – was a disappointment to researchers, and to abandon the chance to apply leading edge technologies appeared to render superfluous much of the hard work that had been done by the cooperative development effort. Convinced that they could still make their techniques work, the process development team fought to keep the autocoater and the electron-beam mastering facility as a pilot operation while the fallback technologies were developed in parallel. But Sonnenfeldt feared that the alternative methods would never get the support they needed if the pilot operation continued to function, and he gave orders that the pilot facility should be dismantled. The electron-beam recorder, so recently installed, was the first piece of equipment to go.

In July 1977, RCA publicly announced that it was discontinuing its VideoDisc development program and shutting down all preproduction activity at Indianapolis. It remained committed, however, to a technical development program with three major goals: a player retailing for $400 or less, well under the price of a videotape recorder, an uncoated disc selling for between $10.95 and $14.95, and improved outside programming arrangements to ensure RCA an adequate supply of software, still a major problem. All personnel associated with the production phase of the project received word that they were laid off or transferred, and the project was formally sent back to the Laboratories. For the time being, Sonnenfeldt remained at the head of the VideoDisc program, and his team continued its activities, focusing on shutting down the development program.

201

System redesign

The decision to adopt the alternative fallback techniques meant a role reversal between Indianapolis and the Laboratories. Now Indianapolis led the development effort, while Princeton restricted most of its activities to analytical support and longer-range developments. Much work had to be done to fashion a new system out of a set of individual pieces that had yet to be integrated. Moreover, one major piece was still missing. Alternatives to the mastering technique and the sapphire stylus had been in the works, but there was no existing alternative to the coated disc. Two external factors influenced the redesign: recent competitive developments and the increasingly stringent consumer safety and product reliability regulations called for by the consumer movement and the regulatory environment of the mid-1970s.

By this time, thousands of discs had been produced and subjected not only to microscopic testing, but to environmental conditions unimaginable anywhere but in the consumer home – extremes of temperature and humidity, and exotic varieties of dust. These tests had greatly advanced the state of materials knowledge in the Laboratories. When the researchers reluctantly accepted the redirection of their efforts, they found that patentable results could be gleaned from working on the new techniques and that some of what they had learned from work on the old techniques could be applied to the new ones. Len Fox, a project head in materials came up with the solution regarding uncoated discs. In the course of performing experimental work with a diamond stylus, researchers tried a simplified coating system which did not require a separate plastic layer. Further experimentation on minimum conductivity requirements for the metal coating led to the "ultimate simplification" – making the disc itself conductive by mixing carefully specified amounts of conductive carbon black in with the thermoplastic disc material. Fox remembered having done earlier exploratory work on conductive thermoplastic but at a time when there was no source of small, uniform, carbon black particles. Since then the available materials had improved. The new conductive disc required new lubricants, but this proved to be no problem.[6] Another change was a switch from injection to compression molding for the production of discs. While injection molding had been the preferred method for the nonconductive disc, the material for the conductive disc was found to have different flow characteristics.

It was already possible to produce discs with two hours' playing time using RCA's approach to signal encoding. The simple expedient of nearly doubling the groove density from 5,555 grooves per inch to 9,541 grooves per inch had already been tried at the Laboratories in late 1976, without affecting the quality of picture to any noticeable degree. The only problem the change then posed was that the stylus had to be half-sized, and the fragile sapphire stylus thus became even more vulnerable to chipping or breakage. This problem was overcome by using a diamond stylus, and RCA researchers patented new methods for working diamonds.

In addition to addressing the central technical goals set for the project to proceed, the Laboratories' staff worked on new, long-term design options, especially for VideoDisc player features that competing products were expected to have. The first VideoDisc models would only include "fast-forward" and "fast-backward" controls so that viewers could locate segments of a program, but would not allow viewers to "freeze frames." It was highly desirable that this feature, and others, be added to later models.

The new effort made startling achievements during the remainder of 1977, some of which exceeded the goals set. The Laboratories demonstrated the feasibility of a two-hour uncoated disc with a total manufacturing cost, including the caddy, of $2. The electromechanical recording technique achieved real-time recording using a simpler process than the conventional audio recording technique from which it had been derived. Ways were found to modify existing compression record presses to produce better results than the expensive computer-controlled injection presses, with greatly improved yields. Radical improvements were also made in the player design. With the change from a sapphire to a diamond stylus, average stylus life increased from approximately 50 hours to over 500 hours, and the stylus breakage and scoring problems

Richard Sonnenfeldt with old and new prototype VideoDisc players in 1977.

were virtually eliminated. To deal with the "locked groove" clearance problem, engineers came up with a new type of electronic circuitry that detected whether the stylus had advanced, and a new encoding program. These called for two custom-designed integrated circuits, but they also made possible such features as rapid scan and freeze frame.

At the end of 1977, even though the budget had been trimmed drastically from $15 million to $8 million at Indianapolis for the year, dropping to $6 million the following year, but with no real cuts at Princeton, Sonnenfeldt could report that much had been achieved. Player redesign had produced a machine that was one-half the size of its predecessor and that contained one-third as many parts. Cost experts assessed its manufacturing costs at under $125, assuming that it could be developed on a gradual tooling cycle of eighteen months. Responsibility for the technical side of the program would shift to Indianapolis and by the end of 1978 Princeton's technical

204

staff would be largely free for analytical support, trouble-shooting, and longer-range product development.

In the programming arena, Tom McDermott had left RCA, but the VideoDisc team planned to have a player and disc package ready by mid-1978 to show to outside program sources in order to convince them that RCA's product was so technically superior that they should enter into program disc production as RCA partners. Griffiths transferred to RCA Herb Schlosser, previously president of a faltering NBC network, to execute this plan. Schlosser received high marks in the entertainment industry and was well acquainted with most of the potential sources of existing programming.

VideoDisc work went on behind the scenes in 1977, away from the scrutiny which had worried Bilby the previous year. The RCA announcement that attracted media attention at this time was the company's intention to sell a two-hour videotape recording system, purchased from Matsushita but bearing the RCA Selectavision label. The existence of a second videotape recorder with a different format from that of Betamax in the U.S. market posed a compatibility problem for consumers, but RCA's enormous marketing strength increased the interest in videotape recorders to such an extent that both products benefited. RCA's VHS system was well received, owing to its having twice as much playtime as Betamax and to aggressive pricing.

New start-up

Journalists interpreted RCA's delay in introducing the Video-Disc as a highly significant and characteristic reversal by Griffiths of the policies of his two immediate predecessors. This was partly because Griffiths in other ways was emerging as the most traditional RCA executive since David Sarnoff. The press made much of his instruction to the RCA advertising staff to resurrect RCA's old familiar trademark, the dog "Nipper" and "His Master's Voice." Ironically perhaps, the RCA tradition most firmly embedded of all was an emphasis on self-obsolescence and risk taking, and the longer Griffiths was in office, the more internal conditions compelled him to support

205

the introduction of a major new business. The coalition within RCA between R&D and Licensing continued to push for decisive action, as videoplayer competitors were intensely and openly active. The Philips–MCA Laservision system manufactured by the Philips' subsidiary Magnavox had surfaced in mid-December 1978, although the introduction of the Magnavision player in a test market in only three major cities (Atlanta, Seattle, and Chicago) was cautious, and the player price of $750 was high. Matsushita had adopted the JVC disc as Sonnenfeldt had predicted and began to make overtures to RCA to negotiate a common disc standard that could be played by either company's pickup. The Japanese electronics companies had formed a committee to negotiate a videodisc standard for the Japanese market, and there was every indication that they would soon be lining up behind one disc player or another. Without an entry for the marketplace, RCA would have no bargaining chip when the standard was decided, and little chance of gaining this very important source of licensing revenue.

RCA had learned the hazards of marketing the inventions of others. In early 1977, RCA had achieved astonishing successes in marketing Matsushita's VHS format player. Despite following Betamax into the market, the VHS was on its way to capturing 25 percent of the market.[7] But fluctuations in the currency markets, and especially the rising yen, soon robbed RCA of much of its expected middleman profit even after it had raised the player price from $1,000 to $1,300. For VideoDisc systems to realize a profit, RCA would have to produce them itself. On the other hand, this experience with videotape recorders persuaded RCA executives that there was good reason to go with a videodisc system. There was still room to differentiate it, based on price, from the VCR, especially with a lower software price.

When Griffiths startled the press with his decision in early 1979 to rush VideoDisc to the market, he had a few surprises up his sleeve. Chief among these was the leadership he had chosen for the crucial final stages. Sonnenfeldt, head of the VideoDisc development for more than five years, was reassigned to special projects and later moved to NBC. His replacement was Roy Pollack, now group vice-president. Pollack was credited with RCA's turnaround in the television business, based on very successful automation of RCA television operations and on improved marketing of RCA's Colortrak products.[8] He had not previously been associated with new product development, nor any form of business venturing. The replacement of Sonnenfeldt signified a near clean sweep of project veterans. While Griffiths acknowledged Sonnenfeldt's able and creative leadership of the technical phase of the program, the press viewed the ouster as an indication that Sonnenfeldt was blamed for delaying the project until the three major issues cited in its delay had been resolved.[9]

Crash plan

Pollack was to call it "RCA's Manhattan Project," in recognition of its size, complexity, urgency, and the caliber of leadership involved. The executives selected to do the job suggested that RCA intented to make VideoDisc as much of an established business as soon as possible, as they were sufficiently senior to command cooperation at all levels. To run VideoDisc operations, Pollack selected the former vice-president for Engineering for Consumer Electronics, Jay Brandinger, an early member of the Princeton research team who had transferred to Indianapolis. As chief engineer at Indianapolis he had improved the working relationship between engineering and manufacturing. Jack Sauter, head of Consumer Electronics Sales and Marketing, took on marketing for the VideoDisc system, hardware and software. In charge of strategic and business planning was Jim Alic, formerly chief financial officer of Consumer Electronics, and recently transferred to NBC where he had been assigned to address NBC's worsening financial picture. Schlosser, already involved in VideoDisc, would stay on as executive vice-president in charge of RCA's Selectavision program catalog.

Staffing was not the only evidence of the VideoDisc level of effort. At the Consumer Electronics distributors meeting in San Diego in late 1979, Griffiths pledged "absolutely massive support," a nationwide roll-out, a huge financial commitment, and a continuing evolution of the technology. He implied that RCA could keep these pledges better than some of its competitors because it was a unified operation, not a loose collection of cooperating ventures. He pointed out that RCA was spending more money on VideoDisc than it had ever spent on a new product, an investment justified by encouraging market research. Because of double-digit inflation, the player price would have to be $500 in 1981 dollars, but all indications were that RCA could expect to sell the 200,000 players it would put in the pipeline in the first year. Overall, VideoDisc looked to be a $7.5 billion business, according to Griffiths:

> In the 10th year, we foresee a business of five to six million players sold annually, and 200 to 250 million Discs – a $7.5 billion annual business. In the first year, 200,000 VideoDisc players, compared to 5,000 color television sets in the first color year.[10]

Speaking in the middle of RCA's most successful financial year in a long time, the credibility of Griffiths' pledge to take over first place and never to relinquish it, and to create a new American industry, seemed very high. In 1979, RCA had finally wrested away from Zenith the leading market position in color television, and the company's financial picture looked solid. Griffiths was also contriving to lay off the risks of the VideoDisc program, substantially increased under the new massive roll-out strategy. To offset the instability that the new business would surely mean for earnings, he acquired CIT Financial in 1979 for a price – $1.4 billion – that raised eyebrows on Wall Street.[11] To raise necessary capital, he also divested some of RCA's less closely related businesses.

Another way to spread the risk and to bolster RCA's position in the coming standards battle was to find other companies who would produce and sell their own players or discs using the RCA Consumer Electronics Division format. In this endeavor, RCA was successful even with some traditional rivals. Zenith agreed in 1980 to manufacture RCA's capacitance player, having chosen to champion Sony's Betamax standard in the VCR contest. CBS also teamed up with RCA for disc production and distribution, and began developing its own disc production capability under the direction of former RCA employee, Donald McCoy. One Wall Street analyst viewed these standardization agreements between old enemies as "of enormous importance because of their marketing power."[12] Retailing agreements with national marketing chains, Sears and J.C. Penney, to sell VideoDisc players under their brandnames underscored the impression of a marketing juggernaut entering the business. Eventually Hitachi would also manufacture the RCA system; it would also be marketed under the brands of Sanyo, Toshiba, Wards, Sharp, Radio Shack, and Hitachi Sales.

Program catalog

On the software side, RCA's plan was to offset the versatile features of other videodisc competitors by offering a larger and more varied selection of programming and to make this easily accessible initially by selling discs through the same distribution channels as players. Schlosser intended to borrow programs from existing media – half feature films, and the rest a potpourri of music, how-to programs, children's programs, sports and cultural events – to form a stable platform from which new forms of programming uniquely suited to the new medium could be developed. It was RCA's intent, he explained, to attract a broad buyer base on fare that had wide appeal, and then gradually to move to "narrowcasting," or more specialized programming for smaller audiences. Ultimately, he explained, the videodisc medium would be closer to the record industry and publishing than to commercial broadcasting, because it would have "greater diversity of programs to attract consumers of different tastes." During 1979, RCA reached agreements with such diverse programming sources as rock music promoter Don Kirshner, Walt Disney Productions, ITC Entertainment, and several film studios.

But RCA's high profile had little effect in achieving better terms from software sources. As Tom McDermott had foreseen in the early 1970s, software suppliers had awakened to the value of their properties in a world of proliferating video media. Since McDermott had first opened negotiations for

Herbert Schlosser (left) and Dr. Benjamin Spock discuss the forthcoming VideoDisc, "Caring for Your Newborn – Dr. Spock Shows You How."

Selectavision programming, pay cable had become available, and other distribution media were jockeying for position.[13] Moreover, the myriad of formats and the prospect of numerous systems continuing to exist side by side made suppliers even more reluctant than they had already been to grant exclusive

210

licenses. As the price of software increased, the number of items RCA had in its introductory catalog decreased, and the time when it would become feasible to produce special programs for VideoDisc alone stretched further into the future.

The last stretch

It took six months to a year to restart the project; this was the penalty that RCA paid for delay. More staff had to be added to the Laboratories, as it once again became the technical center of the project. Recruits were needed in polymer chemistry, physical chemistry, and diamond processing, among others. In Indianapolis a skeleton staff that remained from pilot days grew from thirty people to 300 in the space of eighteen months, and once again the project operated in the Rockville Road facility which housed engineering, manufacturing support, and mastering processes in addition to production facilities. Unlike the days of the pilot plant, equipment was to be modified versions of conventional equipment, which cut the ordering lead time to eighteen months. This time the process was not hampered by the autocoater, which had been the bottleneck of the pilot operation. The only disc coating involved was a thin lubricant that could be applied using a simple spray technique. Fortunately for the project, the hardware operation had a nucleus of process engineers who had recently been involved in automating television lines, an advantage based on experience that the earlier pilot program had lacked. Moreover, Divisional and Laboratories personnel had developed skills at working with each other that made this start-up smoother than its predecessor.

RCA entered the 1980 countdown period amid enthusiastic predictions of success. The massive roll-out planned, and RCA's ability to sign up other leading companies both in the domestic industry and abroad, impressed the press and industry experts. Riding the wave of enthusiasm from their recent successes in television and in magnetic tape, the Selectavision business team seemed justified in its optimism. The respected Wertheim Report of October 1979, for instance, assessed RCA's chances for catching up and quickly surpassing other entrants as high, assuming that there continued to be a substantial different between disc prices and those of magnetic tape cassettes.[14] *Business Week* labeled RCA's CED system the clear favorite while admitting that it seemed to strain at the edges of technological capability. Negative observers posed their question mildly – was there room for both magnetic tape and videodisc systems in the same marketplace? The authoritative consensus was that videotape player sales would soon suffer when well-marketed and well-supported disc systems became available.

For RCA, as the target introduction date approached, some of the developments in the disc marketplace were a bit ominous. The laser disc systems on the market were getting bad press – buyers found the players unreliable, the discs defective, despite claims for indestructibility, and program availability very poor. It would be up to RCA to overcome the negative image that this early experience had created in the consumer mind, though fortunately the number of units sold, so far under 10,000, was small.[15]

The disc business appeared to be shaping into a complex battle of titans as the 1980s began. GE and IBM both announced ventures employing different videodisc formats. GE planned to adopt the JVC standard disc, which had developed into a grooveless, capacitance approach incompatible with the RCA system. IBM chose to join with MCA to form DiscoVision Associates for the purpose of developing, manufacturing, and selling the Laservision optical videoplayers and discs. While both companies had chosen videodiscs of some kind, neither had been willing to join a domestic coalition by backing RCA's standard.

Meanwhile, economic conditions were worsening and 1980 developed into a recession year. Although this should have favored lower-priced items, the VCR business was gripped by a new wave of excitement for prices had been coming down and software was becoming available through clubs and other rental channels. Player sales, projected at some 500,000 units, had exceeded expectations and rose to some 800,000 units for the year.

10

On the market

RCA's Selectavision VideoDisc was finally introduced to the consumer market in March 1981, in the face of continuing recession. VideoDisc sales were a disappointment from the beginning despite heavy advertising and promotion of all kinds. The company quickly refocused its message away from its original emphasis on Hollywood glitter toward motivating the average TV viewing family to buy the product for more useful reasons. New advertisements appeared suggesting that VideoDisc could provide a wholesome alternative to television programs for children or a substitute for a rained-out barbecue.[1] Yet despite a $20 million investment in advertising, first-year player retail sales just topped 100,000 out of 200,000 players shipped to dealers, working out to $200 in advertising costs per player sold.

To stimulate demand in the second and third years, RCA cut player prices drastically, first to $350 and then to $299, and introduced a stereo model. The price cuts cost the company revenue, and only temporarily boosted sales. Consumers seemed to prefer higher-priced versions of all disc players; possibly they lost confidence in the product when its price came down too far. By the third year disappointment became recognition of failure. Few were surprised when, in April 1984, RCA chairman Thornton Bradshaw announced that the company would discontinue production of VideoDisc players and take a $175 million write-off before tax. The total loss to RCA since introduction, including the $100 million per year spent on VideoDisc operations was about $580 million. In three years, player sales had totaled 550,000.

Box office failure

A major cause for failure was RCA dealers' lack of enthusiasm about the new product. In the first eighteen months RCA apparently lost two-thirds of the dealers who had previously agreed to carry VideoDisc.[2] There were a number of reasons for their defection. Many felt they had just begun to master the VCR when the VideoDisc system came along, and they were reluctant to go through the same process again so soon for another product. Since VideoDisc systems were lower priced, and therefore afforded lower dealer margins, it was very much in a dealer's interest to persuade the buyers attracted by VideoDisc advertising to opt for VCRs. Consumers seemed unable to grasp that disc players were not cheaper versions of VCRs. One RCA study revealed that in a test in Atlanta, two out of three players purchased were returned for video cassette players.[3] An additional VideoDisc drawback was that it required dealers to carry stocks of discs, whereas they did not have to carry software for VCRs.

VCR sales increased dramatically just as VideoDisc was introduced and RCA dealers had their hands full meeting this demand. Despite RCA predictions that sales of this higher priced product would continue to be modest, owing to consumer confusion and the smaller market, VCR sales after 1981 were in millions of units per year. By 1984, it was clear that the installed base of VCRs would reach 20 million by 1985. Prices had fallen steadily for both hardware and software and certain types of programs, mostly pornographic films, had sold well even at high prices. In fact pornographic software, both softcore and hardcore, accounted for as much as half the sales and rentals of prerecorded videotapes. Moreover, the entry of chain operations, such as Fotomat, and thousands of independent "video boutiques," into the tape rental business had made it possible for consumers to rent a tape for twenty-four hours for as little as $2. Blank cassettes had dropped to $11 by 1981 and were getting cheaper.

The success of videotape rentals came as a complete surprise to RCA. The company's market research on the subject had for years indicated that American consumers preferred to own

A selection of movie classics included in the first RCA VideoDisc catalog.

something rather than rent it. RCA had not realized that the market was changing as new information technologies proliferated, and that even potential buyers saw rental as a means of deciding what they wanted. RCA had not given itself the option of switching to a rental strategy for discs; most of the programming agreements the company had entered into were

215

for sales only. RCA would be violating the terms of these agreements if it allowed its dealers to lend discs.

For the overshadowed VideoDisc product, only disc sales exceeded expectations and under the circumstances this was a mixed blessing. Owners of players purchased more than the anticipated eight discs per player. In fact, had more players been sold in the first year, there would have been a shortage of discs. In the second and third years, the ratio increased from fifteen to thirty discs per player. VideoDisc owners wanted more programming variety than RCA could afford to make available until the player population justified it. Although RCA added further titles to its catalog, and explored joint programming possibilities, it could not justify an investment in much more dedicated VideoDisc program production. To produce pornographic discs would have violated the company's image and destroyed its family-oriented product concept. RCA would license other companies to produce discs, but the cost of setting up a new disc facility for a market that had yet to materialize was prohibitive.

Some of the companies that RCA had signed up to produce disc players and discs entered the market for a short time, only to find themselves discounting heavily and selling players listing at $500 for $399, with an additional $50 rebate. The Japanese companies that did not license the RCA system, but had announced systems of their own, withheld their products. It was rumored that their intent had been to confuse and fragment the disc player market – U.S. sales of Japanese VCRs were approaching 10 million a year, and Japanese electronics companies obviously had every reason to wish not to undercut that market. Keiichi Takeoka, president of Matsushita Electric Corporation of America, whose JVC subsidiary had announced its own disc system, commented, "I personally think the videodisc business should not be in a great hurry. Video cassette can do so much more."[4]

The press

However favorable the business press coverage had been ahead of time, the media contributed to the VideoDisc market failure. The trade press was quick to excoriate VideoDisc in 1981 for its lack of sophistication. RCA's move to introduce a stereo version in 1982 was a concession to a marketplace that had been converted to the idea of high-tech consumer electronics; its initial monophonic product had elicited "a chorus of derisive jeers, hoots, and hollers" from the audio trade press.[5] The rival Philips–MCA system had stereo jacks that could be attached to a sound system and interactive capabilities that could accommodate video experimentation. These features were valued by videophiles, although the number of Philips–MCA systems sold was less than 100,000.

Thornton Bradshaw, appointed RCA chairman in 1981, cited as decisive in the VideoDisc demise the continuously declining cost of VCRs and prerecorded tapes, and the availability of VCR programming through rental. Pollack explained the failure simply in terms of a lost window of opportunity. "Our mistake was we were late," he said. "Five years earlier it would have been a huge success. If we came out with it three years earlier, it would have been a good success."[6]

Meanwhile Bradshaw discovered that he was faced with the need to pull RCA out of a bad financial situation. After years of steadily increased earnings, RCA reported abysmal profits in the early 1980s. It appeared that Griffiths' attempts to achieve steadily increasing earnings at any cost had seriously undermined RCA's financial position. In 1981 RCA was struggling to service a total debt burden of $2.9 billion at a time of low credit ratings, high interest rates, and low earnings. After a year at the helm, Bradshaw announced his intention to refocus the company on its core businesses, which earlier managers had mistakenly declared to be lacking in opportunity. "Our priority," he said, "is to get to be the technological leader again in our core business of electronics systems communications."[7] To accumulate the necessary cash to shore up the communications, semiconductor, and electronics businesses, Bradshaw sold off several of RCA's unrelated businesses, including CIT Financial.

From early 1982 on, rumors persisted that RCA was a likely target for takeover and, by 1984, the takeover threat was quite real.[8] The company made great efforts to ward off the threat.

Its profitability improved, its credit rating went up, it sold CIT for $1.5 billion, and it was in the process of reorganizing.

The Research Laboratories still had a role to play in RCA's future renewal, for to reemphasize growth in electronics and communications, it would be necessary to bring some of the promising technologies that were under development at the Laboratories to the marketplace.

RCA's long-term future still seemed tied to home information twenty years after David Sarnoff and Elmer Engstrom had first begun to talk about it, although this was a market increasingly dominated by AT&T and IBM. Continuing video-disc research might even play a part in this, for many branches of the work that had been started with consumer videoplayers in mind had since yielded further applications of high-density information storage and retrieval for other fields of electronics. But sustained development of the consumer home information business would require capital, undivided management attention, and an absence of operations that were a drag on the core businesses. Continued support for VideoDisc in its current form would only block progress in that direction.

Postmortem

RCA's VideoDisc strategy had been heavily dependent on a few key assumptions: that the traditional mass-market customer would prefer a low price to more features, that dealers could clear up any consumer confusion about multiple formats, that VCR producers could not substantially reduce the price gap between their players and disc players, that dealers would welcome disc systems as they had VCRs, and that consumers would want to own video programming just as they owned LP records and audio tapes.

There had been no public discussion within RCA of what might happen if the key assumptions failed to hold, or what would be done if other factors that had not been considered influenced the market. If key RCA executives involved in VideoDisc's introduction recognized the uncertainty of their position, that the statements made with such apparent assurance could be arbitrary choices between unknowable alternatives, they did not acknowledge it. Had they understood their position better, they might have provided for contingencies, as Japanese videoplayer makers had when they tried repeatedly during the 1970s to make a go of video cassette recorders. Major innovation had not been a feature of RCA life since the days of David Sarnoff, however, and few understood how to approach it. The people who were chosen to manage it, all heavy hitters in the established business, chose an approach that had only two possible outcomes – complete success or complete failure.

In fact, the outcome quickly revealed that most of the key assumptions on which RCA had based its VideoDisc strategy were no longer valid. RCA's nationwide roll-out, patterned on monochrome television, ensured that the company both raised expectations and left itself little room for maneuver. Had the plan been for a stable product in a familiar business, it would have been well-conceived and well-executed, but for an innovative product in a marketplace destabilized by changing technologies, it was an approach that allowed little room for adjustment and no second chances.

11

Managing R&D: lessons from RCA

The RCA VideoDisc experience sheds light on the difficulties of managing research and development in a large company. R&D has been an institutionalized part of American corporate life for more than half a century, longer than many other corporate functions we take for granted. Yet to the majority of managers, R&D is still an enigma. If no negative consequences arose from this unfamiliarity, R&D could remain unknown territory indefinitely. After all, the typical corporation houses many specialist functions and skills that most managers never understand. It is not, for instance, necessary for a middle manager to have studied medicine in order to seek effective treatment at a company clinic. But R&D's strangeness and remoteness to the rest of the organization affects not only its effectiveness as a support function, but its credibility as a generator and implementor of strategic opportunities. This is a matter of central importance, for without an accessible source of technical support, and without a supply of new technology, either originated or adapted, the technology-based corporation will surely perish.

In too many corporations any business opportunity that originates in the laboratory is automatically suspect. Researchers and the organizations they inhabit are believed to be incapable of sound commercial judgment. An executive serving in most operating divisions will have his opinion regularly solicited. But let him become head of a research organization and he will find himself marooned, his judgment no longer trusted. Often the negative stereotypes cut both ways. Until recently, the engineer who "dirtied his hands" working in a plant could not possibly be a high-class engineer. The stigma that attaches to production environments is still so strong in most long-established companies that technical personnel seldom transfer from plants to laboratories even when the reverse transfer pattern is common. If the widely expressed goal of integrating R&D into the mainstream of corporate operations is ever to be achieved, the state of mutual mistrust between operations and R&D has to be overcome.

The need for general managers to concern themselves with R&D is becoming more compelling. That companies wishing to compete internationally must incorporate advancing technologies quickly and effectively into their products and processes is widely acknowledged in theory. What that means in practice is less well recognized. If advanced and continuously changing technologies are to be incorporated effectively, the strange form of activity known as R&D must gradually invade the ordinary workplace. Though the thought may be unacceptable to many action-oriented managers, the style of management that is necessary in laboratories and pilot plants is likely to become much more familiar in ordinary operating sites. Already the American work force, on the factory floor and in the office, consists of a fair proportion of "knowledge workers," and the activities they pursue involve degrees of change and uncertainty that were once the exclusive preserve of research organizations.

R&D as a form of work

What makes R&D so different from other forms of industrial operation? R&D is a creative and learning-focused activity. It involves two kinds of work, making new knowledge (research) and gathering and applying existing knowledge to the solution of progressively defined problems (development). Although researchers and developers tend to think of themselves in one category or the other – scientists or inventors, discipline oriented or applications oriented – in industrial research the two categories are intertwined. Pursuit of a problem leads to the need for new knowledge; new knowledge finds a problem it can attack. RCA's videoplayer program involved years of such interactive work. In the course of developing the videoplayer, new knowledge was generated in optics and materials and new techniques were developed in such fields as high-resolution recording, vacuum deposition, and photolithography. When a particular applications program was terminated, the people who had worked on it took the knowledge they had acquired with them into new projects. For example, when RCA terminated its electron-beam microscope business, it retained both special equipment and knowledgeable technical people who helped to turn electron microscopy into a high-resolution recording technique. Advanced manufacturing procedures transferred in the same way. It was, for instance, Richard Sonnenfeldt's familiarity with statistical process control techniques in the semiconductor field that led him to introduce similar statistical control techniques into the disc-development effort.

Research staff have different personal goals from most other people in the corporation, and they admire different qualities in people. They care more about intellectual autonomy and about the judgment of their professional peers: other operating division personnel care above all about their chances for managerial achievement and advancement. In the mainstream of corporate life people are measured by their ability to work with others and to follow through on plans in a timely fashion; research personnel, like academics, judge others on the basis of their raw intelligence and novel ideas. Researchers' personal loyalties to their profession are often as strong as their loyalties to their employer, and the opportunities to publish papers and to hold patents may interest them as much as monetary rewards.

The key feature of research work is its uncertainty. Like other forms of creative activity, new knowledge has its own internal logic. There is no predictable correspondence between time and money invested and the quality of output. A creative idea from an ingenious researcher may be worth 300 ideas from people with more mediocre talents. Inspiration may come in a few minutes or a few years. A good research manager knows that, however promising a technical area may appear to be in the abstract, the prospects for a specific technology within his or her own laboratory depend heavily on the quality of the people and on the quality of their interactions. In the early days of RCA exploratory research into high-density recording, William Webster recognized in the Holotape effort all the signs of a fruitful project. If it did not reach its goal, which might in any case change, it would nevertheless spin off much useful knowledge and stimulate competitive energy in the rival disc project.

The key to handling the uncertainty of scientific discovery in industry has been to provide a diversity of potential uses and products that can take advantage of a wide range of new techniques. Like other corporations that set up major research laboratories in the twentieth century, RCA shielded itself from the whimsical side of scientific discovery through a combination of diversity in technology and diversity in markets. If one avenue became blocked, another could be found to produce.

Managers whose sole experience has been in more certain environments tend not to believe the unpredictability of research. They try to force research-dependent innovation as they would an engineering program involving just incremental changes, where all the principles are known, and they believe that efficient organization is the key. They apply pressure and throw money around in ignorance of other stimulating forms of motivation, such as interest, constructive competition, support, and enthusiasm. When a program moves into the realm of certitude, sometimes called a state of "technical readiness," then pressure, money, manpower, and deadlines may be highly effective. But they rarely are at an early stage. The problem for a research manager is to decide when a program has moved out of the first realm and into the second. Many of the rockiest passages in RCA's videoplayer program occurred when managers who did not understand the nature of research-dependent technologies applied premature pressure. David Sarnoff, who in one way was a master at researcher motivation, tried to cross the line in forcing the unforcible in the color television program and again with his anniversary presents. It was hardly surprising, then, that Chase Morsey, coming out of the low-technology environment of Ford in the 1960s, applied pressure cooker tactics to the Holotape program. The fruitless outcome was predictable.

223

R&D as an institution

The institutional character of R&D has never been static. It has evolved over time, influenced by prevailing research philosophies in academia, by government research policies, and by changes in industrial practice.[1] What amounted to a corporate "counterculture" at RCA in fact emerged in numerous companies in the 1950s, especially in the electronics industry, when the percentage of theoretically oriented people on the research staff was very high and their shared values differed greatly from those of personnel in the operating divisions.

Today, other scientific fields are in the building-block phase that electronics was in the 1950s. The corporate counterculture phenomenon is most likely to exist in companies in fields like genetics research and in laboratories like Xerox PARC, where artificial intelligence work is done.[2] A work force in "country club conditions" may be indispensable to the building-block phase of technology. But management must contrive to change the composition of its technical workforce when the technology enters new phases. This is often a difficult proposition. Technical personnel with highly specialized skills are low on the corporate list of fungible resources. Hillier's experience in trying to reform the RCA Laboratories in the early 1960s is the type of situation many companies face when moving from one strategic era to another.

Individual R&D laboratories and engineering centers have large budgets, employ thousands of technical personnel, use expensive capital equipment, and have inputs and outputs like any other operation. But over the past thirty years the operating characteristics of many research organizations have been so different from other forms of industrial operation that corporate R&D has rarely been considered an operation at all. This may have been an accident of history. The confluence of a national policy that favored big science, a few key technologies in their building phases, and a corporate move toward the isolation of research in geographically and organizationally separated divisions may have exaggerated the differences for a time.[3] If it is true that other forms of operation may have to become more like R&D organizations, it follows that the need to understand R&D's peculiar operating characteristics becomes ever greater.

The chief characteristic that distinguished the RCA Research Center from the rest of the corporation, as for most such institutions, was its need for stability growing out of the nature of the long-term work it performed. Few people could handle the degree of uncertainty and ambiguity that videoplayer researchers had to deal with in their daily work without assurance of job security. As it was, the VideoDisc program would have proceeded more rapidly had not plummeting morale cost it months of progress on at least two separate occasions. The critical task for the research executives, Webster and Hillier, as with so many managers of research organizations, was to defend their budgets from the feast-or-famine effect that constantly threatened laboratory stability.

When David Sarnoff ran RCA there was no need for his namesake Laboratories to defend itself. During the era of videoplayer development, however, the research center was never secure. As a consequence, many technical decisions that were made were almost certainly influenced by the needs of the researchers and their institution. When there was too little money to fund exploratory work on high-resolution recording methods for its own sake, for instance, the electron-beam recording technique became the tail that wagged the VideoDisc dog. When the survival of the Laboratories depended on its clear identification with a proprietary, revenue-producing "blockbuster" project, the Laboratories could not be depended upon for reliable judgments about competing technologies. Ironically, it was Edgar Griffiths, not a VideoDisc enthusiast, who defused the Laboratories' collective insecurity and made it possible for this R&D group to become a more cooperative institution. Wishing to live down an antitechnology reputation, he gave the Laboratories the first adequate support base it had had in a decade.

The research center's dearly bought stability may in fact have widened the gap between it and the rest of corporate RCA, which, during the 1970s, was anything but stable. Even if the company had not endured constant executive turnover during the decade, the operating organizations would probably have been unsettled, for RCA, like most professionally managed American corporations during the 1960s and 1970s, placed a premium on mobility. In a relative sense, the Research Laboratories became the most static part of the company, one of the few places where senior employees may have spent their entire working lives at one site, sometimes on projects they could count on the fingers of one hand. When mobility became a badge of honor and a sign of achievement for the ambitious manager, then the sedentary career of a researcher looked like a stalled career.

Paradoxically, the Laboratories' emphasis on stability made the new technology it produced peculiarly vulnerable to historical precedents. Of course, legitimate research could never proceed without frequent checks with the past. To reinvent any wheel would have been an embarrassing and costly mistake; as researcher Len Fox's experience with the conductive disc illustrated, past ideas could become important present breakthroughs. Nevertheless, the "dead hand" of history molded many projects. Who could doubt that the painful memory of losing the videorecorder race to Ampex (still fresh in the minds of people who had been around in the 1950s) influenced the Laboratories' attitude toward magnetic recording in the mid-1960s? Previous battles with CBS colored the response to CBS's EVR. And, as the VideoDisc story shows, this·most future-oriented of institutions was profoundly conservative in its conception of videoplayers. The prevailing interpretation of the relative merits of the black and white and color television imposed a rigid and premature economic goal on the videoplayer. Once the target price was set in 1965, the final price tag changed but RCA's videoplayer project never escaped the straitjacket of the low-cost mass market.

The critical relationship

Protection of his institution's stability must be a high priority for a manager of R&D. This is why charges of political chicanery are often levelled at the heads of R&D organizations. Yet the defense of their institutions by R&D managers is not simply self-interest; it stems from a belief that they must aggressively protect the long-term interests of the corporation. Line managers believe just as strongly that they must protect the practical interests of the corporation against researchers bent on squandering corporate resources. The sad truth is that a fundamental, and ultimately irresolvable, tension lies at the heart of this conflict. Roy Pollack's objection to backing Video-Disc in 1977, however parochial, echoed the frustrations of many managers of mature divisions in countless companies who fear that the lack of immediate technical support and other essential resources in the here-and-now will foreclose any longer-term opportunity.

The relationship between R&D and the rest of the corporation may be the most difficult that a senior executive can face. It is a managerial cliché that in situations where major innovation is required, there is no substitute for top management attention to this critical relationship. At RCA, David Sarnoff embedded this idea in the very fiber of the company: An important innovation in his day had total commitment. None of his successors was able to match, or change, that legacy.

Time and again the most innovative periods for individual companies have coincided with times when senior executives, not necessarily technical themselves, have taken a personal interest in sponsoring the commercialization of particular new technologies. Tom Watson was associated with the IBM 360; Richard Hewlett with a succession of important laboratory generated products; and Frederick Close at Alcoa with the aluminum-clad skyscraper and aluminum can sheet. But senior executives cannot attend to everything, and in recent decades those in large companies have often treated technology as beneath their dignity. Top managers like Polaroid's Edwin Land, who have given their personal attention to research, have been rare and sometimes dismissed as eccentric.

R&D must have strong leadership to achieve effective implementation. David Sarnoff's attempt to build a structure that would innovate after he was gone created an internal logic on the order of "Have Laboratory and Licensing: Will Innovate." But in the case of VideoDisc this resulted in what was more a historic reproduction than a fresh innovation. Without involved, committed, and consistent top management leadership, the only product that could unite warring factions was one that appeared to be able to repeat historic successes. Why else the constant reference to black and white television at moments of strategic uncertainty? And why else associate RCA's historic symbol, the dog "Nipper," with VideoDisc, the company's first innovation in over twenty years? Attempts by other companies to "institutionalize innovation," such as Texas Instruments' elaborate planning procedure called the OST (objectives, strategies, and tactics) system, have also come to grief. No institution and no system can substitute for the fresh vision of a committed leader.

Certain integrative mechanisms can be useful aids in managing the important linkages between R&D and other parts of the corporation. The Selectavision saga, with its interesting comparison between the abysmal experience of the first Bitting venture team and Sonnenfeldt's much more effective later VideoDisc staff, points to some of the crucial elements in an effective linkage mechanism. First, the choice of leadership. Sonnenfeldt had wholly relevant experience in commercial start-up situations; Bitting had managed one-of-a-kind projects for a government system which was probably misleading experience. Second, the scope of the effort. Despite the label, Bitting's venture team never had control of all the pieces of any of the Selectavision projects, and in fact it lost some of the ones that it did have; Sonnenfeldt came to control most of the pieces, though programming under him remained in a kind of limbo. Third, the Bitting effort never had direct access to top management but had merely proximity; Sonnenfeldt himself unified and controlled the information flow to Griffiths. Finally, while neither man won affection from the various constituents of the project, Sonnenfeldt's role was understood, recognized as necessary, and accepted; Bitting's responsibilities were viewed differently by all parties.

What qualifies a manager to be effective at the crucial R&D frontier? Many consider formal technical training essential, and doubtless it helps. But a closer look at top managers who have made their reputations based on successful exploitation of opportunities generated by R&D suggests that the essential qualities may be different. Many top executives who studied engineering sometime in the distant past have been bored or repelled by technologies, while others who have had no formal technical or scientific training have displayed a passion for technology and a receptive attitude. Elmer Engstrom, Sarnoff's second in command for many years, once lamented Sarnoff's lack of formal engineering training.[4] The remark revealed a common but probably misguided prejudice shared by many technical managers. Sarnoff substituted personal field experience at the point where technology met the marketplace for formal technical training. His openness to technical possibility and his belief in its potential counted for much.

Not only have strong managers in technology-based companies that have made good use of R&D been enthusiastic about technology; they have also been willing to provide objective mediation between the parties to technical conflict. Technology-based corporations can be riddled with political conflicts masquerading as technical disputes. In such circumstances, the strong manager may or may not be autocratic by temperament, but he or she must be able to mediate among the partisan views that pervade most companies around the subject of technology. A hands-off approach that allows the "experts" to decide major technological questions is really an abdication of leadership by the only people who can possibly possess the necessary perspective. Although it now seems as though the success of the magnetic VCR had a certain inevitability about it, had RCA been able to resolve the internal conflicts and settle firmly on VideoDisc introduction in 1976, the outcome might have been different. Even as late as 1978, the product might have survived.

R&D and strategy

When R&D allocates its resources and assigns priorities to one area of research over another, it is inevitably predetermining corporate strategy. Faced with a management that supports R&D investment but that does not define and redefine its purpose for the long term, R&D directors tend to fill the breach. As Hillier once noted, the only institution formally charged with the long view must become the corporate entrepreneur. When this happens, as it did with videoplayers, the corporate research center becomes the de facto strategist. When the time eventually comes that the corporation needs lifesaving, top management may find itself with only one life raft available, like it or not.

The alternative, of course, is for top management to integrate R&D into overall strategy, but this is not easy. While R&D can and should be a major source of opportunity, projects that depend on new research cannot be planned, because of the inherent uncertainty involved. From a short-term, bottom-line, point of view, R&D suffers from a time warp. Any research that could produce major new business opportunities for a corporation is not likely to be achieved in less than ten years, and may take fifteen or twenty years to develop. Countless companies have tried to rush the process by throwing money at it just as RCA did in the case of Holotape. This can be done with engineering projects where the effort required is definable, but it cannot be done for projects involving a high degree of new knowledge. Those who try the compression approach are likely to give up altogether on technology-based opportunities.

What, then, is needed to integrate R&D into strategy? The only way to do it is for top management and R&D management to engage in a constant process of mutual education. For R&D management, this is not the same thing as amassing facts about specific technologies; it is providing the kind of information that corporate planners need to make reasonable decisions. Again, the onus for initiating effective information flow should lie with top management. As IBM's CEO, John Akers said when he assumed his post in 1985, a company must learn to apply a suction to its R&D organization.

Indeed, in any company where technology plays a significant role, top management must demand education of substance from its R&D organization concerning the nature of the problems, issues, and opportunities it faces. It is not enough simply to place confidence in a well-chosen R&D management and leave it alone to do its job. No top manager would admit that finance and marketing were subjects too arcane to grasp. Yet top managers of technology-dependent companies routinely confess to ignorance of technological issues, the rudiments of which are not more difficult to grasp than other management disciplines.

The episode that culminated in the first Selectavision press conference in 1969 is too often the kind of encounter that passes for communication between R&D and corporate management. When RCA's marketing staff were given the Laboratories' best estimates for realistic product introduction, the information did not initiate a dialogue. Instead of finding out why the program was expected to take so long, all communication was shut off while the marketing staff manipulated the data into a plausible, though highly optimistic, plan. In the end, when the compressed goals proved to be unrealistic, the R&D organization was charged with misrepresentation and Robert Sarnoff, never personally involved in the preliminary discussions, lost faith in the process. Such miscommunication is much less likely to occur in cases where both sides have taken the responsibility to educate each other.

The other side of integrating R&D with strategy is taking into account the effects of strategic change on the corporate R&D organization. Important changes in corporate strategy must be recognized as having operational consequences for all parts of the corporation. Often the implications for R&D, in particular, are ignored. David Sarnoff had created a pioneering strategy that was wholly dependent on the driving force of technology channeled through the Laboratories and the Licensing Department. It was funded by substantial licensing revenues and the returns for risk taking were the revenues that accrued to all parts of the RCA system when major technological changes required companies in RCA-linked industries to modernize. Robert Sarnoff modified this strategy without changing the technology-centered structure his father had created. The result was not the coordinated system he had in mind, but operating organizations and the Laboratories working at cross purposes.

When R&D has been organized for a single purpose it is very hard to change this focus on short notice. RCA's ambivalence

231

during the Selectavision program between pioneering and following, for instance, points out the different skills, resources, and procedures dictated by the two strategies. Following is not just a less adept version of leadership. Indeed, close following can put more stringent demands on technical functions than pioneering. It requires the ability to transfer technology in an especially timely fashion, and it requires the ability to capture and act upon information from the marketplace in a way that pioneering does not. Caught between the two strategies, the videoplayer research teams expended months of valuable time and effort duplicating other competitive systems.

A major corporate change such as diversification can have enormously positive or negative effects on an R&D organization. Diversification into technologically related businesses allowed RCA's corporate laboratory to achieve very positive contributions in its early years. The RCA experience illustrates the critical role that has been played by many corporate research organizations in transferring technologies between different markets, and between different economic sectors, particularly between defense and commercial applications. Yet a crucial point seems to exist, and beyond that diversification has negative effects on R&D.

What is the red line that diversification must not cross if it is to be constructive to R&D, and why can excessive amounts of it be so destructive? Is it a matter of degree or of kind? The key appears to be operational or technology relatedness and market focus. When a corporate laboratory or engineering facility is asked to support or to provide new product opportunities for too many markets or too many technologies, as RCA's research center was in the late 1950s, it becomes fragmented and ineffective. Communication among different parts of the laboratory and with the operating organizations inevitably breaks down in the face of too much complexity.

Once more, the most destructive effects of diversification on R&D must be assigned to a failure of leadership, the unwillingness or inability of top management to define a new mission for R&D when major changes take place. What, for instance, is the corporate research center of a glass company to do when its senior management declares it to be a packaging company? Too often no planning for this radical departure has been done. Are the leading glass researchers to be let go in favor of plastics chemists? Is the laboratory to do more in support of existing glass businesses and purchase the unrelated technology? Contemporary examples of this problem abound, and the list of companies currently struggling with problems of this sort contains many familiar names, including Western Electric, Bendix under Allied, Owens–Illinois, and Alcoa.

Other influences that can have powerful negative effects on corporate strategy through R&D are the press and the financial community. Premature public exposure disrupts the work of researchers and makes top management overly concerned about the details of a project. As the VideoDisc project demonstrated, R&D personnel naturally react to publicity, and they can often overreact to information in the press about competing innovations in other companies. Such information gains credence because of the market uncertainty that must attend any major science-based innovation. Although companies know only too well how unreliable much of the information is that they give the press about their own innovations, they often act on untrustworthy coverage of a competitor's program. RCA technical managers rightly judged that CBS's EVR was an uneconomic proposition, yet RCA's choice of the Holotape technology to announce and the timing of the announcement occurred because of the favorable coverage that CBS received. In this instance the press influenced the technology and shaped the market. In the case of the VideoDisc race between Philips and RCA, the press also created a competition long before the two products were on the market. Otherwise the "race" might not have occurred, for the Philips and RCA products were initially intended for different markets. It is difficult to say how many other technologies may have been similarly affected, but management sensitivity to press coverage and to the opinions of the financial community has undoubtedly had its influence on other technology-based consumer products while they were still under development. Personal computers and software packages are likely examples of the same phenomenon. Only very decisive management, unswerved by sensational stories and unintimidated by short-term financial market reactions, can protect an R&D organization from public pressure of this kind.

Top management support and direction are essential if R&D is to serve a company's interests. When the purpose of R&D and therefore the mission of the laboratory is not properly defined, it is natural for R&D organizations to respond in two ways. They may try to push for autonomy from the rest of the company so they can limit the demands placed on them, and they may even seek outside funding to maintain their stability. This can prove to be a grave mistake. RCA's policy of continuing to license proprietary technologies to Japan, a policy David Sarnoff had initiated, had the concurrence of a succession of the Laboratories' directors. It was an ultimately self-limiting measure that helped immeasurably to create RCA's most formidable competition and led to sensitivities with regard to overseas licensees that kept the company from developing the international manufacturing capabilities it needed to compete in a worldwide market. When R&D becomes a business of its own, with its own revenue streams and its own new business ventures, the risks of destructive competition with operating divisions and of undercutting the necessary strategic function of top management are very high.

The difficulties of balancing long-term and short-term goals and of managing in-house R&D have led some corporations to try to substitute outside sources of technology for in-house R&D altogether, or at least to limit their activities to development. RCA tapped several outside sources, such as Matsushita's early work on pressure pickup, for the video-player program. But just as farming out the pressure pickup probably initiated premature competition for VideoDisc, there were obvious costs associated with such an arrangement. While current arguments inside many companies for changing the configuration of technical institutions and the relations among them have great merit, there is no way of avoiding industrial investment in research in some form.[5] Nor is it possible to avoid the cost of in-house technical resources. Even purchased technology must be adapted for use, requiring different, but not necessarily less costly, skills than original development.

234

The popular argument that companies should simply rely on purchased technology overlooks the critical point that someone has to produce technology for purchase. For years the Japanese were able to obtain their fundamental technology from leading European and American companies like Philips and RCA. As U.S. sources have fallen behind, Japanese companies have formed their own major corporate research laboratories. Obviously the country, company, or industry that produces the technology has the potential to control it. Little leading-edge technology is ever sold; nor is there any guarantee that other countries or industries will be as willing to sell the technology they produce to foreign companies as the United States has been in the past. Little competitive advantage can be gained from any technology that is available for purchase, for it is available to many. R&D may be a disruptive, uncertain, and expensive exercise, but all creative activity is painful and costly. Without major investment in R&D in some form or other how can any enterprise hope to survive in the modern world?

Companies that remain committed to investment in R&D may still argue the merits of corporate research, and especially of corporate research laboratories. Fashions in organization come and go, and in the 1980s in the United States, centrally located corporate R&D is out of fashion. In certain respects the changes may be salutary, as in the current move to reassociate manufacturing-related R&D more closely with manufacturing divisions. But decentralization of research, putting it once again under the control of operating organizations, is too often tantamount to signing its death warrant. Few operating managers will ever be willing to fund work from which they can expect no outcome for years, even though an in-house stockpile of usable knowledge can mean the difference between developing a new product in time of need and having to wait upon the vagaries of exploration. Unless the managers of operating divisions are rewarded for other activities than immediate output, companies that have been shortsighted enough to do away with their corporate research organizations altogether may well find themselves having to reinvent them.

Appendix: Major interviews

RCA Laboratories personnel

Managers:	*Dates interviewed:*
G. Brown	4/78*
E. Engstrom	4/78*
J. Hillier	2/77, 4/78*
W. Hittinger	5/77, 9/79, 5/80, 10/80, 8/85
H. Rosenthal	11/77, 4/78
T. Stanley	6/76, 10/76, 12/76, 4/78
W. Webster	2/77, 4/78, 10/80, 8/85

Researchers:	
A. Barco	2/77
R. Bartolini	11/76
J. Clemens	11/76, 2/77
N. Crooks	11/76
R. Flory	11/76
W. Hannon	11/76
W. Houghton	4/78
R. Jebens	12/76
E. Keizer	11/76, 4/78
H. Lewis	4/77
M. Lurie	11/76
R. Palmer	12/76
J. Woodward	4/78

Other:	
P. Smith	9/76, 11/76
A. Pinsky	9/76, 11/76

RCA Consumer Electronics and Records Division personnel

K. Lockhart	1/77
J. MacDonald	1/77

D. McCoy	1/77, 4/78, 11/79*
R. Rhodes	1/77
A. Stancel	1/77
F. Stave	1/77
R. Warren	1/77, 4/78

Selectavision venture team

H. Ball	11/77*
R. Bitting	5/77*
G. Bricker	6/77
F. Conaty	6/77

Selectavision special programs

| V. Allen | 3/77 |
| T. McDermott | 11/77* |

Selectavision, other personnel

G. Evanoff	2/78*
P. Feely	3/77
R. Weinberg	3/77

Corporate RCA

K. Bilby	9–12/80, 2–4/81
W. Enders	4/77*, 2/78*
C. Morsey	11/77*
S. Russell	10/77*
R. Sarnoff	3/78*
R. Sonnenfeldt	2/78, 1/80, 3/80, 8/85*

TV industry

| D. Lachenbruch # | 3/78 |

* No longer with RCA at time of interview
\# Never an RCA employee

Notes

1. Selectavision VideoDisc: opportunity and risk

1 This general account of RCA's history draws on RCA annual reports from 1964 to 1981; on *RCA: An Historical Perspective*, a collection of articles from the *RCA Engineer*, 1938 to 1978, published by RCA; and on speeches by successive CEOs to the financial community.

2 Other companies that have effectively maintained monopolies based on technology have been AT&T, Alcoa, Polaroid, and Xerox.

3 *Wall Street Journal*, February 22, 1971, p. 6. The meeting was a special shareholders meeting called to approve the acquisition of Coronet Carpets, and it was this purchase to which the elderly woman in the fur bonnet was objecting.

4 The original concept of a videoplayer was to play back prerecorded material. The concept of "time-shift," recording off the air and playing back over the same machine, was a later development pioneered by Sony.

5 Material describing VideoDisc and the RCA presentation is based on the RCA press kit, dated February 25, 1981; and the special *VideoDisc* issue of *Communicate, The Magazine of RCA*, (May/June 1981). The author also attended the presentation at one distributorship.

6 Interview with Kenneth Bilby, retired RCA executive vice-president of corporate affairs, October 1981. Bilby's own memoir of David Sarnoff and RCA is forthcoming.

7 This account of videoplayer technologies draws on a special *VideoDisc* issue of the *RCA Review*, Vol. 39, No. 1 (March 1978), and on several key articles in the technical and trade press: Michael Blakstad, "On the Video Trail," *Design* (June 1980); David Lachenbruch, "Inside the Video Disc," *Dealerscope* (October 1981), pp. 25–8; David Lachenbruch, "Video Disk vs. Video Disk," *Panorama* (December 1981), pp. 43 ff; Peter Nulty, "Matsushita Takes the Lead in Video Recorders," *Fortune* (July 16, 1979), pp. 110–16; Suzan D. Prince, "The Thinking Man's Guide to VideoDisc Players," *Videoplay* (June/July, 1981), pp. 38–56.

8 The original Philips disc had been designed for one hour programming; and this remained true for the institutional version of the optical disc. For competitive reasons, the consumer version had to offer two hours of programming, and this reduced its interactive capabilities.

2. David Sarnoff: industrial entrepreneur

1 David Sarnoff, "Message to Broadcasters," speech to a convention of NBC affiliates, Atlantic City, September 13, 1947, quoted in Robert C. Bitting, Jr., "Creating an

Industry: A Case Study in the Management of Television Innovation" (Masters Thesis, Massachusetts Institute of Technology, 1963), p. 86.

2 Carl Dreher, who knew Sarnoff as a young man, has written that he was an early IRE president. Organization records are not clear on this point. See Carl Dreher, *Sarnoff, An American Success* (New York: Quadrangle, 1977), p. 23.

3 See Hugh Aitken, *The Continuous Wave* (Princeton, NJ: Princeton University Press, 1985), for a detailed description of the development of wireless technology at this period.

4 See David Sarnoff, *Looking Ahead: The Papers of David Sarnoff* (New York: McGraw-Hill, 1968), p. 30.

5 Ibid., p. 33.

6 This account of the early radio wireless industry draws heavily on several sources: W. Rupert Maclaurin, *Invention and Innovation in the Radio Industry* (New York: Macmillan, 1949); Hugh Aitken, *The Continuous Wave*; Gleason Leonard Archer, *History of Radio*, 2 vols., (New York: American Historical Society, 1939).

7 John Ambrose Fleming, "Telegraph: Wireless Telegraphy," *Encyclopedia Britannica*, 11th ed. (New York: The Encyclopedia Britannica Company, 1911), vol. 2, pp. 532–41.

8 Dreher, *Sarnoff, An American Success*, pp. 32–7.

9 David Sarnoff, "The Development of Radio and the Radio Industry," speech to the Harvard Graduate School of Business Administration, in Harvard University Graduate School of Business Administration, *The Radio Industry: The Story of Its Development as Told by Leaders of the Industry to the Students of the Graduate School of Business Administration* (New York: W. Shaw, 1928), pp. 97–113.

10 United States House of Representatives Committee on Merchant Marine and Fisheries, "Testimony," HR13159 (Washington, DC: U.S. Government Printing Office, 1918).

11 The abbreviation R.C.A. was used until 1968, when Robert Sarnoff changed the company's logo to RCA. David Sarnoff's contemporaries referred to the company as "The R.C.A."

12 See Aitken's detailed account of the formation of F.C.A. in *The Continuous Wave*, and also Archer's two-volume *History of Radio*, which is the classic account of the beginnings of the radio industry.

13 See "Blue Chip, September 1932," for an account of RCA's early business history, in the collection *RCA: The Years 1930–1978 in Selected Articles from Fortune* (Fortune/RCA: 1979), pp. 3–32.

14 Maclaurin, *Invention and Innovation in the Radio Industry*, p. 135.

15 John C. Warner, "Radio Corporation of America, Part One, The Years to 1938," *RCA: Five Historical Views* (New York: RCA, 1978), p. 6.

16 See Federal Communications Commission, *Report of the Federal Communications Commission on the Investigation of the Telephone Industry in the United States* (Washington DC: Superintendent of Documents, 1939); Federal Trade Commission, *The Radio Industry* (Washington, DC: U.S. Government Printing Office, 1923), and "Blue Chip," *Fortune Selections*, p. 32.

17 See Robert Kargon, ed., *The Maturing of American Science: A Portrait of Science in Public Life Drawn from the Presidential Addresses of the American Association for the Advancement of Science, 1920–1970* (Washington, DC: AAAS, 1974), pp. 1–29.

18 Sarnoff, "The Development of Radio," pp. 100.

19 Leonard S. Reich, "Research, Patents, and the Struggle to Control Radio: A Study of Big Business and the Uses of Industrial Research," *Business History Review*, vol. 51

(summer 1977), pp. 230–5.

20 "Blue Chip," *Fortune Selections*, p. 13.
21 Maclaurin, *Invention and Innovation in the Radio Industry*, p. 146.
22 "Blue Chip," *Fortune Selections*, p. 14.

3. Research as prime mover

1 David Sarnoff served as an officer in the Signal Corps during World War II and attained the rank of Brigadier General by the end of the war. After the war he recruited 16 different high-ranking officers to be RCA executives, a tradition that had started when General Harbord became RCA's president, and later chairman.
2 Sarnoff, *Looking Ahead* (New York: McGraw-Hill, 1968), p. 251.
3 This account of the two television innovations draws on several sources: R. Bitting, "Creating an Industry"; George H. Brown, *And Part of Which I Was*, especially chapters 9–13; Maclaurin, *Invention and Innovation in the Radio Industry*; Kenyon Kilbon, "Pioneering in Electronics: A Short History of the Origins and Growth of RCA Laboratories," Radio Corporation of America, 1919 to 1964, Vol. 1, unpublished manuscript; Richard S. O'Brien and Robert B. Monroe, "101 Years of Television Technology," *The Society of Motion Picture and Television Engineers Journal*, 60th anniversary issue (July 1976), pp. 457–80; Francis Bello, "Color TV: Who'll Buy a Triumph?," *Fortune Selections* (November 1955), pp. 52–7; Walter Guzzardi, Jr., "The General Never Got Butterflies," *Fortune Selections* (October 1962), pp. 58–64. Readers who have an interest in a full account of the invention and commercialization of television, including all of the many individuals who played important roles, should consult these sources.
4 See R. Bitting, "Creating an Industry," p. 95 and 94. The second quotation is from a 1963 interview with Merril A. Trainer, at the time Manager of the RCA Broadcast Studio Merchandizing and Engineering Department.
5 See "Blue Chip," *Fortune Selections*, passim.
6 Kilbon, "Pioneering in Electronics", pp. 44–5.
7 "Envisioning the Future: a Conversation with Gen. David Sarnoff, Board Chairman, Radio Corp. of America," *Nation's Business* (June 1966), p. 64.
8 Kilbon, "Pioneering in Electronics", p. 121.
9 Kilbon, "Pioneering in Electronics", p. 127.
10 See James Phinney Baxter III, *Scientists Against Time* (Boston: Little Brown, 1946).
11 Bello, "Color TV," *Fortune Selections*, p. 52.
12 Interview with Charles Jolliffe, quoted in Bitting, *Creating an Industry*, p. 111.
13 Bello, "Color TV," *Fortune Selections*, p. 56.
14 Brown, *And Part of Which I Was*, pp. 228–9 describes in some detail the contributions of RCA and Hazeltine to the final color standard adopted by the second NTSC.
15 Interview with Rex Isom, Indianapolis, January 1977.
16 Interview with Elmer Engstrom, 1977. Engstrom explained that Sarnoff would consult with him as to which general areas of applied research might benefit from his form of stimulation.
17 Brown, *And Part of Which I Was*, p. 268–70.
18 See Brown, *And Part of Which I Was*, pp. 276–80; and Richard S. Rosenbloom and Karen J. Freeze, "Ampex Corporation and Video Innovation," in Richard S. Rosenbloom (ed.), *Research on Technological Innovation, Management and Policy*, Vol. 2 (Greenwich, CT: JAI Press, 1985), pp. 113–85.
19 W. Rupert Maclaurin, "The Organization of Research in the Radio Industry After the

War," *Proceedings of the IRE* (1945) pp. 242 ff.; and Arthur A. Bright, "War, Radar and the Radio Industry," *Harvard Business Review* (Winter 1947), pp. 38–45.

20 See Margaret B.W. Graham, "Industrial Research in the Age of Big Science," in Rosenbloom, *Research on Technological Innovation*, pp. 47–79.

21 Kilbon, "Pioneering in Electronics", p. 179.

22 K. Bilby, forthcoming memoir.

23 Brown, *And Part of Which I Was*, gives this view of Sarnoff. Brown was one of Sarnoff's key technical managers.

4. Laboratory as entrepreneur: videoplayer research begins

1 James Hillier, "New Perspectives for Consumer Electronics," address delivered on October 19, 1964 at the IEEE Consumer Electronics Award Dinner in Chicago, Illinois.

2 This account of the RCA Laboratories in the late 1950s and early 1960s is based on James Hillier, "The Engineer and the Corporation: RCA Laboratories," 1962 company document.

3 Interview with James Hillier, September 1976.

4 Brown, *And Part of Which I Was*, p. 281.

5 The key insight that William Webster hit upon in conversation with Harry Olson was the relevance of a fundamental principle of communications theory, that noise (extraneous information picked up as static) is traded for bandwidth (channel capacity).

6 Internal RCA document, "Prerecorded Electronic Video Systems," November 1967.

5. Selectavision Holotape: RCA's professional innovation

1 Robert Sarnoff made frequent references to the reformulation of RCA strategy, as in two successive speeches to the annual RCA Financial Executives Conference, April 14, 1967, and April 10, 1968.

2 Internal consulting report of the Sorenson Group on Prerecorded Videoplayers, 1969.

3 All the speeches quoted here were distributed as part of the press kit for the Selectavision Holotape press conference, September 1969.

6. Everything ventured

1 Peter Gruber, "The New Ballgame," 1970, quoted in Rick Setlowe, "Everyone's After a Buck on Cassettes, So When is the Boom Going to Start?," *Variety* (October 22, 1970).

2 "Strategy for Selectavision Magtape, 1973–1977", internal document of Selectavision Venture Group, 1972.

3 "$50-mil RCA Vidcassette Bet," *Variety* (October 28, 1970), p. 1.

7. All in the family

1 Internal memos show meetings with Bell & Howell to have taken place in late June 1973, when Donald Frey expressed concern that Philips videorecorder design yielded a better picture.

2 "RCA Selectavision Video Disc Review" Internal report, July 1, 1974.

241

8. VideoDisc in the public eye

1 *Wall Street Journal*, March 21, 1975, p. 16.
2 "The New Television," *Forbes* (June 1, 1976), p. 27. The *Forbes* story was one of two cover stories on the competing videodisc systems that appeared in major business periodicals in 1975–76. *Business Week* also ran a story entitled "VideoDisc, The Expensive Race to be First," (September 15, 1975), pp. 58 ff., and the *Forbes* cover title was "VideoDiscs, the Dawn of Program-Your-Own TV."
3 *Forbes*, "The New Television," p. 27.
4 "The Expensive Race to be First," *Business Week*, pp. 58 ff.
5 Ibid.
6 All further quotations from Richard Sonnenfeldt are from interviews with the author on November 20, 1979, and January 25, 1980.
7 After a few months of using the new statistical method, the Laboratories became one of its greatest advocates. Several statistical experts were hired and the Laboratories carried the new discipline to other parts of RCA.
8 This was a view widely shared by other consumer electronics companies, just as leading companies in other industries at the time vastly underestimated Japanese competitive strength vis-à-vis their own products.
9 Sonnenfeldt memo to Edgar Griffiths and copy of oral presentation dated November 19, 1976.
10 All letters quoted in this section were included in supporting documentation for the review conducted by Paul Potashner in late 1976.
11 Ibid.

9. RCA's "Manhattan Project"

1 John Crudele, "RCA Rushing Video Disk Player Entry," *Electronic News* (January 15, 1979), p. 54.
2 Jefferson Grigsby, "RCA: Off the Roller Coaster, Onto the Escalator," *Forbes* (February 15, 1977), pp. 25–8.
3 "The Peaks and Valleys of RCA's Performance," *Fortune* (December 31, 1978), p. 55. It should be noted that Griffiths was susceptible to the argument that investment had to be made in the long term. He increased the corporate research budget, which had suffered badly during the postcomputer era, from $112 million to $197 million.
4 P.J. Ryan, "Materials and Process Development for VideoDisc Replication," *RCA Review*, VideoDisc issue (March 1978), pp. 87–115.
5 Interview with Richard Sonnenfeldt, New York, November, 1979, and "VideoDisc: A Three-way Race for a Billion Dollar Jackpot," *Business Week* (July 7, 1980), p. 72 ff.
6 L.P. Fox, "The Conductive VideoDisc," pp. 116 ff., and D.L. Ross, "Coating for VideoDisc," pp. 136 ff. in *VideoDisc* issue of *RCA Review*.
7 Peter Nulty, "Matsushita Takes the Lead in VideoRecorders," *Fortune* (July 16, 1979), pp. 110–16.
8 J. Grigsby, "RCA: Off the Roller Coaster," *Forbes* (February 15, 1977), p. 28. Note that a key lesson from the Colortrak experience had been the success that had been achieved when Indianapolis coordinated the technical effort in a joint program with the Laboratories.
9 John Crudele, "RCA to Cut 150 on Video Disk," *Electronic News* (August 1977), p. 14.

10 Edgar Griffiths, "Remarks to Consumer Electronics Distributors," RCA internal script, December 6, 1979.

11 "RCA: Still another Master," *Business Week* (August 17, 1981), pp. 80–6.

12 Robert J. Cole, "Zenith in Pact with RCA to Build TV Disk Sets, "*New York Times*, March 4, 1980, p. D5.

13 "Television's Scrambled Future," *Business Week* (December 17, 1979), pp. 60–4.

14 David J. Londoner, "Like No Business We Know: The Entertainment Industry as it Enters the 1980's," Wertheim "Report", October 1979, pp. 48–62.

15 N.R. Kleinfeld, "VideoCassettes Get a Big Play, Videodisk Sales Face Problems," *New York Times*, December 18, 1980, p. D1.

10. On the market

1 Laura Landro, "Following a Slow Start, RCA Plans a New Push for Its Videodisc Player," *Wall Street Journal*, October 13, 1981, p. 35.

2 "Videodisc Markets Make an Amazing About-face," *Business Week* (September 20, 1982), pp. 119–22.

3 L. Landro, "Following a Slow Start."

4 Edward Meadows, "The Slippery Market for Videodiscs," *Fortune* (November 2, 1981), pp. 82–5. Note that an additional factor that held down videoplayer sales for a while was uncertainty concerning the outcome of a copyright infringement suit filed against Sony by MCA and a few other key entertainment companies. By the time the suit reached the Supreme Court it was clear that any prohibition against recording off the air would be unenforceable.

5 David Lachenbruch, "Video Disk vs. Video Disk," *Panorama* (December 1981), pp. 43 ff., and "Inside the VideoDisc," *Dealerscope* (October 1981), pp. 25–8.

6 "VideoDisc Dead, RCA Eyes New Areas," *Electronics* (April 19, 1984), pp. 52–4.

7 Landro, "Following a Slow Start." See also A.F. Ehrbar, "Splitting up RCA," *Fortune* (March 22, 1982), pp. 62–76.

8 "RCA Buys Some Time," *Financial World* (April 4–17, 1984), p. 16.

11. Managing R&D: lessons from RCA

1 A few of the works that deal with aspects of the evolution of the research and engineering communities at the national level are M. Graham, "Industrial Research in the Age of Big Science," in Rosenbloom, *Research on Technological Innovation*; Daniel Kevles, "The National Science Foundation and the Debate over Post-war Research Policy, 1942–1945," *ISIS* (1976); David Noble, *America by Design: Science, Technology and the Rise of Corporate Capitalism* (New York: Knopf, 1977); and John Servos, "The Industrial Relations of Science: Chemical Engineering at MIT, 1900–1939," *ISIS* (1980).

2 Bro Uttal, "The Lab that Ran away from Xerox," *Fortune* (September 5, 1983), pp. 97–102.

3 M. Graham, "Industrial Research in the Age of Big Science," and Richard R. Nelson and Richard N. Langlois, "Industrial Innovation Policy: Lessons from American History," *Science*, Vol. 219 (February 18, 1983), pp. 814–19.

4 Interview with Elmer Engstrom, Princeton, New Jersey, May 1977.

5 Margaret B.W. Graham, "Corporate Research and Development: The Latest Transformation," *Technology in Society*, Vol. 7, (1985) pp. 179–195.

243

Index

Index

Index